Praise for

The Trouble of Color

"Martha S. Jones is one of our country's greatest historians. Her work has provided us with the tools, the language, and the insight to better understand our collective past. Now, in her book *The Trouble of Color*, she has turned her historian's eye toward her own family, and in the process has allowed us to be part of a remarkable journey of discovery. Elegantly written and painstakingly researched, *The Trouble of Color* inspired me to look deeper into my own family history. I am so grateful to have this book as a model. I am so grateful that Jones has shared her family's story with all of us."

—Clint Smith, #1 *New York Times*–bestselling author of *How the Word Is Passed*

"Through richly descriptive language and revealing personal insight, *The Trouble of Color* invites us to join the prizewinning historian Jones on her courageous quest to recover and confront a troubling racial and family history. This multigenerational memoir is at once moving, surprising, disturbing, and unsettling. Jones presents the multiracial and mixed-race members of a Black family tree branching back to the early nineteenth century, exploring how they 'wore' and experienced their lighter-than-most skin and carried the mantle and advantages of the 'talented tenth' even as they bore private burdens of memory, identity, discrimination, and representation."

—Tiya Miles, National Book Award–winning author of *All That She Carried*

"An astonishing literary feat by an author who combines the scholarly brilliance of a professional historian with the fearless curiosity of a memoirist determined to unlock the family story inscribed in her very being. As she climbs the branches of her ancestral tree through painstaking archival research and the great gathering of stories passed down from one generation to the next, Jones personalizes the color line that Du Bois wrote about so prophetically in *The Souls of Black Folk*. In doing so, Jones traces that line's jagged edges through the bloodlines of an American family whose extraordinary tale of survival reaches back into the darkest corners of slavery through emancipation and the civil rights struggle that made her own story possible."

—Henry Louis Gates Jr., Harvard University

"In *The Trouble of Color*, award-winning historian Jones shares the unforgettable story of her family's travels along the 'jagged color line' of the United States. It is a story of African Americans striving under duress and a testament to the beautiful complexity of African American identity. Jones writes with the intellect and rigor of a superb historian and the heart and soul of a Black woman who insists upon her place in the rugged American landscape."

—Imani Perry, National Book Award–winning
author of *South to America*

"Blending meticulous archival research—the gifted historian's keen-eyed ability to find the luminous details that animate the overlooked and nearly erased past—with the truth-seeker's willingness to ask difficult questions of the self, Jones has crafted a capacious account of a remarkable family's history over five generations. Intimate and searching, *The Trouble of Color* examines what it means to be truly seen, brilliantly excavating the personal in service of a deeper understanding of public history, of American lives shaped—across time and space—by the color line."

—Natasha Trethewey, *New York Times*–bestselling author of *Memorial Drive*

"*The Trouble of Color* most definitely troubles some supposedly still waters. Jones deftly wraps an engaging, suspenseful story around the complicated story of color and complexion in this empire. I'm most wowed by the playfulness of the prose here. Superb writing. Necessary work."

—Kiese Laymon, author of *Heavy*

"The best memoirs tell us something about our shared history and ourselves. Through deep research and masterful storytelling, *The Trouble of Color* does exactly that, with a narrative that spans centuries, regions, unforgettable characters, and shifting social norms around the ever-complex and often-menacing color line. Jones has a knack for making history both accessible and unforgettable. With this powerful exploration of her remarkable family, she has delivered yet another masterpiece."

—Michele Norris, author of *Our Hidden Conversations*

"Jones displays her deft historical acumen in this beautifully written, powerfully engaging, genre-spanning work. As history, it leads readers from slavery to freedom in a nation that remained fixated on color. As memoir, it complicates and deconstructs the experiences of mixed-race Americans in brave and honest prose. *The Trouble of Color* is a mighty book."
— Erica Armstrong Dunbar, author of *Never Caught*

"*The Trouble of Color* illustrates not just Jones's enormous talents as a writer and historian, but also her remarkable generosity. She has shared her family and herself, gifting us an intimate and powerful chronicle of American lives made by the color line. An unforgettable, necessary book."
— Ada Ferrer, Pulitzer Prize–winning author of *Cuba*

"To tell the story of race in America well requires rigor, fortitude, and vulnerability. Jones's evocative and perceptive memoir does that and so much more. *The Trouble of Color* shows how intimately the story of race maps onto our lives and bodies, and the spaces and stories Black families carve for themselves beyond it in order to be whole."
— Salamishah Tillet, Pulitzer Prize–winning critic

THE
TROUBLE
OF COLOR

ALSO BY MARTHA S. JONES

THE TROUBLE OF COLOR

An American Family Memoir

MARTHA S. JONES

BASIC BOOKS
New York

Basic Books
Hachette Book Group
1290 Avenue of the Americas, New York, NY 10104
www.basicbooks.com

Printed in the United States of America

First Edition: March 2025

Published by Basic Books, an imprint of Hachette Book Group, Inc. The Basic Books name and logo is a registered trademark of the Hachette Book Group.

The Hachette Speakers Bureau provides a wide range of authors for speaking events. To find out more, go to hachettespeakersbureau.com or email HachetteSpeakers@hbgusa.com.

Basic books may be purchased in bulk for business, educational, or promotional use. For more information, please contact your local bookseller or the Hachette Book Group Special Markets Department at special.markets@hbgusa.com.

The publisher is not responsible for websites (or their content) that are not owned by the publisher.

Print book interior design by Amy Quinn.

Library of Congress Cataloging-in-Publication Data

Names: Jones, Martha S., author.
Title: The trouble of color : an American family memoir / Martha S. Jones.
Other titles: American family memoir
Description: First edition. | New York, NY : Basic Books, 2025. | Includes bibliographical references.
Identifiers: LCCN 2024031568 (print) | LCCN 2024031569 (ebook) | ISBN 9781541601000 (hardcover) | ISBN 9781541601024 (ebook)
Subjects: LCSH: Jones, Martha S.—Family. | Jones family. | Multiracial families—North Carolina—Greensboro. | Multiracial families—Kansas—Danville. | Multiracial people—Race identity—New York (State)—New York. | African American women—Race identity—New York (State)—New York. | Multiracial women—New York (State)—New York—Biography. | Greensboro (N.C.)—Biography. | Danville (Kan.)—Biography. | New York (N.Y.)—Biography.
Classification: LCC F264.G8 J66 2025 (print) | LCC F264.G8 (ebook) | DDC 929.20973—dc23/eng/20241118
LC record available at https://lccn.loc.gov/2024031568
LC ebook record available at https://lccn.loc.gov/2024031569

ISBNs: 9781541601000 (hardcover), 9781541601024 (ebook)

LSC-C

Printing 1, 2025

To Paul

Wade in the water,
Wade in the water, children,
Wade in the water.
God's gonna trouble the water.
—AFRICAN AMERICAN SPIRITUAL

Contents

THE
TROUBLE
OF COLOR

Who Do You Think You Are?

What did your face look like before your parents
were born?

—ZEN KOAN

WHATEVER HE SAID, I KNEW WHAT HE MEANT: "WHO DO
you think you are?"

Ron pushed back his seat—a small desk-chair combo of
metal and molded plastic. It moaned across the linoleum tiles.
He stood and then thundered, all six-plus feet, long fingers on
elegant hands cutting the air for emphasis. He was a leader of
the Black Student Union: pressed jeans, leather jacket, turtle-
neck. No beret, though my memory nearly sketches one onto
the top of his head. I stumbled backward as his words blew past
me and then ricocheted off the classroom's cinder-block walls.

I rifled through my mind for the right retort, but my tightened throat wouldn't let me speak. This wasn't the rude but
merely curious "What *are* you?" I'd heard that many times

before. Ron, my gut knew, was not demanding a sociological fact or even an answer to his question. Instead, he was leveling an accusation. Perhaps he was unsettled by what he saw: me, as much girl as woman, denim overalls fraying at the hem, buffalo sandals still dusty from days at the beach, faux-ivory elephant hanging from a short chain, chin-length waves parted in the center and clipped back by barrettes. My skin losing its summer glow. Though we faced each other, just a few feet apart, I sensed that Ron could not see me.

—

I'm haunted by this confrontation, though not only because I didn't manage to counter Ron's challenge that day. It's true that I almost withered at his words. What has never left me is something else, and I remember Ron like we do our firsts. Never before had someone so openly demanded, goaded, and nearly shamed me into explaining who I thought I was. For a long time afterward, a persistent confusion plagued me. How could I explain myself when, in the eyes of others, I didn't add up?

That school year, Ron and I sat together through lessons in Black sociology, history, and literature. We were children born into the 1950s promise of the Civil Rights movement, and after that Black Power, while our destiny lay in a future defined by 1980s Regan-era retrenchment. We had a lot to learn. We asked questions of Zora Neale Hurston and E. Franklin Frazier, Langston Hughes and Nella Larsen, Frederick Douglass and John Hope Franklin. We deliberated over one especially prophetic line from W. E. B. Du Bois's *The Souls of Black Folk*: "The problem of the twentieth century is the problem of the color line." I was learning that this boundary—one said to divide Black from white—was neither solid nor sure. It was instead jagged, sharp-edged and threatening. I immersed myself in Black studies and discovered inspiring life stories— ones I'd eventually make a profession out of retelling—all the while quietly searching for answers about me.

—

I hadn't anticipated Ron or much else about college. In spring 1976, my senior year at a Long Island high school, I barely limped to the finish. Physics stood between me and a diploma, so I bent over the lab bench, executed every experiment, and solved each problem until I earned a passing grade. Even with the necessary credits, the approaching graduation was no triumph. Class rankings made the rounds—circulated in our school corridors in purple ink on a single sheet—with my name just a few spots shy of the bottom.

No one in those years much thought of me as a good student. I rarely saw a guidance counselor and instead visited with the school psychologist, who hired me to clean his house rather than study after school. It was a low point in my young sense of self, and I accepted that the adults around me aimed to do little more than prop me up through graduation. I marched with my class—a gloriously sunny afternoon at a nearby university, with my entire family there. I even attended the prom—we called it a gambol, as in "a playful jumping about"—with my boyfriend, a kind, factory-working dropout. I didn't much romp that evening, though I still smile when remembering the dress I wore: sleek fitting, white with large peach flowers, spaghetti straps, all down to the floor. I soon fell into days at work in a Main Street clothes shop, where a deep employee discount had helped me buy that prom outfit.

Summer launched in our small waterside suburb, Port Washington. Set on Long Island's North Shore, it was known in real estate parlance as the Gold Coast. In the early 1900s, Manhattan robber barons—rich from banking, railroads, and real estate—had commissioned colossal harbor-front mansions that symbolized their prowess. Only after World War II did our town become a site for tract-house developments, plotted along winding, newly laid streets and dead-end cul-de-sacs. These became homes for families headed by men like my father who commuted to city jobs each day via the Long Island Railroad.

This description of Port Washington might bring to mind stretches of green, manicured lawns lined by sidewalks and white picket fences. But by the time I finished high school, I knew better. Or at least I knew more. Port Washington was also a fractured place where lines of race and class marred the idyll sold by real estate developers. It was a place where kids like me got lost. As July began, I broke up with my boyfriend and cruised local teen hangouts until late in the night: the town dock, the bandshell, the church steps, and the football-field bleachers. I put scores of miles on my mother's Mazda and, after a late night of skinny-dipping, fell for a boy whom I loved one way and another until he died a decade or so later—of AIDS, they say. Some of the kids around me began to peel off, headed for precollege programs. Soon others readied for fall classes. A twinge of envy hit me when my best friend picked me up in a new used Chevy Vega in which she planned to commute to a local college.

I'd kept a secret in those months, so much so that by August I'd nearly forgotten it. Earlier in the spring, I'd quietly applied to college. Just one school. No one at home noticed when the application arrived. I scooped the envelope up and alone, late at night in my bedroom, filled it out by hand. I wrote a check for the fee, licked the stamps, and dropped it into the bright blue mailbox that sat at the top of our block. Looking back, I believe that words like *afraid* or *ambivalent* might rightly capture my feelings. I'm sure that when I sent off that form, it was my small way of expressing the hope that there was more ahead for me.

I didn't give college another thought until in late, sticky August, a letter arrived: an acceptance to SUNY New Paltz. In an instant, I went from having nothing on deck to being college bound. Surprised, my parents never tried to talk me out of taking a chance. Maybe, like me, they'd harbored unspoken hope for my future. I never hesitated. I'd little sense of where I was going in life but felt sure that freshman year and a fresh start would beat another season in a small, low-end storefront straightening racks and waiting on surly teens.

My dad hustled. In just ten days, he borrowed cash from a friend for the tuition and packed me into his station wagon for a ninety-minute trek up the Hudson Valley. I would come to know the trip by heart: across the George Washington Bridge or the Tappan Zee, up the Thruway to Exit 17. After the toll, west away from the river and along Route 32 to the tiny college town long before colonized by Huguenots, snuggled up against the feet of the Shawangunk Mountains. We pulled into a campus parking lot and began a round of office visits. Admissions. Registrar. Housing. I was giddy, if also mystified, in the way that new beginnings bring on.

The campus was a place of contrasts. Most of it had gone up after World War II, part of a Rockefeller-family vision for public higher education across the state: lots of shiny terra-cotta, brutalist concrete, and angular walkways. The oldest structures were of red brick with white trim, a cheap imitation of the tony Vassar College campus, which sat just across the Hudson. Most buildings bore the names of Belgian immigrants turned colonial landholders: Hasbrouck, Bevier, Lefevre. The library told a different story, named for another early Ulster County resident, an enslaved woman who, as a free person, rebaptized herself Sojourner Truth.

My new college was set on an epic landscape. After she escaped bondage, Truth found refuge with a family in New Paltz and began her journey to freedom. Almost a century and a half later, in 1971, the school opened a library named for her—a place of learning that honored a champion of antislavery and feminism who herself never learned to read or write. It made sense, I see now, that the New Paltz campus attracted so many Black and Brown students from downstate. When we studied in the wake of Sojourner Truth, it was evidence that we'd arrived somewhere that mattered.

At the housing office, few options remained open. Students had claimed most rooms when admitted months earlier. "Either Bliss Hall or Chango," the clerk recited from behind a folding table crowded with paperwork, never looking up from her lists. Bliss was the all-women's dormitory, an arrangement that struck me as old-fashioned. "Chango is the third-world house," she went on. My father stood off to the side, preoccupied by the check he was about to make out for the semester's room and board. I replied with a shrug, having no idea what "third world" meant. "Bliss Hall," I piped up. The only thing left to do was move in. Dad saw to it that my trunk got to the right room. And then he was gone.

Days later, classes started. I pushed my way out of Bliss Hall's glass doors, headed across the sunbaked library plaza and on to class. It was fall 1976, and I had already declared myself a psychology major and Black studies minor. The latter field was in its first, insurgent wave, having surfaced on campuses across the country in courses taught by young instructors who boldly crossed lines between the humanities, social sciences, and radical politics. In Black studies, my personal and intellectual cravings mixed. There was a lot I did not know, and that included how my own family fit into bigger stories of the past.

Professor James Bowen taught Black sociology. I arrived at his classroom, took in the scene, and immediately recognized two students: resident assistants from my dorm, Bliss Hall. They exuded elegance, especially against the backdrop of my hippie-inspired peasant shirts and bell bottoms. Perms, smart outfits—tailored skirts with matching jackets, sweater sets, narrow belts, shoes with low heels—along with careful jewelry and makeup. I was thrilled to share Professor Bowen's course with them and thought of us as sisters of the skin, or underneath it. Perhaps, I hoped, they'd see past superficial differences—and see me.

Among the other students, the standout was Ron. He was suitably brilliant, handsome, and outspokenly confident. We had in common having grown up on Long Island. I can't be sure, but I bet that back home, he'd stood out at the podium, on the debate team or in high school oratory contests. I didn't try to conceal my admiration and hoped it was enough that I would listen to and learn from Ron. For his part, he ignored my presence and looked past me with what I soon learned was barely contained contempt.

Professor Bowen required us to make oral reports on assigned readings, all new to me. I volunteered to present Frantz Fanon's *A Dying Colonialism*, the psychiatrist-philosopher's account of the Algerian overthrow of French rule. Fanon opened my eyes wide to the dilemma of Blackness as bound up with colonialism's psychic evils: inferiority, dependency, status seeking, assimilation. My journey to consciousness was not his. Fanon came of age in colonized Martinique and then through military service and medical training. Instead, my self-discovery began in that cinder-block and linoleum upstate New York classroom.

As I prepared my lesson on Fanon, new anxiety surfaced. I had never before spoken in public, and there, in my first weeks of college, I wanted to appear like I belonged. When the time came, I rose, eyes on my shoes, and walked to the front of the room. Professor Bowen stood just behind my shoulder, leaning back on his steel-and-Formica desk. My resident assistant, Pauline, sat a few rows back; I could see her off to my left. Ron was just to my right. I clutched a small stack of three-by-five index cards outlined with a Bic that gave me what confidence I had. I began to speak, and right away the room grew hazy. My nerves buzzed.

I mechanically recited chapter summaries, eyes glued to my notes. I dared not improvise: The history Fanon recounted was too new to me. I wasn't yet finished when Ron was on his feet. I startled and immediately had two thoughts: He was out of turn *and* I was in trouble. Ron commanded the floor and spoke not to me but to Professor Bowen. "Enough of this," he spat in the professor's direction. "We shouldn't have to listen to this." Ron's eyes swept the room and invited the class to agree: It was offensive to hear me explain Fanon. Pauline looked my way, her eyes wide, and I knew my predicament was real.

"She doesn't even know where the French Antilles are," Ron sputtered.

My brain went into overdrive as I searched frantically for an answer. Ron was, I recognized, in one sense correct. I knew too little about Fanon and his world and did not know the whereabouts of the Antilles. He was at the same time wrong, at least about me. Only now do I have words that express what I felt: Hadn't I earned my place, like every other student in the room? Wasn't I as suited as any of us to question, to speak, to hold in my hands the work of a Black intellectual, to become a student of his ideas? Even to imagine myself to be like him? Ron thought he saw me, while I knew that he'd looked right past me.

To break the tension, Professor Bowen nodded: I should go ahead and answer. I looked from him back to Ron, took in a quick breath, and then said, "Well . . . the French Antilles are in France." After that the scene disappears from my memory.

Whatever came next, all I'm sure of is that I muscled my way through to the end of that report. Class dismissed, I gathered my books, quickstepped out the nearest exit, and made a bee-line for my dorm room. My hands shook all the way home.

There is no consolation, even now, in knowing that my answer to Ron's question was correct, even astute. The French Antilles have always been part of France, despite the chasm that divides the hexagon of metropolitan Europe from the *outre-mer* of the Caribbean department that includes Martinique, from where Fanon hailed. My answer that day was, at best, a good guess. Still, I was not wounded because Ron doubted my intellect. What left an enduring mark was that he doubted me.

Not enough. That was what I looked like to Ron. For him, I was not enough. Not enough for Black studies, for Fanon, for our coursework. My very person—skin too light, hair too limp, features too pointed, diction too suburban—unsettled, perplexed, and even provoked. I might gain command over lessons in the classroom, but I would never be in command of my own body, at least not as others saw it. When I showed up to lectures, at parties, and in club meetings, to rallies and service days, versions of Ron's question surfaced in a glance or a snub, a quip, or occasionally a not-very-subtle suggestion that I leave. I was not enough and too much all at once.

Who did I think I was? My best answer emanates from a single idea: family.

—

It's been a long time since my confrontation with Ron—nearly five decades—and over these years, my feelings have shifted. In the weeks that immediately followed, I stayed awake late into the night. Propped up in my narrow dorm bed, I tried not to wake my roommate while gritting my teeth and clutching my pillow. I boiled with quiet rage and fantasized about a do-over, another chance to give Ron as good as he had given me. *I know how to show him*, I reassured myself and replayed the scene. I imagined puffing my chest a bit: "Who do you think *you* are?" I'd boom back the next time. I'd confront Ron with my outrage, making clear that he had no right to demand a recitation of my family story. No amount of his bravado, I'd say, could earn Ron entry into the precious place where I kept stories about the generations that had fashioned me.

By the next spring, Ron and I had forged a friendship during evenings spent in the lounges of the student union. We debated state politics, higher-ed policy, and nuclear power. We penned editorials for our campus paper, the *Oracle*. Many nights we subsisted on weak coffee and sugary snacks dispensed from a coin-operated vending machine. We never spoke about what had happened between us in Professor Bowen's class, and it was just as well. I wasn't ready to talk. Back then, beyond a few slim branches of my family tree, I understood little about our story. Most of it was, to my mind, in disarray, like the insides of a long-neglected trunk—tucked into an attic corner or underneath the basement stairs, its contents casually tossed atop one another and tough to sort out.

Not long afterward, in my twenties, I joined waves of Americans on the hunt for their family stories. Ron was far from my mind by then. Instead, I was among the many Americans for whom *Roots*—the book and then the television

11

miniseries—sparked an interest in family history. *Roots* fueled genealogical societies, research guides, and a widespread sense that even intimate, everyday stories could and should be preserved. A few years later still, the death of my father's mother, my grandmother whom we called Musie—a nickname that rhymed with her given name, Susie—fueled my curiosity. She'd always shared family lore, but many mysteries remained unsolved. I began to show up at family occasions with a notebook and pen, sketching trees and jotting down recollections. I finished law school in 1987 and organized vacation travel around visits to archival collections. New finds along my family paper trail began to sharpen faded memories.

Today family history is, in a real sense, my vocation. I long ago gave up practicing law to make good on the nascent ambitions that led me to Professor Bowen's Black studies class back in 1976. I teach and write Black history, made possible by getting a later-in-life graduate degree. Those years of training taught me new approaches to uncovering the past. Still, I've never stopped collecting my own family stories, or relying on what I learned as an amateur genealogist. I'm still driven by a hunger that compels me to hunt for every needle in a haystack—or that one person among thousands on a census return. Over the last two decades, I've hunted for my family story while also recovering broader narratives about the law, culture, and politics of the Black past.

I got serious about family history—serious enough to begin writing it down—when I encountered distinguished historians who were writing about us but getting the story wrong. One Civil Rights movement scholar had interviewed my grandmother Musie and used a quote from her to open the first chapter of his book but got her name wrong. He credited her as "Susie B. Jones" rather than her correct name, "Susie W. Jones." I boiled with outrage, and one of Musie's stories came immediately to mind: In the Jim Crow years, she'd battled local white people to be addressed by her preferred name—"Mrs. Jones"—rather than the overly familiar "Susie" or the demeaning "Gal." For people like my grandmother, what they were called mattered. I know that some might judge a misplaced middle initial a harmless slipup, but to me, her granddaughter, it was an intolerable error.

When I discovered yet another historian who had bungled our story, I began to understand what it meant to be caught by the jagged color line. At the start of graduate school, I bought myself a coveted reference work: the *Black Women in America* encyclopedia, two thick volumes slickly covered in red and white. I marveled at the collection's sweep of more than 600 biographical sketches and another 150 essays. Inspired, I splurged on the purchase, opened a space for the books on my shelves, and made myself a promise: Someday I would contribute to histories like those told in the encyclopedia's pages.

Before I put the books away, I scanned the index for any reference to my family. There it was: Bennett College, the historically Black women's school led for three decades by David Dallas Jones, my grandfather known to us as Grandy. I turned to the paragraph on the school's founding, a story I knew by heart: In 1873 Greensboro, North Carolina, formerly enslaved people founded the school in a church basement. Bennett's founders later won support from the northern

Methodist Episcopal Church for teaching from the elementary grades through normal school. The entry continued: In 1926, the school reorganized into a four-year liberal arts college for women. Enter my Grandy, who took over Bennett's leadership that year. I was reading quickly but came to a sudden stop at what came next: "David Dallas Jones, a white businessman living in Atlanta, became the first president of Bennett College for Women."

A chill shot through me, and I sputtered out loud, "'A white businessman'?" Grandy was never in "business"—he'd earlier worked with the YMCA and the Commission on Interracial Cooperation. What unsettled me was encountering Grandy as "white"! Of course, I knew better. His father had been a free man of color living in nearby Orange County, and his mother had been born enslaved in Chowan County to the east. Together they had raised Grandy and his five siblings in one of Greensboro's post–Civil War Black settlements, Warnersville.

It took me only a few beats to surmise what had gone wrong. The encyclopedia author likely had relied on a photograph of Grandy, such as the Bachrach studio portrait reproduced in the college's promotional materials. Renowned for their ability to make everyone from the illustrious to the ordinary appear distinguished, the Bachrach team had posed Grandy perched on a desk. He was outfitted in a three-piece suit, with his Phi Beta Kappa key hanging from a chain at his waist declaring that the love of wisdom is the guide of life. His right hand rested on a book, likely a Bible, and he was relaxed, with the other hand slipped into his trouser pocket. The photograph was taken later in his life, and Grandy was by then at ease with being

Grandy, David Dallas Jones, Fabian Bachrach portrait

photographed, profiled and posing as a representative of the college for women that he led.

To some eyes, I had to concede, he could be taken for white. I also knew that other writers had described Grandy with careful nuance, as had author Lawrence Otis Graham: "David Dallas Jones was president of a society-conscious school. . . . Like many presidents of the elite Black colleges at that time, Jones had a complexion that was light enough to 'pass' for white if he had chosen." He had not, I knew, and the encyclopedia's misrepresentation of Grandy stung. I still don't have words for what it meant to discover that someone had reached into the past and snatched away who he was. I am sure it rhymes with *theft*. Through its error, the same encyclopedia entry also taught me something: Like me, Grandy had known a menacing color line. I remembered what he'd accomplished and knew he must have walked with quick, confident strides while he raised money and reputation for his school.

Like mine, his skin had generated strife. How, I wondered, had he weathered moments when strangers had mistaken him, when he took his seat on a segregated train, entered the lobby of a convention hall or hotel, or shook hands with likely donors in far-off cities like Los Angeles, Chicago, and New York? I let myself fantasize that, while such moments unnerved me, he'd brushed them off with humor-laced swagger. We were not precisely alike. Still, I was beginning to understand that Grandy and I were part of the same story, a family story, about how skin, and the misunderstandings it can invite, troubles. When I discovered Grandy's posthumous mention in an encyclopedia, his past and my present came together. I saw myself in him and him in me.

I started to write our story down, stuck close to the facts, and corrected the record. My experience as an archive sleuth let me recover and then piece together new fragments, and what I discovered about Grandy went well beyond that encyclopedia description. My basement shelves are piled with plastic bins secured by tight lids and labeled "Family photos," "The 1980s," and "Dad's stuff." Grandy's letters to his son, my father, are stored there. I've visited the Amistad Research Center in New Orleans, where Grandy's personal papers, which stretch over decades, are preserved in professional acid-free boxes and folders. I've listened to oral histories, the voices of Grandy's youngest son, my Uncle Fuzz, and my grandmother Musie, who recorded their memories of him. I have discovered news clippings, photographs, Grandy's death certificate, and particulars about his households as recorded by census takers. With these items in hand, I could do my best as a historian and explain how he'd lived. But this scholarly rendering—thorough and rigorous—wasn't all I wanted to say.

It wasn't enough to write his story for other historians. They would, I knew, value Grandy's story if I connected it to bigger histories about the growth of historically Black colleges or the arc of pre–Civil Rights Black activism. Some writers had recounted his story for just these purposes. For my part, I wanted to write down what Grandy meant, not to history but to me and to our family. I knew that he mattered, though not because other scholars told me so. Instead, I knew he mattered because as I immersed myself in the details of his life, my heartbeat quickened, my eyes welled, and emotions like anger, fear, and even pride coursed through me. Yes, I could write a book filled with facts. But what I most needed to put down was how I felt. This sort of writing, prose that goes from the head to the heart, I came to learn, is what writers call *memoir*.

It has taken me this long to understand why Ron's question, back in that Black studies classroom, was so difficult to answer. It would never be enough to reply with raw data about the people I come from. My best answer would need to explain who we have been but also how it has felt to be us. In our first encounter, Ron thought he had called me out: I was someone who didn't belong, with whom he did not want to share

Black studies. I now understand that he hadn't just called me out; he had called *forth* the ages, the generations before me. Ron dared me to summon up our collective past and tell my part of it. Yes, we became friends, but Ron is indelibly part of me because he leveled a challenge. I'll never forget how his voice boomed and his hands cut the air. I'll also never forget how he pushed open the door to a family story that I am finally able to tell.

—

The birth of Nancy Bell Graves in 1808 is as far back as I can trace my family. I'd long before placed her on our tree, but only a dozen years ago did I finally ask who she had been. I pulled a carton from the back of a guest-room closet and fished out a slightly torn manila envelope that I'd held on to since I'd inherited it from my father's sister, Tuppy, years before. It was late spring, and with the blinds wide open, my living room glowed with light, promising that the blossoming of new leaves and tiny crocuses was not far off. I cleared the coffee table—an old IKEA model from my student days—dumped the contents, and gently spread them out. Wanting to get close up, I seated myself between the table and the sofa on the wall-to-wall carpet that ran from the dining room on one end to my office on the other.

I was a professor at a big Midwestern university in those days. It was an ordinary afternoon, but my husband was out of town. Classes had ended, which left me without lessons to prepare or grades to calculate. It was a quiet chance for reflection. I'd lost both my parents in recent years, which gave new significance to keepsakes like these photos and my care of them. More than ever before, I was the custodian of our stories. The only plan I had that day was a practical one: I'd take digital images and upload them for safekeeping. I'd sort through what to save and what to give away. In those hours, I immersed myself in the pleasures of family history.

As I scanned the faces, one portrait stood out as the furthest-back ancestor among them. I knew only that she was my own grandmother's great-grandmother, someone whom no one spoke much about. I flipped over the old cabinet card and discovered my Aunt Tuppy's notation: "Great Great Grand-mother. Last Graves. *Had 7 boys & 7 girls.* Lived in Danville." Nancy was seated in a photographer's studio, her head crowned with white hair, creases, though nary a wrinkle, on her face despite her eighty years. Her eyes were deep set and cheek-bones pronounced; their sharp angles met at a long, square chin. Her clothes were modest, of respectably tailored cotton, a checkered shawl around her shoulders. Resting in her lap was a heavy book, held open to a passage I could not make out.

When I later shared Nancy's photo with friends, they said I looked like her. Some thought they recognized my face in Nancy's. "Something in her eyes," one offered. I held her por-trait up close, pasted it to my computer monitor, and even-tually hung it in a small gold frame near my desk. I became convinced that her skin is the heart of our resemblance. I knew that the photographer likely lacked the ability to capture her true hue. Still, I could see that Nancy was not ebony or deep brown. Her skin was closer in tone to the white bonnet on her head than to the deep, rich dye of her plain, buttoned-up dress.

Nancy Bell Graves

The ties of her cap framed Nancy's face, an almost impercepti-
ble border between her jawline and the studio's light backdrop.

I posed before countless mirrors—bright vanity bulbs, bluish
fluorescents, in green rooms, at the salon, in a yellow-leather-
covered handheld carried in my purse for touch-ups. Everywhere, I began to see Nancy's face in my own: olive, red,
yellow, as I've been termed by loved ones and foes alike. I
wondered what Nancy was called. In her time, long before
colorism and passing, before *white-presenting* and brown-paper-
bag ideals, before antimiscegenation laws and *Loving v. Virginia*,

Nancy knew something of how we came to be women mixed, mulatto, and migrants along the color line. She was an enslaved woman who bore many children, including a daughter who was the grandmother to my grandmother. Nancy bequeathed to us not only her portrait but also the trouble of color—somewhere between too little and too much of it.

—

The next fall, a flight dropped me at Lexington's Blue Grass Airport. I was soon steering along narrow, unfamiliar roads. Nancy's hometown, Danville, Kentucky, was unknown to me save for what tourist literature said about college basketball, thoroughbred horses, and smooth bourbon. Nancy's Danville was home to early Presbyterian religiosity, the launch of more than one college or institute, and the antislavery rumblings of men who included abolitionist James Birney. But my mind was on histories that the local tourist bureau rarely highlighted. Before the abolition of slavery in 1865, the law allowed people to be sold, traded, auctioned, and tracked down openly on the pages of the town's newspapers. Mostly, enslaved people labored in kitchens and fields, in sties and stables, and in trenches and workshops. The regime gave way only after the Union Army opened Camp Nelson nearby. It first housed Black Civil War recruits and later Black refugees from the conflict.

As I anticipated going on a search for Nancy in central Kentucky, I grew wary. This old, familiar fear—of traveling uninvited into southern places—I had learned during childhood summers with my own grandmother Musie. Her home city of Greensboro, North Carolina, was infused with tensions generated by Civil Rights sit-ins and the intimidation and lynchings that preceded them. When in the South, I still lived by Musie's rules: Stick close to home, travel in the company of others, and avoid strangers, especially white ones.

A sound plan would keep us safe, I hoped, and so I charted every detail—flight, car, hotel, meals. Perched in front of my laptop, I searched with a sixth sense about where we'd be at ease, out of harm's way. By "we," I mean me and my husband, a seasoned historian who occasionally signs on as my research assistant. But the fear was mine alone. Jean is tall, pleasant-looking, amiable, gray-haired, French—and white. He was an accomplice on this mission to unearth untold stories in Black family history, but I knew he need not pass. I also knew that, given the shade of my skin, there was a chance I might not.

We woke the first morning in a Shaker village that had been restored to nineteenth-century authenticity. I felt at ease but did not yet know that some of Kentucky's Shakers had kept slaves. Our first stop was a short ride away at downtown Danville's public library. Established in the 1890s, it was a place Nancy's daughters had known of, though they had never stepped inside. (The city's *other* first library—for Black patrons and named for poet Paul Laurence Dunbar—I later learned, was open only from 1919 to 1922.) Just inside, I paused under the domed rotunda and pretended to admire this ambitious addition to the original structure. Really I was finding my courage. The library's color line had been done away with long before, and still, my stomach knotted. I made my way to the Kentucky Room, home to a local history collection. Its shelves of dark wood, walls of deep teal, and subtle lighting all said, "We honor our past." There I immediately met a librarian—youthful, in jeans, bespectacled—who believed she was eager to help.

Words like "family," "great-great-great-grandmother," and "slave" spilled out, a near jumble. I slowed just enough to introduce myself and my husband as historians. Jean and the librarian discovered a shared interest in travel and began to trade adventures. With the reassuring sound of their warm exchange in my ears, I turned microfilm reels, rifled book-lined shelves, and skimmed newspapers. Jean eventually settled in at an adjacent desk and methodically reviewed city directories. We didn't turn up much that was new, however, and I thought it time to be more direct.

Up from my seat, I found the librarian at work nearby and interrupted. "She called herself Nancy Bell," I started. And then clarified, "Bell was not her given name, as in the name of her own parents." Here I simplified, not having much idea at all about who Nancy's people had been. There was no reaction, so I continued, "Bell was the name of the family that enslaved her." I needed help, I tried to say, to understand Nancy's connection to merchant David Bell and his wife Martha Fry Bell. What I did not say was that I wanted to understand my connection to them too.

At my mention of the Bells, the librarian, still behind her desk, got up and then paused for several long seconds. Jean approached us and stood just to my right. I felt expectant and thought she was about to reveal a new key to my search. But I misunderstood. Instead, the librarian drew a long breath, looked into my eyes, leaned in slightly, and deliberately whispered, "Now, be careful." I didn't grasp her meaning but felt the singe of her intensity. "What you're saying implicates some of Danville's most important families." I was puzzled and glanced over at my husband as if to say, "Do you understand what's happening here?" The librarian continued, "Be careful, now, who you talk with about this." I stammered out, "Thanks," but I was shaken.

I'd known Nancy had been enslaved by the Bells. What shook me was meeting up with a librarian who thought she knew more. Without uttering the precise words, she let me know that Nancy might have been a blood relation to the Bells. My presence—and the history it pointed to—sent an unsettling current through the calm of the Kentucky Room, which in turn unsettled me. Was I right to come to Danville? What if my professional demeanor would not shield me from the past or from those guarding it in the present? I stayed only a few minutes more before I signaled to Jean that it was time to pack up. We headed out from the library's shadowed cool into the glare of a warm midday sun. I carried with me new questions and a new awareness about Nancy, her color, and whom she called family.

———

As far back as I can know, my people have been caught up along the jagged color line. Snatched by its teeth—that endless line of gleaming menace, ragged and razor-sharp like the blade of a handsaw—its bends leaving a kerf and then a scar. We've trodden gingerly, approached, even attempted to climb clean over it. Allure has pulled us close to the deep cuts; we've backed away, put distance between our thin skin and a blade designed to skin us alive. We've skipped, hopped, and danced an awkward two-step. Some of us have briefly waltzed. Pens in hand, we've sometimes redrawn the line, at least a short span of it. It has been a journey harrowing and confused, cruel and seductive, personal and perniciously public. We played possum and trickster, stood wide-eyed and defiant, while tragedy in its many guises tracked us, looking to take us out. Approaching the line, I am tethered to the generations before me by ambiguous and even unspoken beginnings—expressed in skin too light, features too fine, hair too limp. I am the heir of misunderstanding, misapprehension, and mistaken identity. Who do I think I am? To begin, I am a daughter of Nancy.

ONE

Family

It was not in the Southland that one could hope
to keep a secret! And the niggers, of course, didn't
try, though they knew their white brothers and
sisters and papas, and watched them, daily, strut-
ting around in their white skins.

—James Baldwin, *No Name in the Street*

I WAS SHAKEN AFTER HOURS SPENT ON THE SEARCH FOR NANCY
in the Danville public library. Nothing had prepared me
for a librarian who discouraged me from digging deeper into
my great-great-great-grandmother's past. During the rest of
that visit to central Kentucky I retraced Nancy's steps. I slowly
steered my car along the winding streets of Duncan Hill, peer-
ing into yards and gardens, only to realize that no sign remains
of the small plot and house that Nancy and her husband,
Edmund, had once called home.

I hoped for better luck at Hilldale Cemetery. I stalked its
acres of sloping green lawns until finally I spied the ornate
monolith that marks her resting place. Back in town, I paced

back and forth out front, then stepped through the shrubs and looked into a ground-floor window of the redbrick, two-story house in which Nancy had been held captive during much of her younger life. I snapped a photo of the nearby historical marker: "The Watts-Bell House circa 1816–1817, was built by William Watts for leading Danville merchant David Bell." David Bell was husband to Nancy's owner, Martha Fry Bell, I remembered. Back in my rental car, I scribbled across the pages of my notebook, jotting down these small glimpses of Nancy's past. I hoped they would add up.

I'd have to rely on Danville's official paper trail if I wanted to make sense of what little I had found. I was distrustful and wondered if I could rely on the men and women who had long ago recorded their stories—on church ledgers, in courthouse folios, in the chapters of local histories, and even between the covers of popular novels. These storytellers had written with their own rather than Nancy's interests in mind. I might rely on their writings, but I needed to resist the pull of their recollections and instead listen for Nancy. I made a promise to her and to myself: I would wade in cautiously and read between the lines until I understood what family meant to her.

The pages of a small twenty-four-page pamphlet were my first window on the world into which Nancy was born. *Slavery Inconsistent with Justice and Good Policy* was authored by the head of the First Presbyterian Church of Danville, the Reverend David Rice. Historians before me, I knew, had admired Rice for his opposition to slavery during a constitutional convention, the first held in the new state of Kentucky in 1792. That spring, Rice stepped to his pulpit with assurance. His home sanctuary, the town's largest venue, was filled with forty-five lawmakers. Among them were Rice's allies: a small faction of antislavery ministers. Still, to speak at a political convention was new for Rice. He mustered enough force to be heard in every corner and above the din of men brokering side deals during the proceedings. His message was clear: Slavery wrecked families and corrupted everyone it touched. It should be abolished by the new constitution, Rice urged.

While he ministered in Danville, Rice learned that nobody there much respected the color line when it came to intimacies. He presided as local households came to church for rituals like admissions, baptisms, and burials. He observed that slavery most degraded the women among them: No one suffered more than "a virtuous woman," and that included "virtuous Africans," who valued their "chastity above every other thing." Rice described a sordid scene in which lawmakers and slaveholders colluded to leave "the chastity of a female slave entirely in the power of her master." Nancy did not herself read Rice's account. But she knew its facts, having heard them from the enslaved women around her. She saw evidence of it written on her own skin. Buried deep in her gut, Nancy lived with a terror that Rice only alluded to: Women like her had "no remedy . . . to redress this insufferable grievance. . . . [They were] denied every small privilege of complaining." Force was ubiquitous in early Kentucky, and against it, women like Nancy and her mother before her had no defense.

Rice was equally frank about how slaveholding men fathered "children by their own slaves, by their fathers' slaves, or the slaves of their neighbors." "How," he taunted, "is the number of Mulattoes increasing in every part of the land?" Family might be a meaningless term in Kentucky, where a "father will have their own children for slaves . . . men will possess their brothers and sisters as their property, have their grey-headed uncles and aunts for slaves, [and] call them their property." A perverse confusion shaped the world into which Nancy was born: "A hard-hearted master will not know whether he has a blood relation, a brother or a sister, an uncle or an aunt, or a stranger of African [descent], under his scourging hand."

When born later, in 1808, Nancy was the child of a mother whose place in a Danville family the Reverend Rice may have understood. That woman, my four times great-grandmother, bequeathed to her new daughter deep-set eyes, a long, narrow chin, and a destiny: Nancy became the newest member of a troubled family in central Kentucky. On the day of her birth, Nancy's mother likely listened for the baby's first cry and then counted fingers and toes. "It's a girl," the woman who attended her uttered. Did anyone remark on the newborn's color? Did they use words like *light*, *bright*, or *nearly white*? There was no need to speak of Danville's open secret: In many households, people crossed the color line. Nancy's birth marked the start of the next chapter during which she too would fend for herself.

—

The Reverend Rice never knew Nancy. But the clergy who inherited his congregation did. A clerk kept the First Presbyterian ledgers, day by day, and recorded who came and who went, who was baptized and buried, who broke the rules and who enforced them. I sat at my computer in the dark, zoomed in on the digitized pages, and squinted to make out the handwriting. It's the sort of work that feels like gambling, the turn of each page a pull of a slot-machine arm. I held my breath and hoped to get lucky. And there she was—the woman whose face mine resembles—noted in ink on paper. Nancy had joined the congregation on the second Sunday of July 1827. She was nineteen, barely a woman, when she stepped out of the Sabbath-day sun and into the cool of a redbrick sanctuary. It was a new day, one that would define her life as a budding Christian. Nancy took her place among the hopeful who sought to formalize a binding covenant with the Lord.

How Nancy made her way to First Presbyterian, the clerk's notes do not say. Likely she did so with the encouragement of Martha Fry Bell, the woman who held Nancy as property. Martha was the daughter of a Virginia slaveholder who'd settled in central Kentucky, made his wealth as a farmer, sealed his reputation as an educator, and, when he died, willed to Martha and his other children his bounty in people. Once a married woman, Martha was the first of her clan to join First Presbyterian; her mother and siblings became members only later. Before them, Nancy was the first to follow Martha and become a convert who, with her baptism, satisfied her soul's cravings. At the same time, Nancy fulfilled Martha's obligation as a church member in good standing. The governing Presbyterian synod directed slaveholding members to ensure that their bondspeople became full-fledged Christians. This was a response to the charge that to hold people as property contradicted religious values. Nancy had her own spiritual commitments, while her study of Presbyterian tenets and rituals also served Martha.

Admission to First Presbyterian demanded that seekers do more than sit on a bench. Nancy braced herself that Sunday, ready to be tested alongside eight other candidates, and stood out as the single slave. When her turn came, Nancy rose. I can imagine her there, still young, slight, and unaccustomed to speaking in public. Nancy gathered herself and recited in response to the minister's demand that she make a "public profession" of her "knowledge and piety," as church law required. She sealed her very own covenant with Christ and looked on as the clerk inscribed her name in First Presbyterian's broad, leather-bound ledger. Her baptism followed that fall. She'd joined a new family, one knit together by faith.

As he noted Nancy's progress toward membership, I could see that the clerk puzzled over how to add her name to his register. Most entries identified members with two names: a family name preceded by a first, or Christian, name. But Nancy had joined First Presbyterian with only one: Nancy. How, the clerk had to ponder, should he distinguish this Nancy from others of the same name? Most days he dipped his quill in ink with authority, marked day by day the congregation's events. But on this day he hesitated and took another long look at the ledger's layout. His was the official record, one that the leaders of First Presbyterian would refer to for generations to come. What he did next was improvise: He noted her as "Nancy _____ (Bell)," and in the column for the names of her parents, he wrote, "Colored." A blank space, parentheses, and a color designation qualified Nancy's connection to the Bells. She

Nancy Bell, baptismal record, First Presbyterian Church of Danville, circa 1827

came to be known as Nancy Bell, a new name that positioned her closer than ever to Martha but also held the two apart.

Nothing in the clerk's ledger reveals what congregants saw when they witnessed Nancy and Martha together. Some details are easily assumed. Both women dressed in their respectable best, long skirts, with hems and shoes wearing the dust of unpaved walkways. Martha's fabrics finer, her skirt longer, her jewelry flashing status. Surely a gesture passed between them when Nancy was baptized. Perhaps Martha embraced Nancy and held her close for a moment. They may have clasped hands. Martha may have sent a deep nod of approval to Nancy across the sanctuary. Harder to know is whether they nestled into a shared bench or sat apart. Did Nancy stiffen when Martha neared, or did her ease admit their familiarity? Were their tones warm or perfunctory? I cannot say whether the two women lingered to visit after the service, one among the free and the other among the enslaved congregants. Headed out, did they walk arm in arm or at a distance? Were their heads bent together as they exchanged whispers in a plan for the afternoon's meal?

What the ledger does admit is that the spiritual companionship of Nancy and Martha was brief. It splintered just ten months after Nancy's baptism. Her exit from First Presbyterian caused the clerk to return to his ledger: "Nancy _____ Bell joined Methodist Church." Nancy abandoned her commitment to the Presbyterians, though not to God. Going forward, Martha and Nancy went separate ways on Sundays, one to First Presbyterian and the other to the makeshift Methodist sanctuary in Danville's old courthouse. The two women continued to share the Bell family name. As for the clerk, his final entry for Nancy was as ambiguous as his first: He dropped the parentheses that set "Bell" apart from "Nancy" on the page but inserted between her names a simple blank line. This was how the clerk explained Nancy's connection to Martha and the Bells.

—

I turned to early Danville storytellers, historians among them, and hoped that they might complete a portrait of Nancy's early years. They had largely ignored her and women like her, I learned, and instead featured the lives of men who had added shine to a small town often overshadowed by cities like Lexington and Louisville. There was physician Ephraim McDowell, who pioneered a surgical procedure that successfully removed ovarian tumors; to this day, medical annals admire his innovation. Writers recounted how Presbyterian minister John Clarke

Young arrived to rescue Danville's Centre College from fiscal troubles and headed the state's governing Presbyterian synod. James Birney, once a member of Danville's First Presbyterian, was celebrated as a journalist, American Anti-Slavery Society member, and two-time Liberty Party candidate for president in the 1840s. When stories about these men noted enslaved people in Danville, they were mere shadows. Readers might never realize that slaves and slaveholders lived together, walked near one another along hard-baked dirt streets, and prayed alongside each other in the city's most important houses of worship.

One figure I'd expected to find was absent from these histories: Supreme Court Justice John Marshall Harlan. He was arguably the most distinguished figure to grow up in early Danville, but Harlan hardly ever appeared in official chronicles. His family was prominent but also troubled. The justice's father had risen from local attorney to Kentucky secretary of state. The future high court justice was born just five miles outside the city in 1813 and attended the local Centre College before studying law. Harlan's years of political leadership, military enlistment, and public service won him, in 1877, appointment to the US Supreme Court, where he served for over two decades. Wasn't his just the sort of local-boy-makes-good story that Danville's boosters would have promoted?

I dug deeper and discovered the catch: Harlan's family. His father had another son—an enslaved boy—born to a woman said to have been "three-quarters white." This boy was raised in his prominent father's home, regarded more as a son than as property. The Harlan family tripped over the color line when, for example, as a youth, the boy was deemed too Black to attend a local school with his brothers, much to his father's disappointment. To the eye, the child might have been regarded as white enough. But to some in Danville, he was also too Black.

Historian Bernie Jones helped me understand that the Harlan family was not exceptional. Records in Kentucky's local courthouses include law-office depositions and trial testimony about enslaved women, their children, and their entanglements with slaveholding men. Skin mattered; it was evidence. A Nelson County jury enforced an 1823 will that favored Narcissa, the daughter of an enslaved woman and a white man, a "mulatto" whose skin confirmed her parents' illicit union. Polly McMinnis claimed to be free despite having been sold as a slave in 1804. She too offered a jury her appearance as evidence and led the court to conclude that "a person apparently white" may, nevertheless, have some "African blood in the veins." Color was one sign of who might be related to whom in central Kentucky.

In Nancy's generation, neither color nor status defined kinship, and judges in Kentucky honored complicated relations. In an 1814 Scott County case, a man who owned Grace and her children freed them all by his will. Grace was named his sole heir, inheritor of his wealth. The deceased's white family members asserted that he had been insane and his will was invalid. Grace insisted that he had not been of unsound mind, and the court agreed: Men "who may wish to marry negro women, or who carry on illicit intercourse with them" could competently execute valid wills. The court was reluctant to upend these all-too-familiar arrangements. Look around, the court urged: Children reared "by a slave without marriage" were "too common, as we all know, from the numbers of our mulatto population."

Narcissa. Polly. Grace. Their color spoke directly to judges about how family worked in central Kentucky. These same sorts of stories shaped everyday thinking on the streets of Danville. Locals came upon Nancy and Martha headed to church or to market, looked the two up and down, and wondered, "Who are they to one another?" Some signs suggested a difference in their status. Clothing and demeanor gave away who was enslaved and who was free. But that wasn't all. People studied their features, their builds, the shades of their skin and then filled in the rest. Resemblances between Martha and Nancy would have been evidence of their kinship. How were they related? Their ages made it unlikely that Martha and Nancy were mother and daughter. Perhaps they shared a father, the two being sisters. Nancy could have been the child of Martha's brother, which would have made them aunt and niece. None of this was wild speculation in Danville.

So much of the historical record was written with silence. If I was going to get closer to Nancy, to her point of view, I'd need to tap another sort of insight. I knew novelists had tried to imagine how women like Nancy saw the world. They went to the heart of what made places like Danville so troubled and invented a protagonist: the tragic mulatto. She was a mixed-race woman, light in appearance, and enslaved. Her white lover's promises of liberty, fidelity, and happiness often were stolen by a world cruelly committed to her demise. An early version of this story landed in Kentucky parlors in 1841, when Louisville's *Courier-Journal* enticed its readers to pick up Joseph Hold Ingraham's *The Quadroone*. Ingraham did not write with Nancy in mind exactly. It's more accurate to say that he hoped to attract white women readers with spectacle and intrigue. Ingraham's pages titillated and indulged deeply held fantasies. He might, if effective, also arouse sympathy for lives wrecked by deceptions of color and status.

In Boston, Lydia Maria Child published her 1842 short story "The Quadroons" in the hope of converting readers to the antislavery cause. Her tale turned on the fate of Xarifa, the daughter of a white merchant, and her mother, Rosalie, herself the child of a white man and an enslaved woman. Innocents, Xarifa and Rosalie exhibit cultivation, grace, pure minds, and fair skin. Rosalie is also, for a time, fortunate in love and bears her daughter under the affectionate protection of her lover. But Xarifa's father abandons the two for marriage and fortune, leaving Rosalie and her daughter alone. Too soon, Rosalie dies of a broken heart and shattered spirit. Her father steps in for a time to raise Xarifa before he too perishes from a potent mix of grief and drink. Xarifa suffers until she too dies.

What did Danville's locals see when they met Nancy at the door of the Bell home, on errands at a Main Street dry-goods store, on a Sunday stroll from church, or as she hauled food-stuffs back from market? Their eyes told them a lot but not everything. What they couldn't make out, the fictions of writers like Ingraham and Child permitted them to imagine. Did they wonder what sort of tragedy awaited Nancy? Did their sympathies bend just a bit in her direction? For her part, Nancy was no fictional character, and when aimed in her direction, the idle pity of others was its own form of cruelty.

—

My last stop on that first visit to Danville was the Boyle County Courthouse. It's hard to miss given its prominent Main Street location. When I first entered, I could not know that I was following in the long-ago steps of Martha Fry Bell, who had visited the place in 1853. I bumped into her traces after I stepped up to the clerk's chest-height counter and asked about where I might search for family stories. Busy with other duties, she cocked her head of teased blond hair to the right, in the direction of shelves filled with oversized, fabric-covered binders. I pulled down an 1850s deed book and needed two hands to manage its weight. Almost immediately, I landed on

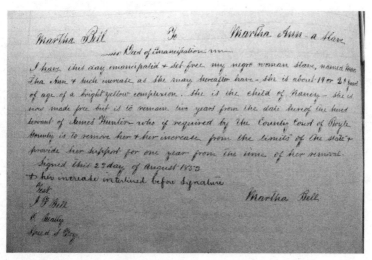

Martha Ann, manumission, 1853

a single-page document, a deed of manumission for Nancy's oldest daughter, a young woman named Martha Ann.

With that page in my hand, I held as much terror and as much hope as I ever had. The document set out how the law separated Nancy from her daughter—terror—and how that same daughter would never again be held enslaved—hope. I stood still and felt my own twoness: elated to discover a small bit about how Martha Ann and Nancy had lived and knocked over by this raw evidence of their years in bondage. I closed my eyes to shut out the clerks' chatter, a friendly mix of gossip and business, and silently prayed for their futures, not sure what came next for Nancy or for Martha Ann.

The document read like a bloodless transcript of a soulless transaction. If I hadn't known better, I might have overlooked its high stakes: Martha Ann's very freedom. Martha Fry Bell had stood before the court clerk with her son, son-in-law, and a nephew and described Nancy's daughter: "About 19 or 20 years of age. . . . Of a bright yellow complexion." Like her mother's, Martha Ann's skin was a sign of troubled origins. She was known as the property of Martha Fry Bell, while she was also her mother's child—"She is the child of Nancy"—distinguishable from others of the same name by that fact. The clerk recorded the bargain that led to this courthouse appearance: a negotiation with a local physician, James Hunter. Hunter had named his price: In exchange for her liberty, Martha Ann would "remain two years from the date hereof" his "hired servant." He was a widower with two small children at home; Martha Ann might provide for their care.

The businesslike terms of Martha Ann's manumission covered up the fears that may have led Nancy and her daughter to see life with Hunter as a best way forward. Martha Ann's niece and Nancy's granddaughter Fannie—my great-grandmother—hinted at this much later, in the 1940s. Fannie spoke with a magazine writer about her own life as an educator and activist but also recalled her grandmother Nancy, who, she explained, had "raised seven daughters in slavery shielding them as best she could from the abuses of that institution." Her words were genteel, but Fannie's meaning was clear: Nancy had striven to protect her daughters from sexual exploitation. In Martha Ann's case, this meant that Nancy encouraged an arrangement that released her daughter from Martha Fry Bell's control and sent her into James Hunter's home as a free woman.

The agreement with Hunter was risky, in law and in practice. Kentucky authorities had the right to require Martha Ann, as a freed slave, to leave the state. Hunter knew this and promised to support Martha Ann if she was forced to depart from Kentucky. She had good reason to fear separation from her family, especially those like Nancy who continued to be enslaved. Once in the Hunter household, Martha Ann was subjected to sexual demands. James Hunter had lost his first wife in 1851 and remarried only in 1858. During Hunter's seven unmarried years, Martha Ann adopted his family name and gave birth to three girls—Julia, Martha Ann, and Louisa—also called Hunter. These events read like the start of a tragedy authored by a writer like Lydia Maria Child, but the misfortune that followed mostly befell Hunter.

It was a tumultuous seven years. After the birth of Martha Ann's first child, Hunter's congregation at First Presbyterian found him guilty of "walking disorderly," a charge that covered a range of sinful offenses, including fornication, or sex outside marriage. Hunter was dismissed from the church. When Martha Ann's second daughter was born, Hunter attempted to right his standing in Danville and placed notices in a local paper: He was "determined to remain in Danville," where he would "devote his attention entirely to the practice of the various branches of his profession." Martha Ann gave birth to her third child in 1857. The following year, Hunter recommitted to an orderly life and married a local widow. Still, his prospects in Danville dissolved, and in 1860, Hunter packed up his household—which included his new wife and children from his first marriage—and migrated hundreds of miles to the south, landing in Texas. Martha Ann and her daughters remained in Danville, where they were never far from Nancy and other relations.

Martha Ann's manumission was laced with uncertainty, but in her case, hadn't the risk been worth it? Hunter left town, while she and her daughters remained behind to begin a new chapter. They bore signs of their time with Hunter on their skin and in their surnames. But this did not define Martha Ann and her girls. They lived decades thereafter in Nancy's company, time enough for all three granddaughters to grow into womanhood before Nancy died in 1889. Like her mother, Martha Ann lived many years and, at eighty, still shared her downtown East Green Street home with her daughter Louise.

When Martha Ann died in 1914, her younger sister Susan completed the death certificate. Susan went to see Danville's Black undertaker, Edward Murrell, at his parlor in the United Brothers of Friendship Hall, which hosted the town's Black fraternal orders. Together Susan and Murrell prepared the official record. It included Martha Ann's vital statistics—born in 1833, daughter of Nancy. Susan made sure that her sister was identified as "Mrs." She added that Martha Ann was a widow. Kentucky, Susan knew, had never allowed legal ties between James Hunter and Martha Ann. Still, Susan made certain her sister's story was recorded just as Martha Ann would have told it: For a time, she and her girls had considered James Hunter kin, bound together by a bargain, by everyday bonds, and by blood.

—

I went back to Nancy's portrait. I lifted it close to my face, looked as deeply as I could into her eyes. I reread the note written in Aunt Tuppy's hand: Nancy had had "7 girls." I remembered Fannie's memory of how Nancy had labored to keep those daughters safe. These clues let me better see the love, fear, and shrewdness that had driven her. But seven daughters? I stumbled. The number seven did not fit with what I had on my family tree. There Nancy had only four girls. For all the time I'd spent digging in official records, I could not name seven. They had never appeared on early census returns or county death certificates. Had first Fannie and then Tuppy guessed or even exaggerated the number of Nancy's daughters? Had they chosen the figure seven in a literary flourish? Seven is, after all, in the Bible an expression of fullness or abundance. Seven could have been a metaphor that remembered Nancy as rich in family, even as she lived a humble existence.

I'd arrived at a crossroads. The historian in me knew well how to rely on the recollections of clerks, census takers, and petty officials. New for me was to listen to the women in my family like Fannie and Tuppy. Which source should carry more weight? Not the record keepers. If they'd ever met Nancy, they had done so only in passing. Their reports—callous and fragmentary—satisfied only the demands of blanks on a form or statistical tables. Fannie, in contrast, had known Nancy for decades during her growing-up years in Danville. She had never met her great-grandmother, but Tuppy had inherited Nancy's stories as later told to her by her mother and grandmother. They were repeated countless times at funerals, while they rocked on the porch, and as they gazed at her single portrait. I joined them when I looked at the same photograph. It was time for me to really listen to these women.

I could not fully account for Nancy's seven daughters if I was not willing to also confront loss. I would need to grieve their absences—three girls nearly lost to me. In her own time, Nancy, I was sure, had understood her own bereavement: preceded by death, disappearance, defection, or the fragilities of small ones barely born. She'd seen children—her own or those of others—bartered, bequeathed, and given over to the auction block. Nancy had hidden her grief away, beyond the sight of record-keeping men whose callousness blinded them to her sadness. Those same men crassly marked her losses in checks, ticks, and statistics. I stared into the chasm that separated

Nancy's time from mine. Its vastness was defined by what I could not know. It was just a start, but I returned to the hundreds of entries on my family tree, and under Nancy's name, I added three "unknown" daughters, a small remembrance of the ones almost forgotten.

——

Nancy's companion through much of her adult life was Edmund Graves. She told their story, one way and another. It depended upon who asked. In one version, Nancy had married Edmund before a Presbyterian minister around 1845. The ritual was not recognized in law but united Nancy and Edmund before their God. At other times, Nancy retold her marriage to Edmund as a freedom story. In 1868, three years after slavery's abolition, the two had appeared at the Boyle County Courthouse and legalized their partnership. The clerk's record told the whole story: "Edm[u]nd Graves and Nancy Graves . . . declared that they have lived together as husband and wife for the past 22 years, and still desire to continue living together as such." Each signed the declaration of marriage with an "X." Unable to read or write, Nancy and Edmund relied upon a printed form and a clerk to record their story.

Edmund was the only man whom Nancy ever claimed as a husband. Before him, she'd had children with other men. One named Penman was father to her oldest children, and a man named Davenport was father to another. I do not know much at all about these men, and Nancy herself never made a record of who they were to her. Her children, however, kept their fathers' names and memories alive. They also passed down recollections of those men to their children. When, for example, Nancy's daughter Susan died, her daughter named Nancy as Susan's mother and Berry Penman as Susan's father. In Nancy's family, not everyone told the same story.

Nancy thought hard about how to tell this story before officials. Her application for Edmund's Civil War pension, preserved all these years by the National Archives, let me see just how she strategized. There, she explained their family, all the while knowing that widows of Black soldiers and sailors faced exceptional scrutiny when claiming compensation for a husband's service to the nation. Pension officials imposed on Nancy and women like her a brand of racism and sexism that assumed they were not chaste, true to marriage vows, or honest. Nancy told a carefully crafted story, one she hoped would win what was due to her.

Edmund had been dead six years when Nancy finally resolved to claim her widow's pension. A quarter century before, he had been discharged from the 123rd US Colored Infantry, Company H. In Danville, anyone who knew the couple also knew the basic facts: Edmund died more than three decades after his discharge, and Nancy became his widow. Nothing was due her in old age from the family of Martha Fry Bell despite the many years she had spent as an uncompensated slave. Nancy needed a war pension to survive the later years of her life. She knew she'd need help if her application was to succeed.

Nancy hired a Baltimore-based firm, E. H. Gelston & Co., one of the country's more notorious pension brokers. "Pensions for soldiers, any disease, wound or injury. Widow and children entitled. Fee $10," read the firm's ad in the *Louisville Courier*. The promise was deceptively simple. Nancy couldn't know that just a couple of years later, in 1883, the US secretary of the interior would nearly disbar the firm for having put forward "false and fraudulent pension claims." The commissioner of pensions interrogated its sole proprietor, attorney Emma H. Gelston, who had inherited the business from her father. Despite how the firm had disappointed veterans and their families, former slaves among them, the company survived the review.

For Nancy, representation by Gelston & Co. got her closer to Washington and a chance to win what was due her as Edmund's widow. She'd rely on the firm to file the paperwork and reply to follow-up questions as they arose. The forms included more queries than Nancy was accustomed to, at least all at once. It seemed to be on the up-and-up; officials demanded the same particulars of all claimants. Still, there was nothing straightforward about the insistence that Nancy recite details about her family. Those matters she ordinarily protected from scrutiny, tucked away close to her heart.

For help with the initial paperwork, Nancy headed to the Boyle County Courthouse, where she'd get help from the clerk. It wasn't a place she knew well, but it was a place that knew her. Shards of her life were stored in the clerk's boxes and folders: her daughter Martha Ann's manumission, her marriage to Edmund, and a deed to the house and lot the two owned on Duncan Hill. Older papers had survived after an 1860 fire had destroyed the structure. By 1862, a new edifice lorded over Main Street: red bricks, white trim, a Corinthian portico, and a two-story clock tower that rivaled nearby churches with its architectural majesty. That same courthouse had been pressed into service as a hospital for those wounded in the battle of Perryville. For years after the war, lynch mobs did their dirty work—terrorizing Black residents with night raids that ended in murder—at the courthouse and the adjacent jail.

Nancy knew that it was better not to enter the courthouse alone. She arrived in the company of men who knew her and Edmund well: two Civil War veterans, one of whom had served with Edmund in the 123rd. Each promised to vouch for the story Nancy was about to tell. They stood before the clerk while Nancy recited the details of her family and the clerk filled in blanks with an elegant script. Nancy explained that Edmund had served in Kentucky's 123rd Regiment. The two had married for the first time in 1845. They had lived as one for thirty years, she told the clerk. Edmund had died in April 1875, of pneumonia.

The application form provided a space in which claimants could list children. Ordinarily it was used to report those under sixteen, as minors might also have a pension claim. In Nancy's case, her boys and girls were already grown men and women. Still, she directed someone to record four names: Mary Frances, Nannie, Marshall, and Woodson, born between 1846 and 1852. Woodson, a marginal note indicated, had since died. The hand of an unnamed third person, not the clerk, worked with Nancy to record these details. Satisfied, she marked her signature with an unsteady "X." Edmund's veteran friends did the same, each swearing to the truth of Nancy's words.

Nancy Bell Graves, application for the veteran's
pension of Edmund Graves, 1881

Everyone knew there was more to Nancy's family than her
pension application admitted. Between her and Edmund, there
were four children, yes. But Nancy had at least ten others that
she did not report, some with fathers named Penman and Davenport. Nancy did not open that door for officials who would
likely ask questions. They would somehow judge her unchaste
and unworthy of Edmund's benefits. She did not conceal her
children out of shame. Instead, Nancy told the story she needed
to tell.

It is not clear why federal officials in the end denied Nancy's application. No one disputed that Edmund had served honorably, and the War Department confirmed just that. He had performed "garrison duty" inside Camp Nelson, rather than in the field, for a full year between 1864 and 1865. The Danville court clerk confirmed that by law, Nancy had been Edmund's wife since 1868. Still, her claim dragged on for years, and eventually, clerks in Washington stamped contradictory verdicts like "ABANDONED" and "REJECTED" on the case record. Gelston & Co. blamed Nancy and implied that she hadn't satisfied the government's "requirements." She never received Edmund's pension, as if they'd never been family at all.

—

Ormond Beatty did me a favor. He was a son-in-law to Martha Fry Bell and, by way of inheritance after her death, became the last person to own Nancy and her family before slavery was abolished. Raised by a slaveholding lawmaker and judge in Mason County, Beatty migrated to Danville to attend college. He made his career as a professor at Centre College and became a highly regarded church leader and educator—a font of wisdom and experience. Late in his life, a local columnist said of Beatty, "A man of varied and profound learning, of acute logical powers, whose whole life has been devoted to the advancement of mankind and of all good works." This assessment overlooked Beatty's many years as a slaveholder, an enterprise that was the best source of his wealth.

That late-nineteenth-century news columnist was not alone in looking away, even when evidence of Beatty's slaveholding was plain to see. I encountered a version of this when I approached the Centre College archives. Beatty's papers are preserved there, and in an email, I asked whether there was any mention of Nancy or her family among those records. The archivist's reply was initially promising: "I am familiar with the Beatty papers. . . . Since we aren't talking about an enormous volume of material, I would be happy to go through the letters to see if there is any mention of slaves or former slaves." After he took a closer look, the archivist wrote again: "[I] didn't find any direct mention of [your family] names." Even then I doubted that there was no trace of Nancy among Beatty's records, but there was no way to second-guess the archivist from a distance.

Since Nancy's time, Danville has proudly been the home of Centre College. Founded in 1819, the school has educated generations of Kentuckians, including men who in Ormond Beatty's time went on to lead in politics. Adjacent to downtown and sprawled across two hundred acres, the campus rolls across greens dotted with red brick and white trim. Its original building, dubbed today "Old Centre," stands carefully restored. Outside the library towers a bronze likeness of Abraham Lincoln, installed in 2012, though Lincoln had no special connection to Danville or Centre. The school is still working through its Civil War–era contradictions; it was occupied by Confederate troops and had students who joined the fight on both sides.

My exchange with the Centre College archivist gnawed at me. I knew from experience that there was no substitute for my own look at the Beatty papers. Often even seasoned library staff are no match for a motivated descendant when it comes to combing through letters, notebooks, and ledgers. I was that descendant, willing to look under each and every rock for Nancy. I finally tested this theory a decade later. In 2022, I showed up at Centre College to look through materials shelved under Beatty's name. I was the only researcher that day in the special collections room; a new archivist greeted me. I set up in a small room with glass walls and shelves crammed with books and papers. Equally crowded worktables filled the space. I was dressed in layers, prepared for a room that was overheated or over-air-conditioned. This room was just right, which let me get immediately to work. I laid my laptop, phone, notebook, and pencil out in front of me and leafed methodically through three boxes, mostly letters written to Beatty, arranged in nearly fifty folders. There was no sign of Nancy or her family, and I was almost ready to concede that the archivist's email from years before had been right.

A final box—gray, constructed of sturdy acid-free cardboard—sat next to the front desk. It was, I knew, a last chance to discover something of Nancy's ties to Beatty. I picked it up, felt that it was heavier than the others, and set it down on my worktable. I lifted the lid and looked down at Ormond Beatty's account books: leather-bound ledgers—covers flaking with age—that meticulously chronicled his personal and business dealings. I forced myself to slow down, suppressing the urge to quickly rifle through. I needed to proceed painstakingly, page by page.

I said that Ormond Beatty did me a favor; he did it in the pages of his ledgers. There he wrote about Nancy, though not with the sweeping generalizations that the Reverend Rice had used in his speech. Neither did Beatty paint florid images of tragic heroines, as had writers like Lydia Maria Child. Beatty meticulously tracked Nancy and her family for more than two decades, from the end of the Civil War until his death in 1890. Along columns and rows, he recorded their comings and goings, their debts and credits, and their hopes and disappointments. I stared a long time at a note in which Beatty summarized what he'd inherited from his mother-in-law, Martha Fry Bell: It included Nancy, Edmund, and their children and grandchildren. Beatty made certain to note their dollar value, a hint about how my family mattered to him most.

Nearly every day over decades, Beatty opened a ledger, pen in hand. Sometimes he recorded household expenses or transactions with local merchants. He marked down fees paid for services and gifts to his children. The pages of his largest ledgers, eight by ten inches, included headings with the names of people, most of them former slaves. Nancy and her family were there. After emancipation, many of them worked in and around Beatty's household. He fastidiously wrote down every cent they earned, along with every penny they owed. I turned to a page titled "Betty. Colored." Beatty managed the woman's moneys and financed the last months of her life in fall 1867: "Paid Tinah for medicines for [Betty]. $10.00." "Paid Dr. Pawling medical services. $20.00." After Betty died, he noted, "Paid Absalom Proctor, digging grave. $3.00." The $55 Beatty paid to Nichols & McGrorty was likely for Betty's funeral casket and perhaps a headstone.

It took until 1871, but Beatty returned to Betty's page to finally settle her account. By then he was president of Centre

College. I pulled my chair closer to the table, used a lead weight to hold the book open, and focused. It was time to connect the dots and read between the lines. Beatty noted a balance due to Betty's family; he paid it to them that spring. Tinah, who'd bought Betty's medicines in 1867, was Betty's sister. She had approved the final settlement, Beatty noted. The balance due, he "divide[d] among the surviving sisters Tinah & Nancy." There she was, in Beatty's tiny script: my Nancy. How could I be sure it was she? Further down the page, Beatty wrote, "Credited to Edmund's ac[coun]t Nancy's portion." Beatty had paid Nancy's husband, Edmund, what was due her.

I gasped, though no one was there to hear me. I'd found Nancy mentioned along with Edmund and two women, Tinah and Betty, her sisters. It was as if a light had come on: I saw Nancy with new color and texture. For so long, my insights into her early life had come from the records of First Presbyterian, which had led me to imagine her alone or in the company of Martha Fry Bell. Now I could rewrite those scenes. There in Danville, Nancy had sisters, kin she'd always known. There she was, walking side by side with Tinah and Betty. On Sunday sitting shoulder to shoulder with them on a church bench. Wasn't it her sisters' gentle hands that tended to Nancy when her firstborn, Martha Ann, came into the world? Their words reassured Nancy when, as a young woman, Martha Ann became entangled with James Hunter. Tinah and Betty grew into women who didn't shy away from calling Nancy theirs and in turn encouraged Nancy to claim them. The sisters remained kin and companions through the end of Betty's life, at least.

I'd learned a lesson. Ten years earlier, an archivist had over-looked what was plainly written on the pages of Beatty's led-gers. Perhaps he'd looked only at the man's correspondence with family and business associates and not at Beatty's account books. Perhaps he'd got through most of them and, finding nothing, assumed the rest were similarly silent when it came to Nancy. Perhaps such ordinary names—Nancy, Susan, Edmund—made it difficult to distinguish which mentions were of members of my family. Many circumstances, includ-ing fatigue, distraction, and time limits, can explain how a researcher overlooks the evidence that is just before their eyes. If I was going to know all I could about Nancy, I'd need to be my most persistent self. This approach was already paying off, and I couldn't help but feel that somewhere Nancy was pleased to know that I was the first to find her and her sisters in the boxes and folders at Centre College.

I left the Centre College archives uneasily. I was thrilled to have discovered Nancy's sisters, Tinah and Betty, and had already schemed about how to learn more. Still, my chest was heavy and my mood dim as I slowly packed up my computer and note-book. I closed its lid and carried the box filled with Beatty's led-gers to the librarian's desk. She'd stepped away, which allowed me to slip out without a word. Back in my car, I watched as stu-dents crossed one way and the other: to class, the gym, a meal. Sadness overcame me. I regretted having abandoned precious traces of Nancy, Tinah, and Betty. I knew that the archivists had those traces carefully filed in acid-free containers and stored in a climate-controlled room. But that was no comfort. I'd left them behind, filed by a twisted logic under the name Ormond Beatty.

I discovered more about Tinah. At first her most distinguishing feature was the many ways she was named: There was Tinah, also spelled Tenah. Sometimes she was Tina and at others Christina. Her last name also varied; in some places she was known as Bell and in others as Miller. When she wrote her will in 1886, Tinah left her house and lot on Walnut Street to her son. To her daughter, Tinah left silver—a tray and a half-dozen teaspoons—along with bed quilts and clothes. Like her sister Betty, Tinah had funds held by Ormond Beatty, and she expected him to settle her account when she died: "I have some money in the hands of Prof. O. Beatty President of Centre College, for which I hold this note, this money I direct to be equally divided between my son . . . and daughter." Finally, Tinah named Beatty executor of her estate, a choice that left me to wonder if she would have been comfortable, more than I was, with notes about her past indexed under his name at Centre College. After all, he'd been the person Tinah had trusted most to manage her affairs after she was gone.

On this visit to Kentucky, I was alone and rented a small cottage at the restored Shaker Village that Jean and I had visited years before. I woke up early the next morning; the view out across the open fields was beautiful in the early light. I made a cup of instant coffee, wolfed down a bowl of cereal, and got on the road, headed north and west along I-64 to Kentucky's capital, Louisville, and the Filson Historical Society. What a contrast to the modest accommodations at Centre

College. The Filson reading room was posh: heavy, solid wood furniture; large windows that let in natural light; an arresting art collection that mixed early American with contemporary paintings. Filson is the repository that has long kept the records of Kentucky's elite. Among them are the papers of Martha Fry Bell's younger sister, who'd spent her married years as mistress of a nearby plantation, Oxmoor.

The papers generated by Oxmoor's occupants are vast. I went through folder after folder for hours at a time. I kept my focus and hoped that in their letters back and forth, Martha Fry Bell in Danville and her sister at Oxmoor had made mention of Nancy, Tinah, or Betty. My eyes strained to adjust to hurried handwriting, faded ink, and cryptic references that only the correspondents, long dead, understood. My hopes rose when a name finally jumped from a page: Tinah! She was an enslaved woman who worked at Oxmoor, and my thoughts raced: Might she be the same Tinah I knew as Nancy's sister? On a break, I spilled out my theory to an interested reading-room attendant who thought she could help: "You should visit Oxmoor," she urged. "It's still there." I made an appointment for the next day.

On a misty fall morning, I landed at a shopping mall of the same name before I found the plantation, or what today is called Oxmoor Farm. I turned off the public road and arrived at what looked like a slightly worn movie set (think *Gone with the Wind*). A long alley lane led up to a main house in the distance, a two-story brick home with a center-hall entrance flanked by east and west wings. To the left, not far off the circular drive, sat small cabins, their bricks and stones painted a gleaming white. They had once been homes to enslaved people and later free workers who for generations made Oxmoor run. I parked, looked out across the grounds, and felt my yearning surge. Was I closer than I'd ever been to solving the mysteries of Nancy's family?

I stepped into the wet cool and took my time walking toward the rear entrance. This was not my first visit to a plantation site. I'd toured many in Louisiana, Virginia, North Carolina, and Tennessee. But standing on the grounds at Oxmoor was different. I was not a removed researcher. I was not a curious tourist. Instead, I was looking for signs of my own family, and my eyes stung as I took in the terrible beauty of Oxmoor. Could I resist the effect of its potent blend of restored opulence and repressed terror?

The caretaker welcomed me into the main house, and we slowly explored bedchambers and parlors, the kitchen and dining room. The oversized library was its own visit—with light from wide floor-to-ceiling windows, bookcases nearly as high in every direction, painted in a deep blend of turquoise and teal. Polished floors, a deep fireplace, ornate woodwork, and candelabra-style chandeliers gave the vast space warmth. The library wing was a new addition to Oxmoor in 1928, I learned. It wasn't hard to imagine it filled with descendants of the plantation's nineteenth-century occupants: ice clinking in highball glasses, polite laughter, short speeches on happy occasions, and perhaps prayers during more solemn gatherings.

From my spot in the library, it wasn't possible to glimpse the slave cabins just outside. I muttered to myself, "Remember the blood on the page," a kernel of wisdom from historian Nell

Irvin Painter that generally reminded me that the documents I sometimes read, though neat and elegantly scripted, had their origins in brutal force. The same could be said of Oxmoor, and I recited in my head, *Remember the blood on the china, blood on the carpet, blood on the fine linens and pristine plaster walls.* Indoors at Oxmoor, enslaved people cooked, cleaned, and tended to the clothing and toilette of their owners, while outdoors, they maintained walks and gardens, cared for animals and equipment, and cultivated hemp from spring to fall. I presented my guide with a neutral face and resolved that I would not allow Oxmoor's luxury to obscure my ability to see that only the labor of women like Tinah made it possible.

I wasn't itching for a fight or a debate and needed to short-circuit my rising anger. It was time to get outside. The day was still overcast, and the sky's gray suited my mood. I zipped my jacket and headed down the rough path that ran beside squat one- and two-room cabins, all in varying states of disrepair. My companions included the eternal voices of rustling trees and crunching fall leaves. The only talk I heard was the sound of gravel under my boots. My eyes played tricks, and I mistook swaying branches for figures in motion. The air was clean but earthy, and I imagined that it had smelled just that way for generations. The sadness I'd felt at Centre College returned, and I shivered, though dressed for the cold.

Stapled to freshly cut wooden stakes, a posted placard explained the promise that today's Oxmoor has made to preserve "all historic structures that remain on this property, including the four slave dwellings dating back to the mid-19th century . . . which are an integral part of our history." This

THE TROUBLE OF COLOR

commitment extended to "the history of 3 generations of enslaved people that lived and worked here." Some of their names, seventy in total, followed. I ran my finger along the sign's cold, slick surface until in the last column I found listed "Tinah," between Beck and Mary. Oxmoor displayed these names in an effort to impress upon visitors the humanity of those once enslaved there. But to my eyes, the list was cool and raw like entries on a plantation ledger, a lawyer's estate inventory, or a census taker's return. I'd come there to learn about their relations: Who was Tinah to Beck and to Mary? Who might she have been to Nancy and to me?

I left Oxmoor with a sliver of hope. Martha Fry Bell and her sister had kept up family ties between Danville and Oxmoor; maybe Tinah and Nancy had sustained their connection to one another across the same distance. I drove back into town and let rosy anticipation take over. I imagined the stories I might finally tell about Nancy, Tinah, and the Oxmoor years. The streetlights came on just as I arrived in Louisville. I steered along a dark boulevard until I finally found the entrance to my bed-and-breakfast. The proprietors eagerly promoted bourbon tastings and warm, hearty breakfasts served in a grand nineteenth-century home that today sits among midgrade condo developments and 1970s ranch houses.

My bedroom was out back, across the parking lot in what had been the stable. Once alone, I picked up a promotional flyer that explained how my bedroom—spacious and elegant—had once been the kitchen. I did not need to read on. I knew that it was a kitchen once worked by enslaved women. Their tasks were demanding, dangerous, and laced with the expectation that every meal would please. As I tried to doze, flames from a gas fire in the oversized hearth flickered from across the room. I couldn't calm my unease and slept only fitfully over the next six hours. I woke early and wondered if Nancy, or perhaps Tinah, had the night before tried to tell me something.

My discomfort only grew in that B&B room. Despite a firm mattress, tufted quilt, and pillows of all shapes and sizes, it was impossible to get comfortable in a room where enslaved women had once completed brutal chores only after leaving behind their beloveds: nursing children, ailing elders, and friends in need. The present day's lavishness covered up the past, but traces of its blood remained. Propped up in that king-sized bed, I went to Oxmoor's website for a closer look. There was no cover-up there. But the unvarnished juxtaposition of the plantation's slaveholding past with the farm's luxurious present—filled with wedding receptions, chamber music recitals, and meetups of the Louisville Polo Club—struck a discordant note deep inside me.

In the days that followed, Oxmoor's caretaker introduced me to a genealogist who knew the plantation's enslaved families, and their living descendants, better than anyone. He was eager to know more about Tinah and how she fit into the Oxmoor story. We went back and forth and traded names, birthdates, and family trees. We tried two or three theories that placed Nancy's Tinah there. But the details never lined up. Yes, a woman named Tinah had been enslaved at Oxmoor. In a letter, Martha Fry Bell's sister recounted details of that Tinah's 1859 wedding on the front porch of the main house. She was not Nancy's Tinah, who was much older than the young bride.

I should have regretted the confusion. I should have felt disappointment when I realized I'd chased a wild goose at Oxmoor. I should have lamented that I'd never see the story of Nancy's sister told there—on placards, in cabins, and in the finely appointed rooms where Martha Fry Bell's sister had once presided. But I did not. Instead, I was relieved. I would not have to leave Nancy's Tinah behind in a place where the groans and sighs of slaves today mix with the strains of violins and the whack of polo mallets. At Oxmoor, voices from the past are nearly drowned out by couples saying "I do" just before nibbling canapés and sipping sparkling wine. The long-ago stench of hemp fields soaked with sweat is nearly overcome by the sweetness of freshly cut grass and spring flowers. I was glad not to leave Nancy's Tinah there and clutched her memory tight like the family treasure it was.

TWO

Amalgamation

I am colored but I offer nothing in the way of
extenuating circumstances except the fact that I
am the only Negro in the United States whose
grandfather on the mother's side was *not* an Indian
chief.

—ZORA NEALE HURSTON,
"HOW IT FEELS TO BE COLORED ME"

THE FIRST STORIES I HEARD ABOUT MY NORTH CAROLINA
family—the Joneses—were pleasing. They pleased us
when they encouraged others to admire an image cultivated by
men like my grandfather's brother, known to us as The Bishop.
By the 1950s, he was in his eighties, balding and slightly
stooped. Still, The Bishop's person, clothed in three-piece
suits, invited respect. He'd long been a man of consequence, a
leader in the Methodist Episcopal Church, North, a long way
from his hardscrabble upbringing in Greensboro. The oldest of six, The Bishop was schooled at Bennett Seminary and
then at Gammon Theological Seminary in Atlanta. He was a
Washingtonian in politics, cerebral in the pulpit, sharp-penned

on the page, and always a power broker when it came to his denomination. As a retiree, The Bishop was preoccupied with leaving a legacy and so agreed to tell our family story for Richard Bardolph's 1959 book, *The Negro Vanguard*.

Twenty years ago, a Detroit cousin gifted me a slightly worn copy of Bardolph's book. It was her way to make certain I read the right texts. She'd first tutored me when I was a teen with *The Autobiography of Malcolm X*. When she passed me *The Negro Vanguard*, my cousin nodded to let me know that I held a key to our family story. His title summed up Bardolph's aim: to explain the roots of a Black leadership class, a premise that flattered The Bishop and aging men like him. Their chests swelled at being cast in high-sounding terms. Bardolph's own pride also shone through. He hoped to be remembered as the scholar who had discovered the secret to Negro greatness.

The Negro Vanguard drew upon interviews that included one with The Bishop. Bardolph's best chance to pin him down was at home in Waveland, Mississippi, where he had retired to Gulfside, the Chautauqua-like retreat that The Bishop had founded in the 1920s. Sprawled across more than six hundred acres, his idyll was rooted in faith, indifferent to the color line, devoted to deep reflection, and invigorated by the waters of the Gulf. The Bishop recounted his family story not long after he'd lost his beloved baby brother, my Grandy. It was up to him to get the story on record for both of them; his earlier attempt at an autobiography had failed. Bardolph, a curious researcher with a book contract, was The Bishop's best chance to achieve posterity.

I regarded *The Negro Vanguard* the way others look to a passed-down family Bible. It contained precious fragments of our origin story. On my first read, I scanned the index, noted "Jones" entries, and began to dog-ear pages and underline passages. The Bishop's words carried weight with me. Though he died in 1960 when I was just two, as a girl, I thought of him as a guiding patriarch, and his stories in *The Negro Vanguard* fueled my desire to become a family storyteller. Today Bardolph's small, Carolina-blue paperback occupies a prominent place on my shelves alongside the books I myself have written: a first book dedicated to my grandmother Musie and a more recent one, titled *Vanguard*, which borrows its title directly from Bardolph. The display reminds me that I've always been a family historian at heart.

The Bishop bordered on boastful when he told Bardolph that the Joneses were "urban Greensboro, North Carolina, folk for generations, remote from the slave environment." I smiled when I read this. It was consistent with a genre of family storytelling that takes pride in having been free rather than enslaved. I knew of at least two books from 1992 alone—T. O. Madden's *We Were Always Free* and Adele Logan Alexander's *Ambiguous Lives*—that recounted families like the one The Bishop described. We had been *urban* rather than country and people *remote*, as in distant from, bondage. We'd not been bent, subjugated, or punished by the lash. This inheritance explained the man The Bishop had become.

"Greensboro Negro Is Elected Bishop," The Bishop's hometown newspaper crowed in 1920. His own position along the color line was unequivocal. Still, the white people in his past had led to many Joneses "with strong white strains." Bardolph suggested that skin color and percentages of white versus black forebears were linked to distinction. The Bishop's looks—tall, light, with a long, narrow nose and receding hairline—had led to no shortage of misunderstandings. He did not doubt who or *what* he was even if, as Bardolph summed it up, The Bishop was "at least seven-eighths white."

The Negro Vanguard still sits on the inspiration shelf in my home office. Most days my eyes are glued to my computer screen. But when my mind wanders, I walk over and pull down the worn paperback—gently because it tatters more with every year—to remember The Bishop's stories about whom we come from. It's like leafing through a photo album or packet of old letters. It's like having a talk with The Bishop. He tells his stories and teaches me what family meant to him.

—

Elijah Jones was The Bishop's "free grandfather." To me, he was my great-great-grandfather on my father's side. Born somewhere in Virginia around 1802, Elijah migrated to North Carolina, started a family, and eventually set up shop as a free man and shoemaker. Two generations later, The Bishop inherited his name, born Robert Elijah Jones in 1872. The story of the name goes further back to the Bible, where Elijah of the Old Testament was a preacher, prophet, and miracle worker. The name was a moniker suited to a child who would one day be a man of the cloth. As for our family's first Elijah, his bride was Mary Haith—a "white woman," The Bishop revealed about his own grandmother.

I don't know how they met or how they chose one another. I do know that Elijah and Mary married in an 1827 ceremony that was not as matter-of-fact as The Bishop made it out to be. North Carolina lawmakers—those determined to fortify the color line—had worried about couples like Mary and Elijah as far back as 1715. Such unions were expressly prohibited from becoming full-fledged marriages: "No White man or woman shall intermarry with any Negro, Mulatto or Indyan Man or Woman under the penalty of Fifty Pounds for each White man or woman." The fine—equal to $1,000 in today's currency— gave the law teeth and those who contemplated breaking it reason to pause.

A legal marriage promised to bestow benefits. Mary and Elijah's future children would be legitimate and entitled to inheritance rights. So lawmakers in the state capital, Raleigh, continued to conspire against them. By 1821, "free people of color" could not testify in court against so-called white persons. When it came to marriage, state law remained resolutely opposed to interracial unions. People might have wondered precisely *what* Elijah was—a Negro or a mulatto; maybe an Indian? In any case, he was clearly "of color," while in contrast, Mary was white. These facts alone made them outlaws.

The couple was not deterred. Just a few days before Christmas, Elijah walked into the Orange County courthouse and right up to the color line. He and a neighbor, Allen Jeffers, spoke with the clerk. Elijah requested a marriage license. In exchange, the clerk had Elijah and Allen promise to pay a bond to the governor should anything "obstruct a marriage between Elijah Jones and Mary Haith." The clerk hurriedly recorded their pledge in businesslike terms on a short slip of paper. Like most workingmen in rural North Carolina, neither Elijah

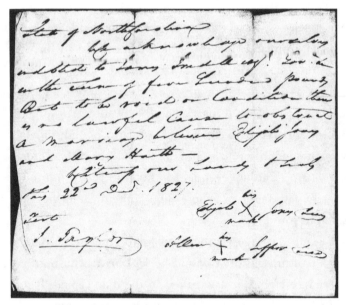

Mary Haith and Elijah Jones marriage bond, 1827

nor his friend could read or write. They relied on the clerk to faithfully make a record of the transaction, and then both men signed by their "X" marks.

Where Elijah and Mary tied the knot, the record doesn't say. If it was too cold for a garden ceremony, perhaps they faced one another in a parlor and exchanged vows. They might have appeared before a local preacher, exposed to God and a congregation, and then recited solemn promises. They may even have visited a local justice of the peace who officiated their partnership. Words adapted from the sixteenth-century *Book of Common Prayer* suited the occasion: "From this day forward," "for better for worse," "for richer for poorer," "in sickness and in health." Love, cherish, and obey until death. Mary and Elijah managed to evade the law when they fooled some and made accomplices of others.

The risky circumstances of Mary and Elijah's marriage reminded me of my own parents. In the 1950s, they also wed across the color line. Mary's story let me see that my mother was not the first white person to join our family tree. That distinction belonged to my great-great-grandmother. I'd heard my parents' interracial union mocked as ahead of its time. It was not: Mary and Elijah had preceded them by more than a century. This gave me one more reason to admire The Bishop. He'd told their story and allowed for no shame when it came to his grandparents' life together. The ignoble and even the illegal were, as he retold them, matters of fact. Transgression was tradition among the Joneses.

When she chose to marry Elijah, Mary gave up her past. She abandoned her family name, Haith, and with it any discernible ties to whiteness. Three years later, a census taker visited their home and encountered Mary, Elijah, and two young children. All of them, the census marshal believed, were people of color. Mary and Elijah must have been anxious. Opposition to marriages like theirs hardened in that same year with the passage of an "Act to prevent intermarriage between free negroes or free people of color and white persons and slaves." At least on paper, their union was "null and void." Mary and Elijah hardly felt the force of these new restrictions most days. But when officials called on them, those laws walked right up to their front door and asked questions.

Mary and Elijah came to expect visits from the census taker. Every ten years, each household in the United States was visited by an assistant marshal. These official dates punctuated their years, like election and tax days. In 1840, Mary and Elijah lived in the same place, now with five children. Again, the enumerator described them all as "free persons of color." In anticipation of the next census, set for 1850, lawmakers in Washington, DC, debated the details of a new, expanded census questionnaire. They would collect data about race and test a theory termed "mulatto degeneracy."

Congress members were perversely curious about people said to be "of color" but neither only white nor Black. People who today are termed *mixed-race* were, in Mary and Elijah's time, called *mulatto*, *quadroon*, or *hybrid*. They were, lawmakers speculated, a distinct class. Hybrid people were said to be more intelligent and capable of civilization than the "pure African." But in physical terms, hybrid people were imagined to be inferior: unable to procreate and destined for extinction. Census data would be used to calculate the relative life expectancy of hybrids. If they lived shorter lives than did pure people, the degeneracy theory would be proven. The census of 1850 was, in part, an experiment in race science. Mary, Elijah, and their children were its unwitting subjects.

Changes to the census were controversial in North Carolina, though not because of new ties between the census and race science. Generally, people opposed the new enumeration system because it would record extensive details about each person in a household. This was akin to an inquisition-like intrusion on the sanctity of homes, some news commentators complained. Others chided officials in Washington: What was next, the ʼnting of geese and chickens? The appointment of local men as assistant marshals in Caswell County fueled the debate.

Mary expected that in June, a census agent would travel across the countryside from one household to the next—by horse, by buggy, or on foot. She might leave him to lean on a porch post or, if the weather demanded, let him step just inside. He'd open a ledger, take a sharp pencil in hand, and prepare to make notes about Mary, Elijah, and their family. He'd work with a new form that, for the first time, detailed everyone under their roof by NAME, AGE, SEX, RACE, OCCU-PATION, BIRTHPLACE, MARITAL STATUS, EDUCATION, LITERACY, and DISABILITY.

Census day demanded that Mary plan carefully. At the front of her mind was not Washington's specious interest in race science. She worried that the census marshal might expose her family, might expose her for who she *was* and who she *was not*. Mary imagined the worst. Could her marriage to Elijah be invalidated? If so, the two would be charged with fornication: sex outside marriage. They could be liable for bastardy because their children were born outside a legal union. Both were crimes in North Carolina. The well-being of Mary's family depended on subterfuge and discretion laced with a measure of luck.

I pictured Mary standing before the census taker and held my breath; I knew she was in danger. William Pinkney Graves, the assistant marshal assigned to Caswell County, was no friend. He approached Mary's home with a bearing that combined the discipline of his membership in the local militia with the arrogance of a planter's son. He was an ambitious man who collected census data as one step in a career that led him to Virginia, where he lorded it over his own slaves and fought for the Confederacy. He policed a social order that he believed in, while Mary and Elijah's family defied it.

I rooted for Mary and her courage in the face of Graves's scrutiny. She was, I knew, inexperienced when it came to public officials. She'd not been there when Elijah had taken out their marriage bond. Perhaps she'd visited the post office, though more likely, she'd let her older boys run that errand. Before the census taker, she dutifully recited a list of family members, which included herself and Elijah, both forty-eight. He was a shoemaker who owned no real estate. Neither could read or write. At home, they had five children, the youngest seven and the oldest twenty-one. Graves marked the entire family "M" for mulatto, likely his own impression. Mary breathed easier as he walked away. She'd kept her secret safe.

How far did Mary go to adopt a new persona as a "woman of color" and later a "mulatto"? No description of her survives. I know that she managed to persuade locals that by law, she and Elijah belonged together. I imagine her with dark hair, kept short but with a wave. Perhaps Mary covered her head with a cotton scarf while she worked around the house. Her eyes were sunken with dark circles, a sign of age or fatigue. Her skin was marked with darker spots from hours working under the sun. I'm less sure about whether she adopted a new style of speech, a repertoire of mannerisms, a sartorial flair, or new cultural habits. I admired Mary for her love of Elijah, her defense of their household, and her fierce mother's instincts.

Mary lived with twoness, and she was not alone. In the county's 1850 census, I discovered scores and scores of residents who, like her, the enumerator marked with an "M." Many of Mary's neighbors did not fit a black-white equation, though none admitted to having married or had children across the color line. In Mary's small world, families held big secrets from census takers and court clerks, while she developed her own ability to read signs of kinship written on neighbors' faces: of blood and affection, proximity and adversity, law and defiance of it. Around her, as at home, white became Black and Black became white. Mary's only reassurance was that in every important way, she and Elijah when they chose each other became one and the same.

—

The Bishop, I was learning, mixed facts with gentle contrivance. To Richard Bardolph, he described his people as urban, by which he meant townsfolk from Greensboro. But The Bishop knew that his father's parents, Mary and Elijah, had spent most of their lives in countryside hamlets. I didn't give much thought to how deliberately The Bishop molded facts until a weekend visit with my Uncle Fuzz. Fuzz was my father's baby brother and The Bishop's nephew. By the time we planned a reunion for spring 2014, he was the last living link in a chain that ran from Mary and Elijah to me.

Our plans gelled when a Boston cousin let me know he'd bring Fuzz to North Carolina for Easter weekend. Jean and I lived there that year. The same months were also time for small family reunions in Greensboro, at Bennett College. My

THE TROUBLE OF COLOR

brother came through by car down from New York, and we
rode one hour west just to take a walk on the campus, our
first in a long time. We were no longer the grandchildren who
biked along the walkways and played ball on the green lawns.
But we carried those memories with us when, as adults, we
finally respected the keep-off-the-grass rule.

As the weekend with Fuzz approached, an uncomfortable
knot grew in my stomach. He and I didn't know one another
all that well, it reminded me. Fuzz and my father, who had
passed eight years before, had rarely been on good terms; Fuzz
and I were likewise distant. Jean convinced me we'd build rapport while we planned a meal. We warmed up over a menu that
included a leg of lamb and roast potatoes. Back in Durham, I
ordered meat from our around-the-corner butcher. That and a
successful hunt for a jar of mint jelly launched the holiday.

It was only minutes into the visit when I realized there
was nothing to worry about. Fuzz put us all at ease with his
storytelling—from his boyhood in Greensboro on the Bennett
College campus to his formative years at Harvard, his distinction as an MIT professor, and finally his retirement to Atlanta.
These tales were long-winded and filled with names and places
I knew little of. Still, each one mixed the funny with the
poignant and let us laugh until we cried that first afternoon.
Immersed in Fuzz's adventures, I lost my self-consciousness.
My uncle didn't mind, it seemed, being served on thrift-store
dishes, sitting on a lumpy secondhand sofa, or dining on
hard-as-stone straight-backed chairs.

I couldn't have said what I hoped for the next day as we piled
into my Volkswagen and headed to Greensboro for a walk at

Bennett. The early-spring lawns and shrubs were just waking up. The smell of moist, pungent soil filled my nose, a sign that the campus gardeners had been at work in the preceding days. Diagonal walks led us from a new learning center to the student union, named for Fuzz's father and my Grandy. The highlight was a stop just inside Pfeiffer Chapel, where Fuzz posed for a picture in the vestibule beneath his father's oil portrait. I pulled out my phone to capture the moment, aware that it already held a shot taken at that spot months before when my brother had been in town.

We may have met briefly with the school's president, but there was otherwise little structure to the afternoon. We all had memories of time at Bennett, often on ritual occasions: Convocation, Founders' Day, and family funerals. This visit was different: no suits, no speeches, no polite chitchat. Instead, we wandered where we pleased and spoke only about what came to mind. All of us, but no one more than Fuzz, knew the way around Bennett. The campus had been his childhood home. When talk lulled, our ears filled with everyday sounds: a bus passed on nearby Gorrell Street, students giggled with heads close together, our shoes on the cement talked some ancient talk with the footsteps of years past.

For the Joneses, Bennett's campus is hallowed ground in which our memories are rooted. Fuzz's recollections stretched back to the early years when every building around us was just going up, brick by brick. He'd watched magnolia saplings—planted in the 1930s in honor of dignitaries and in remembrance—being set into the ground. On our walk, he marveled at how they'd transformed into towering trees. As a boy, he'd looked on as classes of young women in all white paraded through the iron Bearden Gates and on to the chapel for "Convocatum Est." That day marked their debut as Bennett Belles. To our right, I could see the white clapboard house— now an alumni center named for Musie—where Fuzz had been born and raised. The fullness in my chest said I longed to know still more.

Out of nowhere, Fuzz blurted, "Little Texas." I tuned into his words, unsure what he meant. "That's where the Joneses come from," he said, chuckling. Was he amused when the unexpected memory surfaced? Or was he masking discomfort? "We are related to every Jones between Greensboro and Alamance County." I can hear his baritone drawl, even now. He sounded less like a New England academic and more like a son of North Carolina, enunciating every syllable: *E-ver-y*, for instance, had three of them. I fixed this revelation in my mind and, as we continued our tour, murmured to myself, "Don't forget 'Little Texas.'"

That evening, I steered across Durham to drop Fuzz at the downtown Marriott, already having composed Google searches in my head. Back at home, I perched on one of those straight-backed dining chairs, barely setting down my bag and jacket before I powered up my iPad. The screen was my only light. Searches like "Little Texas" and "North Carolina" led to stories about a place where three central counties—Orange, Caswell, and Alamance—still meet. I scanned a few old maps, took a quick pass through some local histories, and then went back to the bits I knew about Mary and Elijah. I began to better understand what Fuzz had shared. It was a chapter that

The Bishop had never revealed to Richard Bardolph. In the decades before the Civil War, our Jones family called Little Texas home.

Still in the dark, I landed on the website of the Occaneechi-Saponi Nation: Little Texas, I learned, was home to Native Americans. Indigenous people then and now claimed the land, some as purchasers with deeds, others as holders of government land grants, and still others whose presence evidenced their indelible ties to the place. No one was sure where the moniker came from; there's no link, for example, to the state of the same name. The phrase *Little Texas* only occasionally appeared on maps, census returns, or other state documents. It was a cultural designation, adopted and then kept alive by community members and descendants who carried it forward—people not unlike my Uncle Fuzz.

The pieces of Mary and Elijah's story began to come together. I looked again at the region's early census returns and recognized that they listed forebears of today's Occaneechi-Saponi people. I'd let the color line deceive me and given too much credit to census takers and courthouse clerks, who almost never acknowledged the Indians who appeared before them as Indians. Instead, public officials imposed labels suggesting that Little Texas was comprised of people who were white, of African descent, or some mixture of the two. Scholars of Indigenous history and culture have since corrected the record. Some Native American families encouraged the state to record them as "of color" or "mulatto," to avoid expulsion from North Carolina during the era of Indian removal from the 1820s through the 1840s. Many Native people were forced west along a brutal trail of starvation, disease, and death. Those who managed to stay put in North Carolina—whatever label they adopted or was imposed upon them—knew themselves to be Indians.

Who then were Mary and Elijah to the people around them? I remembered Allen Jeffers, the man who stood up with Elijah when he went to secure a marriage bond in 1827. On that day, Jeffers took a risk on Elijah and Mary's behalf. If officials later discovered that the couple married across the color line and contrary to law, Jeffers would be obliged to forfeit to the state his five-hundred-pound pledge. Jeffers stood to lose his money, his land, and the roof over the head of his wife and three young daughters. The ties between the two families, the Joneses and the Jefferses, were deep and strong.

I could see a special kinship at work in Little Texas. There were ties of marriage, couples who openly chose one another before God and the state. There were ties of blood, parents to children, passed down across generations. Folks there were also bound together along the color line, many of them living side by side in bald defiance of state-drawn boundaries. Many families survived only by way of subterfuge; they hid who they came from. People white became Black. Native people became people of color and hid behind the designation "M" for mulatto. Their circumstances varied, but what they shared was the risk of exposure. They all feared being found out. As a result, they quietly kept one another's secrets. The only term I have to describe the connection between Mary, Elijah, and their neighbors is *kin*.

I lingered in front of my iPad while in the back of my mind, I rehearsed the timing of the next day's Easter lunch.

I'd discovered what it meant to be from Little Texas. But the realization felt like a curveball, hard to follow and difficult to fix in my sights. I could see traces of Joneses and Jefferses— along with Jeffreys and Jeffries—in the early marriage records of Orange County. Sometimes people pledged bonds for one another, as Allen did for Elijah. Occasionally they married. In central North Carolina, people mixed without much regard for the color line. They made families of choice rather than ones prescribed by law.

It was late. I splashed cold water on my face, hurriedly ran a brush over my teeth, and slipped on the pajamas that hung at the back of the bathroom door. Barefoot, I headed to the bedroom, where Jean was already fast asleep. I stopped just shy of its threshold and, unable to shake my puzzlement, whispered to no one in particular, "I thought we were just plain Negroes."

—

Elijah and Mary chose one another and made a family that eventually included six children. My great-grandfather Dallas was their youngest, born in 1845. For their precious young ones, the best shot at well-being rested on their parents' ability to keep a secret long enough for their three boys and three girls to become men and women and begin families of their own. I could track most of them in the same places I'd first discovered Mary and Elijah: penned on census returns and on bonds secured before marriage ceremonies. That next generation—becoming husbands and wives and parents—was also marked "M" for mulatto. I'd once thought this designation signaled people with ancestors who mixed Black and white. Now I knew better. Mulatto was a designation that hinted at so much more.

Mary and Elijah's oldest boy was Thompson. By 1850, he was eighteen and at work as a shoemaker. Elijah had taught Thompson his trade. He leaned over his son, at a bench or a counter, while together they transformed leather and tacks into shoes. I imagined them there and couldn't help but wonder if my love of shoes had been passed to me by these men. Thompson, at twenty-five, planned to marry Martha Ann Dice and headed to the local courthouse to apply for a license, just as his father had done years before. Thompson brought along a man named Johnston Jeffreys, who pledged the required $1,000 bond, signed with his "X." In 1860, the census taker found Thompson and Mary Ann in their own home with Thompson's youngest sister and the couple's daughter, four years old.

Two of Mary and Elijah's middle children married in 1858. In January, their son Seborn wed Martha Jeffries. Someone I know only as P. B. Sharp promised $1,000, a pledge that there was nothing unlawful about the union. Seborn and Martha settled in nearby Orange County and by 1860 had two children at home when the census taker came around. Over the years, the two had a total of eleven children, and like his father and older brother, Seborn supported his family as a shoemaker. At the end of that same year, Elijah and Mary's daughter Lizzie married Freeman Heath. Ellick Heath, a friend or perhaps a relation, pledged $1,000 so that the couple could marry. Fannie was the last of Mary and Elijah's children to wed before the Civil War began. In 1861, she and Thomas Corn agreed to marry, and a local farmer signed their bond. Fannie bore three daughters in quick succession, filling the home she shared with Thomas.

At first all these names made me dizzy. Without faces or life stories, it wasn't easy to keep track of who was who. I began to imagine. Thompson, the shoemaker, had hands rough and stained from his trade. Seborn raised eleven children in a house that was never quiet. Lizzie was courageous and left her own clan to marry into the Heath family. As for Fannie, Mary and Elijah's baby girl, she began married life amidst the uncertainties imposed by the outbreak of war. On index cards and in the margins of a notebook, I sketched trees and charts along with outlines and graphs. I connected the Joneses to the Jeffrieses and the Corns and felt sure I could see some of what Indigenous storytellers had explained. The children of Mary and Elijah mixed with families that today are associated with the Occaneechi-Saponi Nation.

Long ago, record keepers transformed Mary and Elijah's children from people who lived, loved, and made homes and babies into static, one-dimensional figures. They were trapped in the columns of census returns and the boxes of death certificates. I set their names free: scribbled, drew, marked them across the pages of a notepad. I recited them out loud. I listed them by age and by dates of birth and death. I ordered an oversized map of Little Texas from an online dealer, hung it on my office wall, and stuck pins where I guessed their homes once stood. I charted their migrations from Caswell to Orange, Orange to Alamance, and back again from Alamance to Caswell. Names that had once confused me now delighted.

Most of all, marriages lit up my imagination. Their weddings may have begun in sober encounters with the courthouse clerk and with solemn promises of cash guarantees. But that was just a start. Hadn't there been ceremony, vows exchanged and officiants who dispensed prayer and homespun wisdom? Wasn't there happiness manifest in cheers, embraces, cheeks pressed close, hands clasped, and hearts warmed? Weren't there sweets and libations, some of them of the stronger sort? I was sure there was joy when Thompson wed Martha Ann, when Seborn married Martha, when Fannie said "I do" to Freeman, and when Lizzie tied the knot with her Thomas. Joy isn't easy to see on the cold documents of the past. Still, I became sure I could hear it. Faint but definitely there, I heard strains of joy as I slowly sifted through those old records.

I was still listening for the sound that ran through Mary and Elijah's family on wedding days when I took myself out to hear a bit of live music. I stood in a misty rain and waited to enter a local nightclub where North Carolina's own Rhiannon Giddens was slated to perform. Inside, I stepped onto a wide-open dance floor. A big mirror ball turned overhead. Around me, people clutched cold beer and cheap wine in plastic cups. I made my way toward the stage, the better to stand at Giddens's feet. Soon she was in front of me, wielding her fiddle and banjo when not belting out her distinct brand of folk music with a voice trained for opera and built for a blend of blues, jazz, Cajun, country, gospel, and rock. A marvel onstage, Giddens cried and crooned. We danced.

When Giddens finally spoke between numbers, I remembered that she hails from Greensboro, the same place that my people—the Joneses—eventually called home. If I shouted out "Little Texas," I knew that Giddens would recognize what I meant. She told the audience she is mixed. I saw that written in her features, on her skin, and in the way her hair reclaimed its natural texture at its edges. Giddens's sound reached deep into me, to where the soul, R&B, and rock that I was raised on mix. She stirred a memory of my ties to Mary, Elijah, and Little Texas. She awakened in me the weddings that long ago brought them joy. As the lights above flashed red, green, and gold, I swayed to a Giddens ballad. I was awash in kinship.

After weeks buried in documents and hours of finger-tapping at my keyboard, I was learning to listen for the past. Giddens was my teacher: a storyteller for whom the long-ago becomes present through rhythm and beat, in timbre and melody. She shared a history I needed to hear: the happiness of Mary and Elijah's world written in the strains of bow on fiddle strings and the tight notes of fingertips and picks on the banjo. Giddens does not sugarcoat her journey. As a schoolgirl, she knew Black and white kids, but, as she's explained, "I didn't really fit with either group. . . . The black girls criticized me because I was a hippie. The white girls didn't know what to do with me." In high school, she explored Native culture and heritage, and people called her Pocahontas. In that nickname, I heard one part question—*What are you?*—and another part challenge—*Do you know who you are?* Giddens has never claimed a tribal affiliation, but she does claim a feeling: "When I go to a pow-wow, I know what it is. When I hear that drum, I feel very connected," she told one writer.

For Giddens, Little Texas has been a font. She learned from long-unsung generations of banjo players who developed their craft there. The region's distinct sound defied boundaries. No scheme developed by census officials—who imposed labels like "B" for Black and "M" for mulatto—could contain them. These twentieth-century music makers were enumerated as laborers and small farmers. Giddens explained the rest of the story. Musicianship was passed down, not on the census but in the tunes they composed and the players they trained. Their stories were preserved in the ecstatic bodies that stepped, dipped, swayed, and sweated to their sounds. Giddens credits banjo great Joe Thompson with having passed on to her a tradition that artfully mixes Black, white, and Native into the distinct sound of Little Texas.

For me, the road to understanding the people of Little Texas has been long. I am always learning. Years ago, I wrote to a scholar of the Occaneechi-Saponi Nation to ask for help with my family research. I made clear I was a historian, with a need for professional advice. I received a one-line reply: "Who were your people from Little Texas?" *My people?* Even though I knew where they fit on my family tree, I didn't yet think of Mary and Elijah that way. I hurriedly tapped out a reply that listed them and their children as if they were data points and not *my people* at all. I never received a reply. It was possible that I'd caught that expert at a bad time or that other responsibilities had left him unavailable for queries like mine. I didn't bother him again. Only now do I understand that before we went further, he'd likely wanted to know who Mary and Elijah were to me. His point was not to discover where they sat on a tree or a chart. Instead, he was pressing me to confront what I meant when I termed them *kin*.

I shared what I knew about Mary and Elijah at professional meetings. As with my query to the Occaneechi-Saponi scholar, I hoped to elicit research help. I presented their story in a hotel meeting room, sweating pitchers of water and tiny hard candies in front of me on the dais. I absorbed sharp criticism: Rather than emphasizing blood, I needed to focus on community ties when approaching Native American kinship. How were the lives of Mary, Elijah, and their children knit to others in Little Texas—through marriage, ritual, and everyday life—in their own time and across generations?

Once, after a similar presentation, a stranger came close enough to whisper in my ear: "They—the Occaneechi Saponi—are a made-up tribe, you know. They aren't real Indians." Then they were gone. I stood still, speechless, but my mind raced: *Could it be that the Indians in Little Texas weren't Indians at all?* I fumed, not understanding why someone had tried to pull the rug out from under me. I'll never know. But I taught myself the rest of the story. The Occaneechi-Saponi campaign to win legal recognition was always opposed by skeptics. They won formal standing from the state of North Carolina in 2001, but only after the nation faced down those who doubted the ties between today's residents of Little Texas and the Indians of Mary and Elijah's time. Those who doubted them, I learned, were still among us.

By the time I met up with Rhiannon Giddens, I'd learned something about my sense of kinship. It was constructed out of family stories like those that The Bishop told about Mary and Elijah. It borrowed from official records like the census, though it didn't regard them as gospel. I knew that the bonds formed in the chores and rituals of everyday life—birthing babies, harvesting crops, praying over the dead, and bartering for the necessaries—mattered too. Added to that were scenes of joy—the ones we cannot see and can only feel. The homes of Little Texas were filled with tricksters: men, women, and children who dodged the census taker and fooled the clerk. Families owed their survival to an ability to pretend to be who they were not while never forgetting who they were. This made Mary, Elijah, and their children kin to their Native American neighbors. This makes me kin to them still.

—

My great-grandfather Dallas Jones was Mary and Elijah's youngest son and The Bishop's father. His early life is to me a mystery. Though he was already five when his mother, Mary, spoke with the census taker in 1850, she didn't mention him. Ten years later, in 1860, Dallas was fifteen, and still there's no sign of him on the censuses of Little Texas. I can see only his older siblings, married and in their own households. I've spun out speculations. As a small child, was he raised by a relative or bound out to work as an apprentice? As a young man, did Dallas have the spirit of a wanderer, an adventurer, or even a rebel, which led him to try life alone, apart from kin? Nothing added up.

Finally, Dallas surfaced. I sat squeezed in front of a microfilm machine in the North Carolina State Archives. Frame by frame, I turned through a long reel of land deeds, records of who had purchased which parcel from whom in Greensboro.

Sidney D[allas] Jones from George Albright, land
deed, 1864

I slowed down to have a closer look at the filings for September 1864, and there was Dallas along with his brothers.
He had paid $128 for just over one acre of land on the east
side of Greensboro. The plot was bounded by stone markers
to the south and, to the north, by a parcel already owned by
Dallas's brother Seborn. Soon their brother Thompson joined
Dallas and Seborn and bought a larger lot of nearly two acres
just south of Dallas for $220. I still had unanswered questions,
including why they'd left Little Texas and where they'd gotten

so much cash. Still, even with the Civil War unsettled, I finally understood how the three Jones brothers—Elijah and Mary's sons—had become the "urban" people described by The Bishop. They'd exchanged cash for land and left Little Texas behind.

THREE

Bastardy

In looking back, calmly, on the events of my life,
I feel that the slave woman ought not to be judged
by the same standard as others.

—HARRIET JACOBS,
INCIDENTS IN THE LIFE OF A SLAVE GIRL

I MIGHT NEVER HAVE LOOKED FOR FAMILY AMONG THE PAPERS
of the federal Freedmen's Bureau. The Bishop, after all, had
said we'd always been free, while the bureau's work concerned
former slaves. After the Civil War, it had taken over from the
army responsibility for people displaced, destitute, and headed
toward freedom. Reams of reports—personnel, finances, and
day-by-day minutes—survive. They recount how the bureau
used the lure of subsidies as well as the force of law to see to
it that former slaves became free workers and citizens. A California cousin was the first to search for us among the bureau's
complaints, contracts, and account books.

My cousin and I shared a passion for family history, which
meant that when her email included an attachment, my heart

leapt. It was a sign that she'd turned up something new. And she had. Among the documents long ago filed with the bureau's Greensboro, North Carolina, office was a two-page complaint dated June 1867. I clicked open the file and saw a name—Isabella Holley. She was, I knew, my great-great-grandmother. The air stilled. I felt her look back at me from a document that she had signed with her "X." Isabella had gone to the Freedmen's Bureau office to demand satisfaction: William J. Holley, the father of her children, had reneged on a bargain they'd made.

Isabella was also The Bishop's maternal grandmother. I'd first learned her name from him, and I knew that she was sometimes called Belle. He'd been her oldest grandchild and someone who visited her home on the outskirts of Greensboro in the Black enclave of Warnersville. The Bishop described Isabella for *The Negro Vanguard* as "a handsome, light-skinned Negro." He also spoke about William Holley, his "maternal grandfather" and "a white man who had four children" with Isabella. Holley "maintained but never married" her. The Bishop regarded them both as family.

Once again, I was about to discover a story that The Bishop had never shared. Isabella was his grandmother, but she had not always been free. I read through the details of her complaint, and a chill of recognition shot through me. William Holley, before the war, had called Isabella his property—she'd been enslaved and admitted as much to the Freedmen's Bureau. I worried that I was exposing a secret that The Bishop had long kept to himself. Might he, if he could, admonish me to leave the story as he'd told it? Would he want me to leave Isabella's memory alone? I filed away her complaint to the Freedmen's Bureau, unsure where it might lead me.

—

Isabella was a girl of twelve when William Holley paid her price and brought her to his Bertie County plantation in eastern North Carolina. His land spread across three hundred acres, all inherited from Holley's father. Already wealthy in land and slaves, Holley for a time dabbled in local politics. By the time Isabella joined his household around 1850, Holley was preparing to move across the Chowan River to a plantation he called Bandon. The riverfront property was valued at $10,000 ($400,000 in today's money), and Holley forced eighty enslaved people to work the place. Bandon was situated in a world of waterways, of the river and its tributaries, of fisheries, and of commerce plied north and south by boat. Holley purchased Bandon for the potential of its wharf, where goods changed hands along the route of the Albemarle Steam Navigation Company. He grew wealthier by controlling commerce at that busy depot. Holley's wife with their four children resettled with him at Bandon. Isabella was with them, already mother to her oldest daughter, Jennie, who grew up to be The Bishop's mother.

At Bandon, Holley owned lots of land, but his business was the river. He used the hands, the backs, and the know-how of enslaved people to extract wealth from the water. Aboard boats and skiffs, they trapped fish and then prepared the catch for market in sheds that reeked of scales, bones, and skin. In the family home, Isabella may have scrubbed and dusted, taken charge of children, helped those cooking in the kitchen serve meals, or learned to fire the pots, mix the lye, and stir garments of lighter cotton and heavier wool as a laundress. She may have taken her turns processing fish. But Isabella's labor at Bandon always included reproduction, bearing children—Holley's children.

Bandon was then home to two families that regarded William Holley as father. His wife, by the time of her death in 1857, was mother to five. Isabella, who had been pregnant many more times, had at least four surviving children of her own. "She is the mother of nine children . . . five dead," Isabella told the Freedmen's Bureau. About their relationship to Holley, she spoke plainly to officials: "These children were all his, he being their father." Beyond this, Isabella said little about life at Bandon. There was enough acreage there to imagine that Holley's wife and Isabella, with their respective children, lived separate existences. A census taker in 1860 underscored this. He recorded the name of each child borne by Holley's wife, along with sex and age, while Isabella and her children were mere statistics: age, sex, and color. The census did not give them, as enslaved people, names. These two families painfully coexisted during many years at Bandon.

I needed to see the place where Isabella had been enslaved for myself. It was time to visit Chowan County. First, I followed the well-marked trail of its best-remembered enslaved woman, Harriet Jacobs. I also read the account of Harriet's life published in her 1861 memoir, *Incidents in the Life of a Slave Girl*. As was true for Isabella, Harriet encountered men—white men—who insisted on knowing her intimately, even if they stopped short of using brute force. Step-by-step, Harriet bargained her way to freedom. First, she chose a lover—a free white man with property—and bore two children with him. Then she won his promise to free their children and her beloved brother. Harriet then disappeared for seven years, hidden in the attic of her grandmother, a freedwoman. It took that long for her to devise a route out of North Carolina, and finally, Harriet escaped to the free soil of the North.

When I arrived in Chowan County's capital city, Edenton, I knew I'd encounter plaques and markers remembering Harriet; one sits prominently at the corner of Broad and Gale Streets. I picked up a self-guided tour map, slipped on a comfortable pair of running sneakers, and set out to walk in her shoes. It was a clear, sunshine-filled day. Along Broad Street, I paused in front of the Episcopal Church where Harriet's children were baptized. Two blocks farther down, on Eden Street, once stood the house in which Harriet had been held as a slave. On West King Street, I lingered for a moment where her lover had lived. The site of Harriet's grandmother's home is today a parking lot. I took a moment to stand there and remember how Harriet had crouched under its roof, undetected for seven years. I saw Edenton's ten square blocks for myself and better understood how difficult it had been for her grandmother to keep Harriet's secret. It made her escape seem all the more remarkable.

I planned to retrace Isabella's steps and carried with me an old photo postcard of William Holley's Bandon: a two-story, white-shingled house with four sets of front-facing shuttered windows and a portico held up by twin columns. But there was nothing left to see. The main house had burned to the ground in 1964, a local guide explained. I was "in luck," she continued with an upbeat smile, though I did not feel lucky at all. After the fire, preservationists had moved two of Bandon's surviving structures—an office and the kitchen—to downtown Edenton. I could glimpse what little survived of Isabella's world if I retraced my steps down the same streets along which Harriet's early life had played out. I would not see Bandon, but I had discovered how the lives of Harriet and Isabella were intertwined in memory. This partly soothed my disappointment. As enslaved girls turned freedwomen, had they met, Harriet and Isabella would have understood one another.

I took the drive up toward Bandon anyway, steering along country roads dotted with mailboxes marked "Holley." Only later did I learn that like Isabella, others had kept the Holley name after freedom came. A 1950s visitor to Bandon described spending time with Bandon's last owner, during which he

Bandon plantation, circa 1933

observed how the farm was kept up by "one horse, one mule, and one man." That man was "Art Holley, whose name comes from the antebellum owners of Bandon." Art had inherited his name from his parents and theirs before him, going all the way back to William Holley's time at Bandon. Art's wife, the same visitor explained, was Bessie, who cooked at Bandon, the fourth generation of women to do so. Bessie's family line also stretched back to William Holley's years. Families like those of Art and Bessie had stayed put even after slavery ended. Isabella and her children had gotten away. For all of them, I let myself feel glad that the place had finally burned to the ground.

———

A constitutional amendment abolished slavery in 1865. The freedom of former slaves was secure, but no one was certain about the future. Nothing in the amendment said whether they could travel, work, own property, vote, sign contracts, or sit on juries. Isabella was among those who made a new life amidst uncertainty: Could she head a family, raise her children, and keep a roof over their heads? It took nearly two years, but in winter 1867, she and William Holley devised a plan. Isabella and her children would leave Bandon, with Holley's support. She explained to the Freedmen's Bureau, "Said Wm J. Holley is a man of considerable means, and abundantly able to provide for the children." The two schemed, probably haggled a bit, and then came to terms: "He agreed late last March (the 24th) to purchase a house and lot for her." Isabella and her children, she and Holley agreed, would leave Chowan County for good, their futures secured by a roof over their heads.

It's likely that William Holley, who knew Greensboro, rec-ommended that Isabella head that way. Years before, he had invested in land there but later sold it at a loss. With four chil-dren in tow, Isabella set out to travel two hundred miles west to the Piedmont region. A hired carriage or wagon carried her family to the nearby train depot, Tarboro or Rocky Mount, where rail lines carried them the rest of the way to Greens-boro. Isabella was immediately disappointed. Instead of a house and lot, she explained to officials, "the full extent of assistance rendered her since the [war's end] has been [for Holley] to pay the rent of a small one-room tenement in which she and the children live."

Isabella endured difficult days, and the climate in Greens-boro only added to her troubles. Nothing about the future of families like hers was sure. The prospect of Black men at the polls, for instance, set city residents against one another. On one side, friends of the Union called a mass meeting to explain "WHO CAN VOTE" and urged that Ku Klux Klan violence must be replaced with the "law and order" of elected representatives. On the other side, a news story mocked Black voters. A former slave, Henry Gwinn, was said to have declared Black people not yet ready for the vote; they should put their next years in the hands of white southerners.

Mixed families like Isabella's especially vexed North Car-olina's leadership. Newspapers warned against their poten-tial. In Fayetteville, it was said that a white man had married a Black woman. The union was nothing short of revolting, "committed at times to shock and paralyse a whole commu-nity and astound men with the development of the occasional unnatural and monstrous degradation of human nature." This was a reference to the couple's mixed-race children. Their "indignation and abhorrence" not only upended family life but also threatened the political order. The husband was a radical who welcomed Black men at the polls and in party meetings, thereby threatening to render the state's politics "mongrel." Politics, marriage, and race made for a volatile mix that left even white men wondering if they were safe. The message to people like Isabella was plain: It was risky for families to openly cross the color line. If found out, they became targets.

By that June, Isabella was in dire straits. She grew certain that Holley would do little to relieve her family. On an early-summer morning, she woke up in that one-room tenement. It was a small, rundown building shared with other renters. Isabella put her children in charge of one another or a neighbor. There's no way to know precisely what she wore, but she surely pulled together her best frock, neatened her hair, and stiffened her back. She expected to be sized up by officials and, in her head, rehearsed the story she'd tell about her ties to Holley, their bargain, and what he cost her children when he short-changed them.

Isabella was headed to the Guilford County Courthouse on East Market Street, at the city's most important crossroads. From whatever direction she may have come, Isabella was surrounded by hallmarks of the city's elite: grand homes, fashionable shops, and imposing churches, including those of the Episcopalians and Southern Methodists. Carriages came and went, and patrons filed in and out of hotels like the Southern, with its white columns and second-story gallery on West Street, and the Planter, which boasted a restaurant, bar, and stables on East Street. The courthouse was Roman-Corinthian style. Constructed with stucco-covered brick, the building imposed like a towering stone structure and its spire-topped clock tower drew attention from nearly anywhere in downtown Greensboro.

As Isabella stepped into the ground-floor office of Superior Court Clerk John Payne, she steeled herself. He had run for office as a Civil War veteran resolutely loyal to the Confederacy.

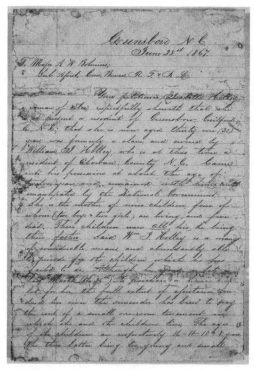

Isabella Holley, Freedmen's Bureau complaint, 1867

She may have been made to wait and cleared her throat before speaking. Still, she had come, cash in hand, to secure Payne's assistance. Experienced with the law and with drafting formal documents, Payne offered this service to everyone in Greensboro. Isabella's type of complaint did not appear on his fee schedule, but even the clerk's lowest quote of $5—$100 in today's money—was a burdensome sum for a woman unsure of how to feed her children. Perhaps Isabella had worked to save up for the visit; just as likely, she'd borrowed cash from a friend. Payne listened as she recited her story, then translated it into words on paper in his deliberate, inelegant hand.

Isabella kept score of Holley's infractions and explained that as a girl, she "came into his possession." She did not share the wretched details of what precisely Holley had entitled himself to; Isabella left the clerk to imagine the specifics. But she made the results plain enough: "She is the mother of nine children, four of whom (two boys & two girls) are living, and five dead." In the back of her mind, Isabella likely recalled that nine times her flow had stopped. Her belly had begun to swell. Of the five who had not survived to see Greensboro, she alone recalled their names and burial spots. Holley must have kept a record of how Isabella had come to increase his bounty—with her four children who lived—though no one had troubled to preserve it. Isabella, however, needed no ledger or account book to recall what had transpired—in a bed or a barn, in the light of day or under the cover of nighttime shadows.

With Payne's work done, Isabella drew her "X" on the document, but only after he had recited it aloud: "She heard read the foregoing petition and knows the contents thereof and that the same is true of her own knowledge." Her mark on the page was unsteady. There is a slight blotch where Isabella set down the quill, a sign of her inexperience with ink and paper. It was a solemn scene: Isabella left behind the compromises of life with William Holley and stepped into an even more uncertain future. Still, with her complaint in hand, Isabella wasn't yet done.

As she left the courthouse, Isabella headed west past the Odd Fellows fraternity hall and then crossed Greene Street. There she entered the Garrett Building, home to the Freedmen's Bureau. Officials at the bureau distributed rent subsidies and food rations, arbitrated labor contracts between former slaves and their employers, cataloged the violence that suppressed political rights, and adjudicated the many sorts of complaints that surfaced as Greensboro transformed from a slaveholding village to an urban laboratory of freedom. Isabella couldn't mistake how the bureau's office was far less imposing than the county courthouse. It was a modest walk-up that shared quarters with a cabinet shop, a billiard saloon, a liquor store, a dentist's office, and a dry-goods dealer. The courthouse enjoyed an air of permanence, if not timelessness. The bureau offices let on that its officials were both newcomers and transient.

Major Adolphus Bolenius greeted Isabella. Responsible for oversight of the branch and freedpeople's claims in Greensboro, he accepted her complaint as written out by Payne. An immigrant from Germany, Bolenius had lost an arm at the Battle of Bull Run. Isabella watched as he copied the account of her grievance into his ledger in a styled script, evidence of how his years as a gentleman and merchant ranked him above the court clerk, Payne. Perhaps Bolenius had questions for Isabella, but if so, his notes don't include them. His task was to send her demand on to William Holley at his Chowan County plantation. Bolenius did not promise any more than that—but still, Isabella had made him an accomplice as she elevated her story and let her interests be known.

Isabella, in her complaint, comes across as frank, a tone likely enhanced by Payne's legalese. She never characterized her bond with Holley beyond their connection as enslaved person and slaveholder: "She is now aged thirty-one years; was formerly a slave and owned by William J. Holley." Isabella never gave Holley a label or title. Over decades, the two had shared life at Bandon and she had been nine times pregnant, but Isabella didn't disclose the quality of those years. I searched for a term that best captured the ties between her and Holley. Was she a slave mistress or concubine? Between them was there favor or affection that I might call love? Perhaps there was little more between them than violence: Holley was a rapist by twenty-first-century terms. In her recent novel *Let Us Descend*, Jesmyn Ward uses *sire* to refer to a man like Holley. The double meaning fits: *sire* as in both a male who participates in procreation and a superior who commands submission.

Isabella chose the term *father* and aimed to win all she could for her children. "The ages of the children are respectively 16-11-10-9 years, the three latter being too young and small to contribute to their own maintenance, by her own unaided labor and efforts, she finds it difficult and almost impossible to provide for herself and their children." Their bonds to Holley mattered, she insisted: "These children were <u>all</u> his, he being their father." When she used the term *father*, Isabella urged the Freedmen's Bureau to see Holley's obligations as self-evident, specific, and enduring.

I resisted the idea that Holley had been *father* to Isabella's children, that he had been *grandfather* to The Bishop. I regarded such titles as more than biological facts. They were honorifics. Still, I also could not impose my judgment. I knew that many others, including the lawmakers of Isabella's time, had wantonly done just that. Some wrote laws suggesting that when Isabella resisted, Holley had committed rape: "If any person shall ravish and carnally know any female, of the age of ten years or more, by force and against her will . . . he shall suffer death." Others concluded differently and deemed Holley's power over Isabella unlimited. The state's high court had in 1830 ruled that the authority of men like Holley was unqualified: "The power of the master must be absolute, to render the submission of the slave perfect." Lawyer Thomas R. R. Cobb in 1858 wrote presumptuously, as if he knew the inner lives of women like Isabella, recommending that legislators outlaw the rape of enslaved women but reassuring that prosecutions would rarely take place: "The known lasciviousness of the negro, renders the possibility of [rape's] occurrence very remote." The act, Cobb went on to conclude, was "almost unheard of."

All around her, men told stories about Isabella and women like her. Eventually Freedmen's Bureau officials told one of their own. A clerk inked his pen and marked down a single word in the margin of her complaint: "Bastardy." Federal officials did not conclude that Isabella had been sexually assaulted. Holley had committed no offense against her. The only victim in their eyes was the state of North Carolina. Bastardy was a charge that accused both Isabella and Holley with wrongdoing. Together they parented children outside marriage but had failed to pay the bond that doing so required. Children born outside wedlock, state officials judged, became public burdens. Bastardy bonds obliged someone, often a father, to bear that expense. Isabella would have agreed that Holley should be bound to support their children. But had she also done wrong? Unequivocally, no.

I don't know how the contest between Isabella and Holley ended. I am certain that officials forwarded the charges to him at Bandon, but there's no record that he provided any additional support to Isabella. Still, she and her children survived and then focused on the future. Six months after filing her Freedmen's Bureau complaint, Isabella attended another official occasion: the marriage of her oldest daughter, Jennie, to Dallas, the youngest son of Mary and Elijah Jones. The ceremony was officiated by the Reverend Matthew Alston, minister of a newly established congregation for former slaves, St. Matthews. Isabella and her family had not only found a home but had also become part of a community. And on Jennie and Dallas's marriage bond form, where the court clerk might have named William Holley as Jennie's father, he left the space blank.

———

In Greensboro, as in many places across the onetime slaveholding South, the evidence of coupling between slaveholding men and enslaved woman—illicit, clandestine, and exploitative—was everywhere. Former slaves like "light-skinned" Isabella

wore this story on their faces, and they captured the imagination of one among Greensboro's best storytellers, Albion
Tourgée. He was a Union Army veteran from Ohio who had
carpetbagged his way to Greensboro in 1865 with his family,
business partners, and a vision for remaking the South's economy and politics. Over more than a decade and a half, Tourgée
was a Republican Party stalwart, an ally to freedpeople, and
eventually a superior court judge.

Tourgée, though tough and outspoken in politics, may be
best remembered today for his novels. In fiction, he harnessed
what he knew, what others told him, and what he felt, all
to make sense of the chaos around him. He composed hundreds of pages, fictionalized accounts of Reconstruction-era
Greensboro, most famously in his 1879 *A Fool's Errand*. Troubled truths ran across Tourgée's pages. Isabella's adopted home
was, after the war, plagued by unbridled, organized violence
that nearly engulfed the city. Too many North Carolinians,
among them members of the Ku Klux Klan, honored no limits as they sought to defy Congress and its efforts to foster a
new, interracial democracy. Violence in Greensboro and the
surrounding county targeted Republican radicals like Tourgée
and their Black compatriots. Tourgée's stories privileged and
at times overstated the role men like him played in the fight
against white supremacy. Still, his depictions of Greensboro as
a city nearly besieged by opponents of Black citizenship ring
tragically true.

If Isabella and Tourgée ever met face-to-face, it would have
been in Warnersville, the Black neighborhood Isabella called
home. Located on the southwest edge of Greensboro proper,

the community began in 1865 when northern Quakers part-nered with Black residents to develop more than thirty-five acres, subdivided into small lots that encouraged freedpeople's homeownership. Tourgée spent time in Warnersville as early as 1869 to "organize for the Republican cause." He was a keen listener who harvested characters and stories from the people of Warnersville for later inclusion in his books.

In those same years, Tourgée was at work on his first novel, *Toinette*, an exploration of what drove North Carolina's anti-miscegenation politics, first published in 1874. His protagonist, Toinette, was an enslaved young woman who loved and bore a child with her owner. She was beautiful, light-skinned, and of noble character. Toinette adapted to adversity with grace and ingenuity in a world dominated by the companion ills of slavery and racism. Absent those burdens, Tourgée suggested, she and her child would have enjoyed ideal lives. In the end, Toinette overcame, happily married to the man who had once owned her. The story promoted the possibility of intimacy and even love across lines of status and color in the postwar world.

Tourgée's story was also incendiary, especially in its por-trayal of white southern men as those who initiated and even desired interracial intimacy. He directly countered North Car-olina lawmakers who had long blamed such offenses on Black women's "lasciviousness." Tourgée pointed a finger at men's predatory inclinations, ones that women like Harriet Jacobs and Isabella knew well. Open acknowledgment of such liaisons rankled southerners who, just after the war, were reinforcing the color line. A new law that regulated marriage and defined who was a "Negro" stated "that negroes and their issue, even where one ancestor in each succeeding generation to the fourth inclusive, is white, shall be deemed persons of color." Women light in appearance, like Tourgée's protagonist Toinette, might trick the eye. But their parentage defined them.

Tourgée sympathized with the situations of women like Toinette and Isabella but knew he wrote against the tide. In 1866, North Carolina had once again outlawed marriage between white Americans and persons of color. It was an emphatic gesture given that such unions had long been void there. Judges did their part, affirming what legislators did in an 1869 high court decision that upheld the state's long tradition of barring "intermarriage" between white and Black people as "against public policy and . . . unlawful." The drumbeat of antimiscegenation law and policy continued into 1871, when the state again outlawed marriages between a white person and either a "negro" or an "Indian."

It isn't likely that Isabella read *Toinette*, though she may have heard about how some locals in Greensboro received the book. Initially, Tourgée published under a pseudonym. In 1879, he reissued the novel under his own name but, hoping to mitigate criticism, changed the ending to omit Toinette's happy marriage to her former owner. Critics pummeled the second edition of *Toinette* anyway. In Greensboro, an editor of the *Patriot* condemned the book's suggestion that white southerners ever desired intimacy and even families with Black Americans. The moment provided a lesson for Isabella and women like her: Some stories went down easier than others. Isabella and Holley had been intimate. They'd had children together. Together they had planned the future, though that had meant going separate ways. But to regard them as family was for many unthinkable. When she insisted upon Holley's culpability, the Freedmen's Bureau charge of bastardy was likely as much as Isabella could expect.

—

In 1876, Isabella erased the last vestige of her connection to William Holley: She gave up his name. That year, she met and married a widower, Albert Dunn, who had migrated to Greensboro from Virginia and was probably, like Isabella, a former slave. Albert and Isabella made a home together. Her children had married and had their own small ones to raise, and she stepped in to care for Albert's three: one boy and two girls. Their mother had died years before. I've found only snippets of their life together. Albert worked at the railroad depot, while Isabella earned her part as a nurse. They prospered enough to purchase their own house and lot in Warnersville for $144, cash. Their time together was brief. Albert died suddenly in 1880 of apoplexy, what today is termed a stroke. He was forty-five. Isabella and members of Albert's fraternal lodge saw to it that he was buried with full "Masonic honors," and in a tribute to him, Isabella kept Albert's surname for the remainder of her life.

She turned to her own children in later years. Isabella's oldest son—who went by his father's name, William Holley—saw to his mother's well-being as she aged, welcoming her into his home on South Elm Street. Isabella's younger daughter predeceased her mother and left behind a daughter of her own. Also nearby was Isabella's oldest, Jennie. Each of Jennie's six children—from her first, The Bishop, to her last, my grandfather Grandy—knew their grandmother. I had to consider that it was from Isabella herself that The Bishop first learned her story, though I cannot say which version of that story she told.

To keep these relations straight, I kept an online family tree where I plotted out those presumed to be kin—by blood, by marriage, or by law. What I puzzled over was how I should record Isabella's relationship to William Holley. At first I improvised and marked him as the first of Isabella's two husbands, although this was a fiction in the eyes of white men's law, then and now. It was not a relation that even Isabella claimed. Some years later, my family-tree program expanded its options. Adult relations grew to include "spouse," "partner," "friend," "single," "other," and "unknown." I considered marking William Holley as "unknown," but in the end, "other" seemed closer to the truth. After all, Isabella knew what her relationship was to Holley. She knew what it had meant to her, even if she never shared that with The Bishop or with me.

FOUR

Freedom

Freeing yourself was one thing, claiming owner-
ship of that freed self was another.

—TONI MORRISON, *BELOVED*

SUMMERS WITH MY GRANDMOTHER MUSIE WERE TIMES FOR
making and sharing family memories. I was only a few
weeks old the first time my parents packed me up for the long
car trip from our Manhattan walk-up to Musie's white clapboard house in Greensboro, North Carolina. Everything I
remember about that visit comes from my father's snapshots:
My mother cradled me in her arms while we gently rocked in a
wide canvas hammock under a big shade tree. The main Bennett College campus was visible just across the street. I have my
own memories of the summer I turned four. It was 1962 when
my parents dropped me with Musie and turned right around.
Back in New York, they would spend the summer buying their
first home and welcoming my sister, who was due in July. I
passed those months as my grandmother's small companion. I
can feel the rough wood of Musie's back steps under my skinny

butt. I watched her from that perch as she tended her garden, unloaded groceries from her car, and set tables and chairs for my birthday party. It topped off with the best gift ever: a puppy that I named Susie, in my grandmother's honor.

I continued to make summer treks to North Carolina for the rest of Musie's life. These journeys brought me into a family tradition that her grandmother Susan had begun. As a girl, Musie herself had been sent by her parents from their home—in Louisville and Covington in Kentucky—to Danville, where Susan had welcomed her granddaughters each summer. This time shared with elders—Musie in Danville and me in Greensboro—was a respite for our parents, who won a brief escape from the work of child-rearing. During the same breaks, our grandmothers left their marks on us. We came home reciting family tales, craving homestyle cooking, and lifted by the gift of seeing ourselves through their adoring eyes.

Musie taught me about her girlhood visits to Danville. I'd be nestled in a wicker chair on the front porch, in fresh pajamas after a bath in her deep, cool tub, or tucked into the narrow twin bed of an upstairs room as I listened to Musie paint pictures of her past. During car rides—Musie behind the wheel of her silver-blue Chevy Impala—she passed the minutes with memories of her grandmother between stops at the library, a market, or a friend's house. Sitting in her downstairs den, its walls decorated with dozens of family portraits, Musie explained that she'd been born in her grandmother Susan's Danville home. When she reached school age, Musie returned each July and August and passed the weeks on Susan's shady porch when she wasn't running errands downtown.

Musie settled on the steps or sat cross-legged on the porch while Susan presided, her head of white hair like a crown. Susan's bearing was regal, Musie explained, and my grandmother beamed as her memories spilled out. Susan arranged for new dresses, parties, and reunions with cousins who visited from Lexington. Danville was a small town when compared to the cities where Musie lived with her parents during the school year. Still, Susan did all she could to ensure that Musie's time with her was thrilling, full of family and fun. By winter, Musie pined for a return to her grandmother and Danville, just as I, as a girl, longed for the next summer's visit to Greensboro and Musie.

Slavery was the only school Susan knew. The daughter of Nancy Bell Graves, she was, like her mother, the property of Martha Fry Bell. Bell had no use for Susan's labor. Instead, as a young person, Susan earned cash for her owner by working in the home of the Reverend John Clarke Young, head of Danville's First Presbyterian Church and president of Centre College. In Young's household, Susan acquired her lifelong love of literature. Each night, the minister read to his wife with Susan seated nearby, absorbing it all, Musie explained. Young, when he exposed Susan to literature, was also conducting an experiment. He wondered how much an enslaved girl could learn. A lot, he discovered. While Susan mastered reading and recitation, she also built up her sense of self. Susan's body was enslaved. But her mind, Musie let me know, struggled to be free.

Musie was a deliberate woman who carefully worded her story about Susan's youth. I can picture my grandmother seated at her desk with inkwell and stationery set out for an afternoon of letter writing. The sun beaming in through her west-facing window and the Bennett College campus just to the right, Musie anticipated my upcoming summer visit. She wanted to be sure that I knew how Susan, despite living for years in bondage, had survived and even thrived. By the time I, as a grown woman, wanted to know even more, I was seated at my own desk as Musie had once sat at hers. My grandmother was gone, having left me to discover the rest of Susan's story on my own. I began with the clues right in front of me. I had a cache of old photos, including images of Susan, that Musie had left to my Aunt Tuppy, who gave them to me. Displayed in my dining room cabinet are Susan's dishes, ones she'd long ago used to serve visitors to her home in Danville.

—

Susan's young years were spent working in the home of Reverend Young. Musie, with her serene descriptions of that scene, downplayed the accompanying hardships. In the Young household, Susan labored to suit the needs of a busy patriarch; Young was both a working minister and a college head. She took direction from Mrs. Young, whose expectations were formed in the elite, slaveholding home of her own father, Governor and US Senator John Crittenden. Susan also tended to the Youngs' small children. When she could, she took comfort in the company of her mother, Nancy, who lived nearby. But her days were laced with fear that her family would be separated. She knew that for enslaved people, kinship ties were fragile.

By the time Susan was thirteen, Martha Fry Bell had given Susan's older sister, Martha Ann, to James Hunter with the understanding that if a court demanded it, Susan's sister would be sent out of Kentucky. The next year, Susan's cousin Cary also was freed by Martha Fry Bell, but only because he agreed to migrate to the West African colony of Liberia. In spring 1854, Cary was among nearly 250 people, most of whom were former slaves, bound for Monrovia. Slaveholders gave while also taking, and Susan had reason to fear that someone she loved might end up a long way from Danville. By the time her first two children—Susan's precious boys, John and Edward—were born at the end of the 1850s, keeping them with her was a primary concern.

When the Civil War turned central Kentucky upside down, and Susan's life along with it, she witnessed how the conflict remade Danville. Centre College, which she'd known as home to the Young family, became a makeshift hospital for wounded soldiers after the Confederacy invaded the state. The next fall, in 1862, the city's mood changed again. The Battle of Perryville played out just a dozen or so miles due west of downtown until, after tremendous bloodshed, Union forces decisively brought Kentucky under their control. Confederate troops retreated, and federal men streamed into Danville. One resident described the scene: "The courthouse, seminary buildings, every church and unoccupied house, private dwellings and all are full to overflowing." Susan, like many people in Danville, learned how to assess allies, avoid rapacious soldiers, and keep her family warm and fed. Nothing insulated her from the dangers of those years.

Susan endured threats from without and also from within the Bell clan. In summer 1863, Martha Fry Bell died, and soon

Susan and her children faced the uncertainties of an estate proceeding. Enslaved people—as belongings of Martha Fry Bell would be distributed, like other property, among creditors and heirs. Susan clung to her boys while she listened for news of their fates. She may have lingered in the parlor or the dining room as the Bell family conferred. She might have listened in as letters between the Bell heirs were read aloud. She huddled with her mother, Nancy, and her sister Martha Ann as together they assessed what was possible and what was likely. They endured the long months it took to settle Martha Fry Bell's affairs.

Bell's heirs wrangled over the future of Susan's family in callous terms. They privileged the interests of their pocketbooks over the human ones that preoccupied Susan. Finally, it was decided: Susan and her children would remain in Danville. They would not be sold or bartered away. Instead, they would join the household of Martha Fry Bell's son-in-law Ormond Beatty, a man whose prominent nose and portly middle never much changed over the many years he sat for formal portraits. Beatty was at the time a professor of chemistry and natural philosophy at Centre College. He was also an experienced manager of enslaved people, having served since 1857 as administrator of his own father's estate and the enslaved people attached to it.

Beatty recorded Susan's fate. Opening a leather-bound account book, he noted the settlement of his mother-in-law's estate: "Distribution of Mrs. Bell's property. Negroes. Susan & two children Ed and John . . . $600.00." In yet another ledger, Beatty detailed how he also took legal charge of Susan's mother, Nancy; Nancy's husband, Edmund; and three of Nancy and Edmund's children: "Slaves. Susan & two children. Edmund, Nancy, Woodson, and Nancy, jr. & Betty. Estimated altogether at [$]1,100." As Bell's heir, Beatty kept Susan and her family enslaved. He also kept them together.

During the war years, despite President Lincoln's Emancipation Proclamation and wartime acts of Congress, enslaved people in Kentucky remained in bondage by state law. News of a new Thirteenth Amendment to the US Constitution traveled unevenly across the nation, but by June 1865, the merits of the change were being debated openly on the pages of the *Central Kentucky Gazette*. "The world," one local leader urged, "is moving." Susan was among the many who watched and waited in Danville while too little felt sure. Hearts sank when Kentucky's General Assembly refused to endorse the new amendment and then lifted when the necessary two-thirds of all states approved it, bringing abolition to Kentucky over the objections of its legislators.

In Beatty's household, it was clear why men like him opposed slavery's abolition. Without his property in persons, the professor's wealth nearly evaporated. Like his father and mother-in-law before him, Beatty had prospered by relying on enslaved labor in his home. He had paid no wages for the upkeep of his household or its grounds. He had earned cash when he'd hired out slaves to friends and neighbors and then collected their wages for himself. The abolition of slavery ended these arrangements. It also established some distance between Beatty, Susan, and others like her. A new future was possible. Susan—with her boys and a new daughter born in 1863—set up a household and anticipated her children's futures: their lessons to learn, vocations to pursue, and freedom dreams to invent. Old tethers that had once bound people like Susan and Ormond Beatty to one another stretched, strained, and threatened to break.

—

My great-aunt Sweets was Musie's sister, and she had her own stories to tell about Susan. "Grandmother did marry a Negro man," she recalled during an oral history interview. I knew Sweets as a petite woman who dressed in smart suits and spoke with a sharp tongue. After studying at Mount Holyoke, the New York School of Social Work, and the University of Chicago, Sweets learned politics as a YWCA field organizer and at the NAACP's 1933 Amenia conference. By the 1940s, she was based in Washington, DC, and served on the NAACP board while also holding posts in federal agencies, on a presidential civil rights commission, and as a congressional staffer. Behind the scenes, Aunt Sweets was an adviser to men like Civil Rights leader and NAACP head Walter White and Claude Barnett, the journalist who founded the Associated Negro Press news service.

In our family, Sweets was among the best storytellers. In the 1970s, a researcher from Harvard University's Schlesinger Library interviewed her for an oral history collection, and Sweets eagerly went on the record. Not long into the conversation, she recalled her grandmother Susan and her forty-six-year-long marriage to a man named Sam Davis. As Sweets told it, Susan's life illustrated how in Danville, even after slavery,

families continued to cross the color line. A cousin in Lexington first pointed this out to Sweets when she commented,
"[Susan] had the nerve to marry a Negro man and start a family." This puzzled Sweets. "I never thought about Grandmother
that way," she admitted. "I thought of her, I thought what kind
of person she was to have picked that path."

That "path" was her grandmother's marriage to a "Negro
man," Sam. In one important way, Susan and Sam were the
same: Both had lived in central Kentucky, enslaved before the
war. But there the similarity ended. While Susan spent the war
in Danville, waiting to learn the result of Martha Fry Bell's
estate proceedings and the fate of her family, Sam enlisted. The
Union Army had established a Kentucky depot for the con-
solidation of troops and supplies, Camp Nelson. It sat about
sixteen miles northeast of Danville. A total of eight "colored"
regiments organized there—nearly ten thousand men, with
Sam among them. By 1868, when Sam and Susan decided to
marry, both were free. In January, Sam headed to the county
courthouse to secure a marriage bond. The $100 fee, guaran-
teed by Sam's brother-in-law, promised that nothing barred
their union.

When she married Sam, Susan already had three children:
Edward, John, and Fannie. The next year, their daughter, Lils,
was born. By 1870, the census taker found the six of them living together. Sam worked as a hotel waiter, Susan was at home
"keeping house," and the older boys were at school; all were
marked "M" for mulatto, as per the bureau's directions: "Be par-
ticularly careful in reporting the class Mulatto." The term had a
broad meaning: "[Mulatto] is here generic, and includes so-called

quadroons, octoroons, and all persons having any perceptible trace of African blood. Important scientific results depend upon the correct determination of this class." The enumerator carefully reported Sam, Susan, and their children as mulatto, while the boarders living in their home he marked as "B" for Black.

Aunt Sweets noticed how Susan and Sam differed in their demeanors. Susan cloaked herself in middle-class pretensions when, for example, serving her ladies club on fine French china. Sam did not. He "didn't have the refinement," Sweets remembered. "He was quiet," by which she meant that Susan took charge of things at home, called the shots, while Sam

Susan Penman Davis

attended to her needs and handed over his pay each week as a matter of course. Sweets also understood that Susan had married a Negro man, while Susan's sisters had not. Her oldest sister, Martha Ann, briefly made a home and bore three daughters with a white man, James Hunter. Susan's younger sister, Fannie, stayed long enough with another white man to have four children before she packed them up, left Danville, and resettled alone in Lexington. Sam was Susan's "path," a difficult one, and her "nerve" won Susan her granddaughter's admiration.

The most remarkable difference between Susan and Sam was not demeanor. Nor was it how their marriage differed from those of Susan's sisters. What most distinguished Susan from Sam was how she regarded the slaveholding household in which she'd been raised. Sam cut his ties, left his past as a slave behind, and clearly marked the start of his new life as a freedman. He changed his name. When he enlisted, Sam went by Kincaide, using the family name of his owner. By the war's end, he had deliberately adopted the name Davis, that of his own father. Susan, in contrast, never broke with the Bell family. She kept Bell, using it as a middle name for the rest of her life. She also regarded the family of Martha Fry Bell and Ormond Beatty like her own.

—

After the war, Susan held on to the Bell name and her ties to Ormond Beatty. His biographers—some associated with Centre College and others part of the Presbyterian Church— uncritically admired him. The esteem of these institutions was bound up with Beatty's reputation. They never mentioned that before the Civil War, he had grown prosperous by exploiting the labor and the lives of enslaved people like Susan. They also did not admit how, even after slavery's abolition, by managing her money, Beatty lorded it over Susan's life.

In the same ledgers where I'd found her mother, Nancy, I discovered a record of how Susan had worked in Beatty's home until summer 1867, many months after she'd become free. That season, it looked like she'd finally got clear of him. Beatty closed her account: "I made a full settlement with Susan and paid her all I owed to her up to August 1st 1867 at which time her service with me expired." Susan was on the verge of a new chapter, about to break with her past. Liberated from Beatty, she married Sam just a few months later. But her independence did not last. Five years later, Susan and Sam turned to Beatty, who opened a new account in Sam's name. He lent the couple $435.82 for the purchase of a lot. The next summer, he lent

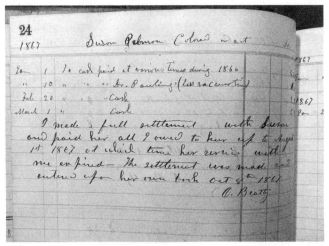

Ledger of Ormond Beatty, entry for Susan (Penman) Davis, 1867

Susan and Sam another $320.32, likely to finance the construction of a house for their family.

I sat alone in the Centre College library, going line by line over Beatty's ledgers. Each time I turned a page, I willed Susan to get free of him. But she never got far. Susan and Sam often had money trouble—as in too little of it—and went deeper into debt. Goosebumps ran up and down my arms when I read an 1876 sheriff's notice that threatened to claim their land for $4.39 in overdue local taxes. That small sum was a fortune for Sam and Susan, but they caught up on what they owed the town and kept their home. Getting there required relying on Beatty, whose grip on Sam and Susan tightened with each small loan. They submitted to servitude of another kind as they worked to slowly pay off what they owed. Each month, Beatty opened his ledger to Susan's page, toting up debts and credits all the way to 1890. When he died that year, Susan still owed Beatty $17.

Beatty's ledgers are a cold source. They never give away what people felt or reveal their intimate circumstances. On many days, Beatty gave only a brief thought to Susan as he marked down what she'd earned or owed. He never went beyond dollars and cents, making it difficult for me to discern the emotional terms of their dealings. Likely these transactions were tense and even demeaning for Susan, as the record of Beatty's transactions with another former slave, Mary King, suggests. Mary's former owner died and left Mary $500, which Beatty managed. He maintained his grip on her inheritance, controlled her moneys, and stingily doled out bits of cash over many, many years. Mary's notes to Beatty, saved among his papers, tell the story.

Mary pleaded with Beatty for what she needed. A letter dated February 22, 1877, was typical: "Mr. Beatty. Kind [sir] I would be pleased if you [would] send me four dollars. My condition has [been] so that I will have to ask you for [some money.] times is so hard that my husband could not get out to get any work. I had to sow with ten pigs But that [are] all dead. I [expected] to make money off of them but [they are] dead I will have to ask you for some money. Mary King." Again and again, Mary asked Beatty to release small sums, sounding like a supplicant rather than the modest heiress that she was. When he kept her account, Beatty held on to his power over Mary. My heart hurt as I saw Mary's dignity wither in the face of Beatty's paternalism. I hoped that Susan's negotiations with Beatty were less demeaning, though I'd no reason to think they were.

—

Ormond Beatty was not the only member of his family with ties to Susan. During her years working for him, Susan grew to know Beatty's daughter, Pattie, born in 1853, when Susan was a teen. She watched Pattie grow into a mediocre student but a vivacious socialite. Pattie married at the age of twenty-nine, on a Tuesday evening in February 1882. The couple gathered with friends and family in Ormond Beatty's home in the Centre College president's mansion. Set on a bluff overlooking the campus, the house had a brick facade grandly appointed with a portico and four stately columns. Guests walked up from the nearby carriage path and filled two front parlors.

The afternoon was carefully orchestrated. Pattie's wedding, like many among the local elite, was influenced by merchants and marketers who promoted an elaborate etiquette. Danville's local newspaper warned against wedding unreformed grooms, men who would not give up their bachelor habits. Readers learned who was to bear which expenses and how a widow's nuptials should be more modest than those of a first-time bride. It also prescribed what unfolded in the Beatty parlors. On one side stood arrayed the bride and groom, their families, two ministers—one Presbyterian, the other Methodist—and "five little girls" for attendants. Pattie was the centerpiece of this tableau. Her dress reflected the "white wedding" tradition inaugurated by England's Queen Victoria in 1840: "white embossed velvet, with jabots of real Spanish lace and Roman pearls, and court grain of gas-blue satin surah," the *Danville Tribune* breathlessly reported, all complemented by a "customary" veil.

Pattie displayed her gifts, which, guides suggested, were generally intended for the bride alone. Only close family and friends presented personal items; most offered a check or an adornment for the home. Everyone took care to avoid gifts that suggested that the bride was entering marriage without an adequate trousseau. Pattie carefully noted each item received on a handwritten list that today is preserved among her father's papers. Fashionable choices included china, clocks, lamps, a sofa pillow, and a book—Milton's *Paradise Lost*—with gilt details. Silver items predominated, signifying the wealth of the givers and reflecting how goods from companies such as Reed & Barton and Tiffany had become synonymous with better gift giving. Her brother-in-law presented Pattie with a carved walnut table, and the groom marked their marriage by offering her flowers and diamonds, the former ephemeral and the latter everlasting.

Susan presented the bride-to-be with a bell. She might have given Pattie a lace spread, as Susan's sister did. She could have done the same as her brother and given Pattie an old-fashioned plaque. Sophy Campbell, the Beattys' cook, offered two antique plates and a silk scarf. Susan knew of many possibilities, and from among them, she chose a bell. Glass, too delicate for everyday use, was an attractive trinket to display atop a bureau or writing table. Silver was an extravagance, though perhaps Susan chose a silver-plated example that could be bought for as little as 50 cents, the equivalent of $30 today. A bell of hearty brass would have had many purposes during Pattie's days as head of her own household. Having served on and off in the Beatty home, Susan would have heard a bell used as a summons that brought a servant to a master's side. Only Pattie would ring a bell, while Susan was obliged to answer it.

The gift of a bell had a second meaning when exchanged between Susan and Pattie. Bell was their shared family name. Both of their mothers had at one time been called just that: Pattie's mother, Mildred, until she married Ormond Beatty in 1848 and Susan's mother, Nancy, until she married Edmund Graves. The bell was both a suitably polite and intensely intimate gesture. More than years of service bound Susan and Pattie to one another. Whether it sat on Pattie's nightstand or by her elbow on that new walnut dining table, when rung, the bell delicately sounded a family's past.

Not all signs of how Susan's family was tied to that of the Beattys were subtle. Some were, for me, unexpected. Susan's

sister Martha Ann never worked for Beatty. She never borrowed money or asked for credit. Martha Ann did not send
a gift to mark Pattie's wedding. She did, however, appear in
Beatty's account books. When short on cash, he asked Martha
Ann for a loan, funds that helped finance Pattie's costly wedding. Marriage manuals warned that it was easy for families
to spend too much on a wedding. They would be tempted to
spend on dresses, meals, carriages, jewelry, and flowers.

Pattie's ceremony indulged in all this and more. Just five
weeks before the day, Ormond Beatty signed a promissory
note to Martha Ann: "Danville Ky January 1 1882. Twelve
months after date for value received, I promise to pay Martha
Ann Hunter fifty dollars with interest from date, at the rate
of 8 per cent per annum until principal is paid. O. Beatty."
This loan equaled $1,500 in today's money. Relations ran in
two directions between Susan's people and Beatty's household.
Beatty remained indebted to Martha Ann through to his death
in 1890. When his estate was finally settled, she received a final
balance due her: $146.90.

—

For all her life, Susan remained learned in a way that reflected
her early years bound to Reverend Young's household. Musie
made sure her own children knew Susan for themselves,
sending them to see their great-grandmother in Danville. She
recounted for an oral history, "When my two oldest children
were about three and four, I took them to see her, and she
recited for us, sitting in her rocking chair on the front porch,
all of Byron's 'Prisoner of Chillon.'" I looked it up: 392 lines

composed in the early nineteenth century. For Musie, Susan's mastery of Byron's narrative poem exemplified how her grandmother managed to eke out dignity from years spent enslaved.

When I finally read "The Prisoner of Chillon" for myself, my admiration for Susan initially swelled. She had learned the poem early in life, in the 1850s, in Reverend Young's home and then held on to each and every word for more than seven decades until the end of her life. As I worked my way through the stanzas, I felt a weight grow in my chest. Byron imagined for his readers a man who, after years detained, nearly preferred the squalor and solitude of his cell to the open-endedness of freedom. Through Byron's words, I felt Susan come through in a way that no photo, or even the recollections of her adoring granddaughters, Musie and Sweets, could convey. I sensed that the prisoner's story was a version of Susan's own. She too was someone who never completely got free of her chains.

Byron's poem was inspired by his visit to Lake Geneva's Chillon Castle, where, in the 1530s, a monk had been held as a political prisoner. Byron then composed the saga of a man who, unjustly detained, languished in a dungeon. His "keepers" remained callous but eventually loosened his chains. It was a gesture that felt empty: "A kind of change came in my fate, / My keepers grew compassionate; / I know not what had made them so, / They were inured to sights of woe." When finally liberated, the prisoner sensed how time in detention had changed him. He no longer craved freedom: "At last men came to set me free; / I ask'd not why, and reck'd not where; / It was at length the same to me, / Fetter'd or fetterless to be, / I learn'd to love despair." The prisoner only reluctantly emerged from confinement and lamented abandoning the friends that had kept him company: spiders and mice. He even missed his chains: "My very chains and I grew friends, / So much a long communion tends, / To make us what we are: even I, / Regain'd my freedom with a sigh."

The parallels between Susan and Byron's prisoner struck me. For Susan, enslavement's chains were long, durable, and twisted. And she loved them. Susan never gave up her ties to the Bell-Beatty family. They had been her companions in confinement, and, not unlike the prisoner's "mice" and "spiders," they became dear. Though no one ever came right out and said it, Musie believed Susan's connection to the Bells and Beattys ran deeper still. They were family, as Musie explained: "I am quite sure," she began, "we never knew exactly what connection we had with the white people in our grandmother's home that might have been part of her, really part of our, family."

Susan did not directly tell Musie that she and the Beattys were kin. Instead, she showed her. Each summer, Susan dressed her granddaughter in her best, and then they loaded into Susan's buggy. She took the reins and steered toward Pattie's grand home on Danville's Lexington Avenue. Once parked out front, the two headed up the long front walk. Susan knocked on the front door, and after another moment, she and Musie stepped inside. Pattie welcomed them into the parlor, where they took their places on her finely upholstered seats. It was an exceptional scene. Nearly all Black visitors to Pattie's home entered at the back, a reflection of their subordinate status. Musie noted that she and Susan were different: They "always went to the front door" because they were making what Musie termed a "formal call." Formal as in social. Formal as in a reunion of kin.

On a visit to Danville, I retraced Susan's path, discovering that Pattie's home still stands. The late-Victorian two-story brick house—added to the National Register of Historic Places in the 1980s—is today mostly obscured by mature trees. It is a long trek from the curb to the front door, and I sat for a good while, my rental car in park and the engine running. The courage to approach the house, ring the bell, and ask if I might look around never materialized. I didn't have the nerve to open that door to the past. That brand of courage was Susan's alone.

—

The closest I came to knowing Susan and her husband, Sam, on their own terms was the day I visited their burial sites in Danville's Hilldale Cemetery. The place is miles from their home on the other side of town. It was a fitting site for their final rest, and not only because Hilldale was Danville's principal Black cemetery. Most of Susan's people—her mother, Nancy, and some brothers and sisters—are also buried there. Sam's kin, including his sister, rest nearby. Technically Hilldale sat outside Danville proper, in the Black enclave of Duncan Hill, where many folks, including Susan's mother, Nancy, and her husband, Edmund, wound up settling on small plots after the war.

I pulled up to the cemetery gates and parked just outside the entrance. Affixed to a stone pillar was a large bronze plaque placed there in May 1948 by Danville's Domestic Economy Club. It was a tribute to Susan, who was credited as their "organizer." An old news article explained the rest of the story. More than two decades after her death, a crowd gathered at Hilldale to recognize Susan's leadership. The club she had founded continued to meet long after she passed. Among those who honored her were nurses, ministers, and the next generation of Domestic Economy Club leaders. No one from the Bell-Beatty clan was there.

When I saw the plaque, it occurred to me that I was not at Hilldale only to ferret out clues to the past. I was also there to pay my respects. I flushed, embarrassed to be underdressed in a fleece pullover, a cheap, faded blue-and-gray windbreaker, and shoes better suited to mud than to a formal visit at Susan's resting place. Nobody needed to remind me that whenever Musie or Sweets had visited Hilldale, they'd taken care to choose the right ensemble, a sign of respect for the dead and a demand for respectability from the living. That morning, I had hurriedly pulled back my hair before heading out for a day's sleuthing. All I could do was put away my camera, slow down, and take in the whole of this quiet memorial that our family and others like them had made.

FIVE

Reconstruction

Their faces, like all faces, are time batteries, and
maybe even works of art.
—RUTH OZEKI, *THE FACE: A TIME CODE*

JENNIE WAS ISABELLA'S OLDEST CHILD AND THE BISHOP'S
mother. It was 1902 when she sat down during the daylight
hours in her Warnersville home. She held a pencil in her hand
while in the air, coal fumes mixed with the stench of drying
tobacco leaves and the sourness of liquor poured in nearby
saloons. Her home was not yet connected to the city's electric
grid, and Jennie relied on the sun or a gas lamp and candles
to help her aging eyes find their way. She poured out wor-
ries about her youngest boy, Davie, with a dull point on paper.
That boy would grow up to be my grandfather.

She'd recently sent Davie to New Orleans, where he lived
with his older brother, a young minister and journalist who
only decades later would be a head of the Methodist Church,
The Bishop. Greensboro was a long way from New Orleans,
but word about Davie's troubles had reached Jennie. "I am so

sorry that [D]avie will not do right . . . his nature is rough," she wrote. Should she arrange to bring Davie back to Greensboro? "I rather you would send him home than to worry." He might be too much trouble for her daughter-in-law, The Bishop's wife, Valena, to handle. A new mother, she had her own small child to tend to: "My dear dau[gh]ter Valena . . . I have been a mother so long I know something about house keeping it is not [an] easy job . . . do not worry about David I will take him home." Jennie fretted. Was she the mother she'd hoped to be? "No one know[s how] much I study about my children." These like all matters, Jennie left to God: "I trust that god will help me."

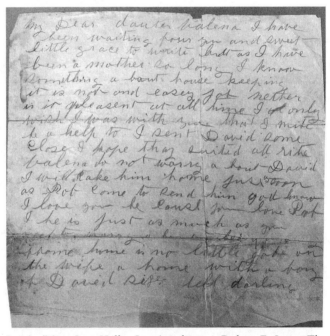

Jennie (Mary Jane Holley Jones) to her son Robert E. Jones, The Bishop, circa 1902

This is how I first encountered my great-grandmother Jennie: with her heart spilling across a few precious sheets of paper. Among The Bishop's materials preserved at the Amistad Research Center, I found two of Jennie's missives. It took me a while to make out the words and realize that Jennie was their author. It was an unexpected discovery that left me nearly breathless. Of all the women in our family who began their lives enslaved, Jennie is the only one whose unfiltered words, written in her own hand, survived. Jennie's script, spelling, and grammar are uneven. Some people might call it a scrawl. What I saw, however, was her soul, wholly apparent as she wrote down her fears about Davie. Her devotion to family—"My da[r]lling son Rob," "I remain your Devoted mother"—hovered above every page. I slowed down and breathed Jennie in.

The Bishop proudly remembered his mother, Jennie, as one of Greensboro's first Black schoolteachers. She was part of those years in which Greensboro, the South, and the nation were being remade during the period that history books call Reconstruction. Former slaves of all ages, eager to learn, gathered around others like Jennie who could read, write, or calculate. I can't say how Jennie learned what she did. She may have stolen the lessons taught to William Holley's white children. She might have picked up a primer and secretly taught herself. What Jennie knew, The Bishop explained, she shared with the people around her. Later, formally trained educators came to Warnersville and opened a schoolhouse. Before they arrived, Jennie was one of Black Greensboro's first and best teachers.

—

Jennie married Dallas Jones in December 1867, and her mother breathed a small sigh of relief. Isabella was nearly overcome by poverty after William Holley abandoned her household. When Jennie set out to make her own home with Dallas, she lightened her mother's load. Isabella had one less mouth to feed, one less body to keep dry and warm. Dallas was a young man of some means, owning a small rectangle of land just east of Greensboro's downtown, alongside plots held by his brothers. He earned his living making shoes, a skill handed down by his father, Elijah. Dallas and Jennie set out to build a future on land, a livelihood, and by 1872 children. That year, their first baby arrived, and over the following years, a total of six small ones went from first breaths to standing upright under their roof.

Their parents before them had built families while dodging jagged boundaries of color, class, and status. Jennie's parents, Isabella and William Holley, had been slave and slaveholder and lived a crude bargain that failed once slavery ended. Dallas's folks, Mary and Elijah, were free people whose marriage defied the color line. Their origin stories differed: Jennie had been born enslaved, while Dallas had been born free. He owned a small plot of land, while she had little more than the crude cotton dress on her back. In Warnersville, these differences did not matter. There and across North Carolina, the color line was being redrawn. It was bright and stark. Officials might occasionally mark them by shades of skin, such as mulatto or Black. But on most days, officials grouped Jennie, Dallas, and their neighbors under the same category. They were colored.

In North Carolina's capital, Raleigh, the legislature was at work redefining the color line. In 1866, a new statute aimed to define who was colored: "Negroes and their issue, even where one ancestor in each succeeding generation to the fourth inclusive, is white, shall be deemed persons of color." Using terms like *issue*, *ancestor*, and *generation*, lawmakers adopted formal, pseudoscientific language to set in place a fictional line. Jennie and Dallas sat on one side: colored and kin. Their white parents, nearly erased by law, were relegated to the other.

In Warnersville, much of life was defined by the hardships of violence, poverty, and meager political rights. Still, when I looked back, I was comforted by how Jennie and Dallas had lived. Around them, at home in small cottages along muddy lanes, were people of all shades, from alabaster to ebony. Their families crowded into identical shacks and made their way each Sunday to one of the sanctuaries built just for them. When schools came, children crowded in, divided only by age or what learning they brought with them. Sometimes people ventured elsewhere, but usually to labor for the day or overnight. When a newcomer recited the names of their kin, everyone knew to whom they belonged. Jennie and Dallas were parents, churchgoers, and friends. They were Joneses. They were colored.

In two small rooms, Jennie spent decades keeping house and worrying. Could she calm her youngest son's restlessness or comfort her oldest daughter's fussy infants? She fretted over the dangers of military service when the army sent her son-in-law to war in the Philippines. She barely withstood the shock of her younger daughter's sudden death. By the time Jennie sat down to write to her oldest son in New Orleans, she was bent from shouldering a tremendous lot. She prayed for The Bishop as he made his own home so far from Warnersville. He'd surely shared with Jennie his love for the majesty of its waterways, from the Mississippi to the Gulf of Mexico. She might have known that in New Orleans, the color line had its own irregular shape, an artifact of centuries-old mixing of people said to be French, Spanish, American, and African. In contrast, Greensboro was a tiny landlocked town of little distinction. There Jennie worried about many things, but color wasn't one of them.

———

Jennie's husband, Dallas, exuded ambition from the start. He impressed some but alarmed others as he moved through Greensboro as a "proud, restless, forceful man," as The Bishop remembered him. His range of vocations dazzle: a cobbler who in some years set up shop in the family's McCulloch Street shack. Everyone at home lived to the tip-tap rhythms of his small hammer on tiny tacks and the smells of leather being shaved, stretched, and rendered suitable for everyday wear. At other times, Dallas poured spirits in the downtown saloons that sat just behind Greensboro's federal building, where his son recalled working out his first math problems on the floor. Dallas unloaded flats and stocked shelves at his brother-in-law's grocery on East Market Street. Later he made the rounds as a city lamplighter, a job that paid a welcome wage.

I think of Dallas as a small-scale hero in a drama that, after the Civil War, looked to reconstruct North Carolina into an interracial democracy. It was always an uphill fight. Factions there splintered and faced off: Republican versus Democrat. White versus Black. Radical versus conservative. Segregationist versus integrationist. The battle took Greensboro and the whole of the South from the optimism of Reconstruction through a reign of white supremacy, and all the while, Dallas was in the mix. A man shuffling through a succession of jobs, he had only one genuine calling: politics.

Dallas was "a Republican politician who could divert enough votes from an organization candidate to his own man to elect a Democrat when his party leaders slighted him," The Bishop told Richard Bardolph. Dallas was among the wave of Black men who registered to vote for the first time in 1868. New laws had finally erased the long ban against Black votes in North Carolina. It was October when the county clerk inscribed Dallas, along with his brothers, on the voter roll. Those were dangerous days. The local, pro–white supremacy *Greensboro Patriot* seethed as Black men began to exercise their newly won political rights. Dallas thrived during rough-and-tumble political campaigns, stump speeches, and club meetings while enduring threats and violence. He became known as an independent, unorthodox politician who openly debated opponents and organized for whatever party might win him an advantage. Until the 1890s, his allies included white men like Albion Tourgée. But eventually Black men in Greensboro were left to stand alone as the scourge of terror crushed any possibility of interracial alliances.

Jennie had reason to worry as she waited for Dallas to come home from nights at Republican club meetings. In

THE TROUBLE OF COLOR

their tight quarters, he could not slip in unnoticed. The door creaked. The floorboards moaned. The stench of his work clothes and the smells from the alley filled the space. Jennie held her breath many nights, and for good reason. Whether out of bravado brought on by the whiskey he poured or tensions wrought by his willingness to confront political foes, she knew that Dallas might wind up in the mud, in the gutter, or on a sawdust-covered floor before the night ended. One clash, just before Christmas 1876, earned him an assault conviction. Relief came only when the mayor's court suspended the judgment. Dallas was lucky to make it home that night, sleeping in their bed rather than on the dirt floor of Greensboro's jailhouse.

Jennie became only more anxious as Dallas grew into a notorious Republican Party leader. No longer just a reliable cobbler or jovial barkeep, Dallas became a target. In 1880, a local newspaper excoriated him as one member of a "spike team," a term that generally denoted beasts of burden—horses and oxen—powerfully harnessed together. In politics, the connotation was that men like Dallas—in strong, tight alliances—cleared the field of opponents during election season with brute force. Dallas relished his reputation, but it was a risky one in a city dominated by Democrats who craved white rule.

Dallas juggled his other activities with the challenge of parenting three, then four, five, and finally six children. His youngest—my grandfather Grandy—was born in 1887. In the next years, Dallas's adversaries pinned a target to his back. I'm not sure how to feel about the risks he took. I am proud to learn that he fought against the segregation, disenfranchisement, and violence that descended on Greensboro. He courageously insisted on a more just future for the city's Black community. I am also terrified to think of how Dallas risked his own safety and with it the well-being of his children. Back in Warnersville, they slept most nights piled together in their shared beds. He and Jennie had our family's next generation in their care.

Jennie didn't need to attend party meetings to know that Dallas was running in important circles. In late-night whispers, he could recount for her how contests over political power were heating up in Greensboro. Local newspapers put the changes unfolding in North Carolina into a national context. In Washington, DC, Congress and the Supreme Court had abandoned Black southerners, leaving them without recourse when local white people looked to take away their rights. Republican Party heads appointed Dallas to the leadership: On a committee of credentials, he judged which men were in and which were out when it came to candidates for office. He was the sole "colored" man among the committee's members. Most of his life with Jennie—at home, school, and church—was segregated in those years, while in politics, Dallas shared power with white men.

Sometime around 1890, Dallas's political career hit a wall: a phalanx of white Democrats determined to crush Black voters in Greensboro. In advance of election day, anonymous men circulated a broadside that directed poll officials to refuse nearly four hundred men their ballots. Each was identified by name on a perverse who's-who list of Black Greensboro, Dallas among them. It read, "The following is a correct list of the COLORED VOTERS registered at Greensboro. . . . If any of them are on your book let us know AT ONCE, through a letter from

Broadside, circa 1890

your Registrar, that we may challenge them here and we may urge you to do so at your place: *but don't challenge until the day of the election.*" The city's Black voters were on notice.

Word reached Dallas. A fellow party member might have caught up with him at home and shared news of the looming threat. Perhaps he first read the notice pinned to the wall of a nearby saloon or coffeehouse. Warnings must have spread quickly by word of mouth in the days that followed: from neighbor to friend, from brother to brother, and from father to son. Men gathered throughout Warnersville, on corners, on porches, and in parlors. They gauged risks, weighed responses, and took stock of the few white allies who remained. Women like Jennie—wives, mothers, sisters—weighed in too. Everyone balanced concerns about personal safety against the principle at stake. As election day approached, things in Greensboro heated up. They threatened to explode.

Local papers reported nothing about what happened next. There's no record of widespread violence or mob attacks on that election day. The threat may have been enough to keep men like Dallas at home. They stayed away from the polls, forced to give up casting ballots. Some felt defeated and others relieved. Some held on to their fighting spirit, while others turned inward and safeguarded their jobs and their homes. There were those who abandoned politics altogether. For Dallas, the incident marked the end of his political career. What it meant to be colored in Greensboro had a new meaning. Violence wrenched their political rights from Dallas and men like him.

Then Dallas disappeared, at least from the public record. I searched for any sign of him in the days, months, and years after that fateful election day. It netted me nothing. The silence that surrounds his end still puzzles me. Was it so ignoble that no one—not a local paper, public officials, or even our family stories—dared make a record? Did he continue to oppose the rise of Jim Crow politics so adamantly that his opponents did Dallas in? Perhaps, with his political prospects crushed, Dallas drifted away from his family, his work, and even his adopted hometown. I've only seen one photo of Dallas, distorted now by time and the elements. Maybe he left Greensboro—disappeared into his fair skin, pointed features, and bushy mustache—taken for Spanish, Portuguese, or French rather than colored.

I remembered The Bishop. He was curiously quiet about the end of his father's life. Neither his interview with Richard Bardolph nor his personal papers hinted at why Dallas disappeared from Greensboro. Was The Bishop hiding something or shielding his feelings from a difficult truth? Was he ashamed by how Dallas left behind his family or as confused as I was about how a man with roots, kin, and a reputation gave it all up? Was The Bishop protecting someone—his mother, his siblings, himself—from the memory of a betrayal? All I can say for certain is that by whatever terms, Dallas had definitively crossed over by the late 1890s. Not a trace of him survives.

Dallas had been larger than life. Now Jennie had to assume his place. In 1899, she called three generations of her family together in Warnersville. A photographer arranged them in a cluster: a grandmother, her children, their spouses, and the family's newest members. She sat at center right, her daughter Jessie to the left. Each woman held a small child. They were Jessie's babies and Jennie's grandchildren: Jennie Louise, named for her grandmother, and Valena, named for The Bishop's future wife, who waited for him back in New Orleans. The Bishop was seated at his mother's feet alongside Jennie's Davie, my grandfather.

The simple houses of Warnersville were faintly visible in the background. The family appeared to be fixed there as everyone but little Jennie Louise dutifully held a pose for the camera. But outside its frame, Jennie's family was in motion. Her oldest, Minnie, had moved on to live with her new husband's

Jennie Holley Jones and family; David Dallas Jones (Grandy) and Robert Jones (The Bishop) in the foreground

family. Daughter Jessie, married with two girls, kept her own house. Jennie spent most days at home with her two younger daughters. Shortly after this gathering, The Bishop boarded a train for Louisiana, where over the next year, he married, had his first child, and lightened his mother's burden by arranging for his troublesome baby brother to join him there. My copy of this family portrait, passed to me by my father, has been handled many times. It has been shared among us, evidence of where we began and of who we once were.

—

Jennie had always attended to her family while also building up the institutions that sustained them. She was there when, shortly after her marriage to Dallas, Warnersville's Methodists founded their own church. The congregation blended new converts with families expelled from the white-led West Market Street church. They named the sanctuary St. Matthews, and a migrant from Georgia, the Reverend Matthew Alston—the man who had married Jennie and Dallas—led them. It took decades for Jennie and her neighbors to raise enough funds for a new brick-and-mortar building. But their first, modest house of worship commanded Sundays in Warnersville when in fall 1872, a newly installed bell summoned congregants to prayer.

The main floor at St. Matthews was reserved for those forging their relationship to God. All of Jennie's children learned lessons of faith there, especially The Bishop, for whom the Methodist church became his vocation. The basement, the congregation determined, would have another purpose: a school. There the lessons were reading, writing, and calculating. This modest start became, in 1873, Bennett College. The school educated generations of students, from new learners to those training to become teachers and ministers. A benefactor from New York helped Bennett purchase ten acres just across the railroad tracks from Warnersville. Buildings went up, lawns were cleared and trees planted, and students enrolled. At Bennett, Jennie's daughters became schoolteachers of the credentialed sort. The Bishop was trained to ascend within the church hierarchy. In 1926, more than a half century after Bennett's founding, Jennie's boy Davie took charge of the school as its eighth president. He reorganized it into a liberal arts college for women.

I knew this story of Bennett's founding by heart, and I might have continued to tell it just that way. But in 2015, I stumbled onto a news report that changed my thinking. A writer for a Greensboro paper reviewed a biography of Albion Tourgée, the carpetbagger activist who, after the Civil War, settled in Greensboro. The article told a different story about Bennett's founding: The school began not in St. Matthews Church but rather on Tourgée's farm. He and his wife were credited with organizing the "area's first 'colored' school. (It became Bennett Seminary in 1873.)" I blinked hard and read the line again. How could it be right that Tourgée, rather than Jennie and the St. Matthews congregation, had given Bennett its start?

A Bennett alumna, class of 1955, was also unsettled and challenged the Tourgée story in a letter to the editor. She recited the same tale I knew: "Bennett College was organized by the Rev. Matthew Alston, minister of St. Matthews Methodist Episcopal Church, in 1873 in the church basement." There was, I began to understand, a real dispute about the school's founding and, I thought, Jennie's part in it. One line in the alum's letter stood out to me: "Nowhere in the history of the college does the name of Albion Tourgée appear." Was Tourgée never there, or was he present for Bennett's founding, only to later have his name dropped from histories of the school?

It was not very difficult to find Tourgée there during Bennett's early years. Jennie, the St. Matthews congregation, and the school community knew him well. Tourgée was a featured speaker during Bennett's spring 1875 commencement. In 1879, he delivered the school's annual address on the theme "Courage the keystone to success." Educator Charles Moore, who formally incorporated Bennett as a college in 1889, recalled Tourgée. Under cover of night, Tourgée and others instructed former slaves about their rights at the Warnersville school. Perhaps Jennie, Dallas, or even their older children studied with the lawyer turned judge.

Tourgée not only took part in the school's early rituals. Once upon a time, he was also part of Bennett lore. Jennie would have known these stories, which were still being told while her son The Bishop was a Bennett student in the 1890s. One source was James Corrothers, later a noted poet, journalist, and minister, who was one of The Bishop's closest classmates. Corrothers recalled having been told that Tourgée had written his most popular book, *A Fool's Errand*, in the Bennett library. Corrothers even believed that he had studied at the table once used by Tourgée. It was among the young poet's most cherished memories. I read Corrothers's 1916 autobiography, *In Spite of the Handicap*, and believed him enough to make a call to Bennett's current president. She had never heard tell of the Tourgée table, but I still hold on to hope that today it is somewhere in the school's library.

Tourgée had been forgotten, and I could only speculate as to why. Then I remembered Dallas. He and Tourgée were, when it came to politics, two of a kind. Each, I could see, made his mark and earned enemies by insisting that the Black men of Greensboro must have equal rights. The two denounced the color line when it came to political parties, votes on election day, and office holding. Both knew the thrill of enthralling a crowd or besting the opposition at the polls. They also knew the danger of published recriminations and late-night mobs.

Both Dallas and Tourgée regarded themselves as representatives of Warnersville. Tourgée, when he left North Carolina in 1879, was admired by some and reviled by many others. He left the work of radical politics to the men who remained behind, Dallas among them.

Albion Tourgée and Dallas Jones met different ends. Tourgée lived a long life—long enough to reprise his alliance with Black activists when he represented Homer Plessy in a challenge to segregated street cars in New Orleans at the century's end. It was about that same time that, back in Greensboro, Dallas was warned to stay away from the polls and then disappeared. Still, in memory, the two men suffered a similar fate. They were erased. I cannot say why The Bishop left memories of Dallas's end out of our family story. I better understand why, at Bennett College, Tourgée was forgotten. The politics he stood for only grew more reviled in the years after Tourgée left Greensboro. To be associated with him, even with his memory, invited scrutiny, unwelcome heat, and organized violence. Bennett's leaders distanced the school from Tourgée and, as Jim Crow became the dominant regime in Greensboro and across the South, chose moderation and negotiation over radical politics. Along with his writing table, Bennett College tucked away its connections to Tourgée.

It became dangerous to repeat stories like those about the radical politics of men like Tourgée and Dallas, especially in admiring terms. Jennie must have turned them over in her mind. She had been there during the years Tourgée spent in and around Bennett. Her years with Dallas had taught Jennie that terror perpetrated by men called conservative Democrats by day and hooded riders by night could end a career, if not a life. She knew that if Bennett was going to thrive, it needed to avoid the wrath of such men. It needed time to erect a few buildings, manicure a good stretch of lawn, expand some minds, and set young, hungry genius loose on the world. None of that would be possible if the school were associated with Tourgée, Dallas, and their radical politics.

Jennie was settled at home, getting in a last bit of mending before the light was gone. Her son, after a day spent in classes at Bennett, entered quietly. His bright eyes said he was eager to speak. His buddy James Corrothers had repeated an old yarn about Tourgée writing his book in the Bennett library. Corrothers had beamed as he excitedly recounted an afternoon seated at Tourgée's table, editing a poem he would later title "Ethiopia." The association with Tourgée had inspired Corrothers, The Bishop told his mother. At the same time, The Bishop wondered aloud about his own father. Shouldn't he too be remembered and even admired? In reply, Jennie gave him a stern look that said, *Leave such memories in the past. When it comes to the future of Bennett, nothing good can come from them.*

———

Jennie never claimed William Holley. Her mother, Isabella, had told the Freedmen's Bureau that Holley was Jennie's father. Jennie herself never looked back, at least not to the years she and her mother had spent with Holley at Bandon. When she did reach for the past, Jennie skipped that chapter altogether. But history did interest her. Jennie "believed herself a granddaughter of John Jacob Astor," The Bishop told Richard

Bardolph. What she meant to say was that her mother, Isabella, was Astor's daughter. The first time I read this story, I'd already heard of Astor. Like me, most New Yorkers have. He was a German immigrant to the United States who, trading first in furs and later in New York real estate, became the richest man in early-nineteenth-century America.

This story about our Astor ties still makes the rounds today. My Detroit cousin explained that her mother, who as a girl for a time lived with Jennie, learned that her Astor roots were a source of pride. She even quoted Jennie: "Hold your head up high. The blood of John Jacob Astor is running through your veins." A California cousin set up an entire "Astor's Bastards Family Tree," where she keeps track of her own sleuthing into Jennie's story. I've pondered this cousin's alternative theory, which involves a "poor enslaved woman" coupled not with John Jacob but with his son William Backhouse. I've collected these tales, unsure what to make of them.

My father believed Jennie's story, at least for one summer evening. He was still single and working in New York City when he tested it. With friends, he rode the elevated subway from Manhattan up to the Bronx until they arrived at Yankee Stadium. It was one of the first major-league fields to install lights for night games. My father's reserve seats were on the field level. Nearby were the pricier boxes that were held mostly by season subscribers. In old Yankee Stadium, the best seats were wood-slatted chairs, set apart by rails but open to the elements, foul balls, and curious onlookers. My father glanced toward the boxes, and there sat members of the Astor family. Once upon a time, they'd practically owned the joint as holders of a deed to the very land on which the stadium sat. They were at home.

My father also felt at home. In the 1950s, New York's high and low all mixed it up at Yankee Stadium. A dollar or two and a subway token were all it took to witness the greats up close. His group was in high spirits, likely fueled by Ballantine beer—a foamy, pale draft served in wax cups by barkers carting the drink up and down the aisles. They may have started the evening in one of the dark, shallow bars that lined the surrounding streets. Settled in his seat, my father spotted the Astors a few rows ahead and shouted, "Hey, cuz. Over here, cuz." He never said whether anyone responded. Likely his voice was soon drowned out by the next roar of the crowd.

"We are Astor bastards," my father told me, grinning widely. I was ten and learning to like baseball at least as much as he did. He turned from the television set to me during a commercial break. I loved how, when he said it, the phrase rhymed: "Asta bastads." I understood. More than a century before, an enslaved woman had briefly crossed paths with a rich and powerful man. The result was the birth of a girl child named Isabella. Isabella had Jennie. Jennie had Grandy. And Grandy along with Musie had my father. It was the closest he ever came to explaining why we looked the way we did. It was not a tragic tale, as he told it. It was simply another story about how we came to be us. That night in Yankee Stadium, he was young and struggling to know himself. For those few moments underneath a Bronx summer sky, my father grabbed on to Jennie's story and ran with it.

My chance to try on her account came not in a baseball stadium but in the archives. Like my father before me, I believed

Jennie at least enough to have it in mind when I opened boxes, unfolded letters, clicked on images, or turned reels on an old microfilm machine. I gripped the handle while my arm turned round and round—churn, chunk, churn, chunk. I rummaged in the back of my bedroom closet until I found an old triptych portrait of Jennie and her sons, The Bishop and my Grandy. I hung it on the wall above my desk and waited. I hoped for a sign, something that would connect Jennie and her mother, Isabella, to John Jacob Astor. Sometimes successful research grows out of faith mixed with patience.

It arrived. The sign I was hoping for turned up on the pages of a narrative written by a man who, like Jennie, was once enslaved in Chowan County: John Jacobs. He'd begun his life just where Isabella and Jennie had started theirs. He was also brother to a more well-known author, Harriet Jacobs, who published her story in the book *Incidents in the Life of a Slave Girl*. John, when he published his own saga, explained that while Harriet had spent years in hiding, he had served as valet to her lover Samuel Tredwell Sawyer. Sawyer was elected to Congress in 1836, and John accompanied him to Washington, DC. They roomed in an Alexandria, Virginia, home where Sawyer met and fell in love with the daughter of his slaveholding landlord. The two courted, and by summer 1838, Sawyer and his fiancée were planning to marry in Chicago at the home of her sister.

In those same years, John Jacob Astor—a land-speculating tycoon—was in New York City, helping downtown recover from the Great Fire of 1835. Among his contributions was opening the Astor House hotel in 1836. At the corner of

Broadway and Vesey Street, the Greek Revival building occupied four square blocks and contained more than three hundred guest rooms on five floors and a sixth level for servants.
The city celebrated Astor for spearheading lower Manhattan's
revival. Less talked about was how, just a few years before, Astor
had helped an enslaved young man, William Henry Johnson,
to evade slave catchers. Astor had secured Johnson's passage by
ship to New Bedford, Massachusetts, and out of harm's way.

Back in Alexandria, Sawyer and his wife-to-be readied for
their wedding voyage. John managed Sawyer's personal affairs.
An enslaved woman, her maid, attended to the bride's packing.
Sawyer, his betrothed, and their entourage—including John
and the same maid—traveled by train to Chicago. I assume
it was a grand affair. When their celebration wrapped up, the
party headed back to Virginia by way of a three- or four-day
stopover in New York City. They took quarters at Astor House.

The hotel was already a favorite among southerners who
passed through New York. John recalled that most members of
the Sawyer party took in the sights. He remained behind at the
hotel, searched his soul, and resolved to escape. John secreted
the removal of his clothing and trunk from the hotel by pretending to send out laundry. He then boarded a ship bound for
New Bedford and never turned back. Some historians believe
that Astor helped John as he had aided William Henry Johnson. Perhaps Astor made the right introductions or financed
John's passage; John's memoir does not say.

John got away, but Mrs. Sawyer's maid remained behind.
To complete the story, I had little more than my imagination.
Perhaps that maid had her own encounter, a sexual one, with

Mr. Astor. It might have been that he assaulted or coerced her. Possibly she invited Astor's attention. After all, the man was known to help people get free of their owners. Would he help her get to New Bedford, like John? Perhaps she hoped their brief liaison might blossom into fidelity. It was true that years before, back in Chowan County, Harriet had managed to win Samuel Sawyer's help in just that way. The Sawyer party's time at Astor House came to an end. Soon they were all, except John, back aboard a train headed south to Sawyer's home in Chowan County. What no one yet knew was that Mrs. Sawyer's maid was carrying John Jacob Astor's child, a girl.

That girl was Isabella, who was born the next year, in 1839. By 1840, she and her mother, Mrs. Sawyer's maid, were among the twenty-eight enslaved people in the Edenton household of Samuel Sawyer. At twelve, Isabella moved up the Chowan River to the home of William Holley. About how that happened, all I can say is that he somehow bought, traded, or otherwise bargained for her. Before Isabella boarded Holley's wagon, she said goodbye to her mother, the maid who had briefly met up with John Jacob Astor in New York. Not long afterward, Isabella began to bear William Holley's children. Jennie was her firstborn. After civil war and a constitutional amendment, the two left Bandon as freedpeople in 1867. Isabella and Jennie carried with them Holley's name along with the legend of Astor.

Even as I've connected the dots, I can't say for certain that Jennie was Astor's granddaughter or Isabella his child. I am sure that I've given Jennie's story the serious consideration it deserves. When she spoke with her children and grandchildren about the past, Jennie did not recount her years at Bandon or her connection to William Holley. She did not claim Holley as her father. Perhaps those memories were too painful, too sordid, or too devoid of pride or pleasure. Instead, to illuminate who she was, to explain whom we became, Jennie reached further back. She claimed her grandmother, the woman who was also Mrs. Sawyer's maid. She claimed John Jacob Astor. She carefully crafted the story of her past, of our family past. It was the story she needed to tell.

—

Jennie erased William Holley from her family story. She never returned to Bandon and instead made a new family in Greensboro with her mother, her siblings, and, just a bit later, Dallas and their children. Jennie lived another six decades in Warnersville, and with each year, her memories of Bandon faded a bit more. My research, in contrast, nearly brought Bandon to life. I saw it on maps and in descriptions written on deeds, legal notices, and even a postcard. Searches in census returns, death certificates, and old newspapers transformed members of William Holley's white family into characters with their own life stories. I didn't exactly think of the Holleys back at Bandon as my kin. But I let myself consider that they might be.

William Holley had a total of five children by 1852. His first wife was mother to four. Her oldest daughter was Mary Elizabeth, known as "Bettie." With the arrival of Isabella's Mary Jane, known as "Jennie," there were five. I imagined them at Bandon: Jennie and Bettie. Maybe they were rivals, proxies for the tension that ran between their mothers. They might have been, when young, playmates who shared secrets and games. It is possible that adults kept them apart, allowing little more than furtive glances between them. But as Jennie grew old enough to do housework, she and Bettie might have shared a bedchamber, one a servant and the other served. For all the ways in which lines of color and status dissected a plantation household, their statuses as slave and slaveholder may have led Bettie and Jennie to know one another well.

They last saw each other in 1867 when Isabella and her children left Bandon for Greensboro. Still, Jennie and Bettie remained companion characters in the myth of the South's Lost Cause. That story lamented southern defeat and slavery's demise. Slaveholders like Bettie's family had been, it was said, benevolent caretakers of families like Jennie's. Slaves were people aptly suited to bondage and were content on plantations. Bettie, in this tale, was the heir of a kindly regime, while Jennie, as she strove to be free, equal, and independent, lived beyond her capacities and defied a natural order. To quell the troubles that followed slavery's end, the myth went, a white-supremacist order must be restored. Jennie must again be Bettie's subordinate.

She never was. Bettie and Jennie were not mythical characters. But they were women who lived, in broad terms, parallel lives. Both married in the 1860s and raised families, Jennie with a total of six living children and Bettie seven. By the close of the century, both were nearly fifty and widowed. Neither remarried; instead, each spent her remaining years in the company of her adult children. Jennie lived on McCulloch Street, next door to her daughter Minnie. Bettie lived on her family farm in Murfreesboro with two sons, Sidney and Clinton. These are the sorts of facts that, between another set of sisters, might have drawn them closer. For Jennie and Bettie, history and myth both ensured that they would never know and never have a chance to transform their commonalities into kinship.

Both women left legacies: their children and grandchildren. Among them were educators who indelibly shaped the South. There was Jennie's youngest son, David, about whom she'd worried so much during his boyhood. He found his footing and, while under the care of The Bishop, excelled in the public schools of New Orleans and then at Wesleyan University in Connecticut. Into adulthood, he did graduate work at the University of Chicago and Columbia University in New York. David aspired to lead and spent his early adult years organizing for the YMCA in St. Louis, Missouri, and then for the Committee on Interracial Cooperation in Atlanta. When the Methodist Church reorganized Greensboro's Bennett College into a liberal arts school for women, David got the call. He returned home, assumed the presidency of Bennett, and remained there for the balance of his life, thirty years.

Bettie's grandson Colgate Darden, Jr., like Grandy was a leader in higher education. He also left his mark on politics. With a law degree from Columbia University, where Grandy would study later, Darden went on to graduate work at Oxford. He was chosen to serve in the Virginia state house and then the US Congress. He was elected governor of Virginia in 1942 and served one term. Darden took over as president of the University of Virginia in 1947 after a short stint as chancellor at the College of William & Mary.

By the early 1950s, both Jennie's son David Jones and Bettie's grandson Colgate Darden were at the peak of their careers. As influential and respected educators, they were soon called upon to help the South navigate its greatest challenge since Reconstruction. The Civil Rights movement was pressuring southern states to desegregate public education from professional schools down to elementary classrooms. In 1954, in *Brown v. Board of Education*, the US Supreme Court ruled segregation in public education unconstitutional. Both David Jones and Colgate Darden responded to the challenge, but their positions set them as far apart as Jennie had once stood from Bettie during their years at Bandon. In Greensboro, Grandy quickly pressed for the integration of the city's public schools, moved by *Brown v. Board of Education*. Darden, in contrast, remained unshakably opposed to desegregation in Virginia, defending the state's "separate but equal" regime even after *Brown*.

William Holley's daughters—Jennie and Bettie—were not sisters if the term *sister* implies that they shared bonds of honor and affection. The two were much closer to adversaries, on opposite sides and set against one another during the wars over slavery and Jim Crow that ravaged their lifetimes and then those of their children and grandchildren. I might be able to point out parallels between them, but those are little more than eerie coincidences. Not even a slim thread ran between Jennie and Bettie after they were separated for the final time in 1867. Likely neither regretted how the other receded into an increasingly remote past. Jennie was teaching me about how in families, there sometimes can be as many reasons to forget as there are to remember.

I knew Jennie's face from family photos. I finally saw a portrait of Bettie much later when I allowed myself to visit a family tree posted by one of her descendants. I studied Bettie's face, framed by a black mat and a gilt oval. She wore a finely tailored dark dress with a white collar. She was of mature years, her gray hair and sunken eyes signs of age. With the full-ness of youth gone, Bettie's long chin and narrow, pronounced nose were prominent, even striking. She was not beautiful, but her long neck and straight-backed pose gave her a dignified appearance.

I was alone in the dark at my desk and could hear the tick-tick of the kitchen clock and the hum of the fridge. The light above my head was the only one still on; the rest of the house was only

Jennie (Mary Jane Holley Jones)

dimly lit by the streetlamp just outside. Bettie's portrait arrested me. I could not turn away from it. I knew her face because, I realized, it was also Jennie's face. Jennie's portrait—the one in which she was positioned between her two boys, The Bishop and Grandy—hung just over my left shoulder. It was a bit faded, but her features were clear: a long chin and narrow but pronounced nose. The shadows under her eyes, a trait a dermatologist once told me I'd inherited, were there too.

What did it mean that during all the years they spent apart, Jennie and Bettie wore the same face? Each woman, as she fixed herself up for work, for church, for a trip into town, saw the other in her looking glass. As she pondered how to style her hair or angle a collar, she saw the face of the other. When she studied her own smile or watched her teeth yellow, she was learning the other's changing face. Neighbors recognized her as she headed out of the house or to the market, the shoemaker's workshop, or the dressmaker's salon. She was familiar in the pew on Sunday or in a parlor paying her respects after death had come calling. On the porch or along a walkway, people recognized that face as Jennie; they knew it as Bettie. They put on their best faces in trying moments and faced the future and its uncertainties. Jennie, like Bettie. Bettie, like Jennie. The one she'd last seen in the yard at Bandon and whom she'd seen nearly every day since in her dressing mirror. I don't have a word for a woman who was not quite Jennie's sister but whose face she would have known almost as well as her own.

SIX

Passing

I feel a little guilty saying how much fun I have
had being a colored girl in the twentieth century.
—ANITA THOMPSON DICKINSON REYNOLDS,
AMERICAN COCKTAIL

I WAS RAISED TO LOOK UP TO FANNIE. SHE WAS SUSAN'S FIRST
daughter, born in Danville in 1863 on the cusp of slavery's abolition, and my great-grandmother. By the end of the
century, Fannie was mother to her own children, including
my grandmother Musie and her sister, Aunt Sweets. Fannie was our family's first college graduate. After finishing at
Kentucky's Berea College in 1888, she spent her adult life
as an educator, teaching Latin, and as a civic leader devoted
to the YWCA and the NAACP. She was a matriarch whom
her grown children in their letters called "Ma" instead of
the more formal "Mother" or "Mrs. Williams," the term
of address she preferred in public. She spent sixty-two years
married to Frank Williams, whom we called "The Professor." It was Great-Aunt Sweets who encouraged me to

see Fannie in myself and made sure I had reminders of the great-grandmother I never met.

Toward the end of her life, Aunt Sweets was left to clear out her family's St. Louis, Missouri, home. In that three-story redbrick house, Fannie had presided until her death in 1956. Around 1990, the mementos accumulated over three-quarters of a century sat waiting to be distributed. Sweets had her moving company ship me two boxes. The smaller contained a piece of jewelry, gold with a floral-like design and a tiny diamond set at its center. "This is from a pair of Fannie's earrings, now a pendant and keepsake for you," Sweets wrote to me in her small, careful script on good paper stock. The second box was big enough to hold the two upholstered chairs packed inside, one wing-backed, the other a vanity stool. "These chairs," Sweets wrote, "are especially suited to women like us, with tiny frames." By "us," Sweets meant me, her, and Fannie.

I was like Fannie, Aunt Sweets wanted me to know. I soaked up words and ideas at home, sitting in her chairs. I was grateful that, like me, Fannie chose furniture styled to keep short legs comfortable. When after the end of high school, I teetered on the edge of skipping out on college, I like to think that it was Fannie who, from the other side, nudged me onward. In challenging times, I hung Fannie's pendant on a chain around my neck like an amulet, hoping to borrow from her strength. My great-grandmother was not a hand-holder. Still, she generously shared her steely determination with those whom she loved. Sweets was sure that I was one of them.

———

Fannie's Danville upbringing prepared her for the world and kept her safe from it. With just over 2,500 residents, the city further swelled when classes were in session at the local colleges. From across the county, people arrived in Danville to see Court Clerk Jonathan Nichols, a man at the start of a long career spent authorizing estate claims, land sales, and marriages. Down the hall, judges listened to disputes from the commercial to the everyday. In the company of her mother, Susan, Fannie peered into the storefronts through plate-glass windows. It was an exciting world that included a photo studio, a boot and shoe seller, more than one dry-goods outlet, a paint shop, a jeweler, and one department store: a one-stop shop for clothes, accessories, home décor, and linens, with a dress-making department that promised the "latest and most fashionable styles."

A casual visitor to Danville might find its downtown ordinary. But along its streets ran violence. Susan, Fannie's mother, kept her daughter close. There were good reasons to take special care with a girl in the years after the Civil War, especially as viciousness engulfed Danville and its environs. "There is a mob in Boyle county, Ky., that has shot, outraged or hung nearly fifty persons. . . . [They] are over 100 strong, well-armed, and mounted," a Louisville newspaper warned in 1867. Men like Fannie's stepfather, Susan's husband, Sam, took special care when on isolated roads and anywhere after dark. So too did women like Susan. Mobs committed "outrages"—a genteel way of referring to acts of sexual violence—against mothers, daughters, and sisters. These scenes from Danville helped me better understand why my own grandmother insisted, even a century later, that I not go out alone after dark. Only our own vigilance would keep us safe was wisdom that Susan passed on to Fannie, who handed it down to Musie, from whom it came to me.

Fannie's mother committed to seeing her children educated, but the same mobs that lynched men also targeted schools. In August 1866, her family woke to news of an overnight act of terror. Fannie's older brothers were already students when arsonists burned Danville's "freedmen's" schoolhouse to the ground. A few years later, Fannie's slim advantage came from studying in a small Presbyterian church school where her mother was a member of the congregation. Each time Fannie stepped into a classroom, took her seat on a bench, buried her head in a primer, or put chalk to a slate, she invited the wrath of vigilantes. When Susan left her daughter behind with class-mates and teachers, she knew the risks they all faced. Seeing to Fannie's education demanded intelligence along with raw courage.

Susan eventually sent Fannie away to school, and this helped me better understand why she'd kept working in Ormond Beatty's home. She had tuition and travel expenses to cover: Fannie was headed to the Allegheny Institute, today's Allegheny College, in Meadville, Pennsylvania. Susan's brother, living there, promised to keep an eye on Fannie, who in 1883 packed her few things and boarded a train. She left Danville behind, heading first to Cincinnati, north just across the Ohio border; then on the Pennsylvania Railroad between Cincinnati and Pittsburgh; and finally on to Meadville, about ninety miles north still. Fannie landed amidst the bustle of her uncle's home on North Main Street; he ran a thriving barber's parlor by day and brokered power in town politics by night. Fannie made a place for herself with his wife, three young children, and their boarders.

In Meadville, Fannie was far from the Jim Crow customs that had ordered her days in Kentucky. For example, there the county court had just decreed the desegregation of the city's public schools. At Allegheny, Fannie fit in. It was a Methodist Church institution that had never barred Black students, though Fannie was the only former slave in her preparatory class. The 1883–1884 Allegheny *Catalogue* published Fannie's name alphabetically—between McQuiston of Meadville and Perry of Malden, West Virginia—without any reference to color. When she came upon the class of 1880 stone, inscribed "Spes sibi quisque," or "Everyone is their own hope," Fannie was encouraged to believe that this was as true for her as for any student.

After one year at Allegheny, Fannie returned to Kentucky. She was ready to be in charge of her own classroom and accepted an assignment to a schoolhouse in Lincoln County. She also served the state's Colored Teachers Institute as its secretary. To occupy her leisure time, Fannie joined the Danville Social Club. Run on middle-class terms, it rivaled the city's Young Ladies' Social Club, which welcomed white women only. Attending the club's social affairs, Fannie was among those "who occup[ied] the best positions in colored society," as a local newspaper put it.

Being among the best was not all fun. In Danville, it also invited ridicule. Fannie was among dozens who one evening turned up at Danville's Central House, a downtown hotel, in spring 1885. The crowd whirred to the sounds of Baughman's Orchestra as the city's "young colored people" gathered for "an elegant and delightful Hop." A highlight was the dancers and their costumes, and Fannie stood out in her "white silk" and "crème draperage." The evening was marred when the next day, a local paper mocked, "One young girl's outfit cost $100, including diamonds, and another wore a similarly expensive 'crushed strawberry' dress." The newspaper derided: Who did Danville's Black residents think they were, going out in such costly "good style"? When color crossed with class in Danville, Fannie and her friends were labeled excessive and even crass.

Fannie didn't stay long in her hometown. Perhaps it had grown too small or she'd gotten too big. Following what likely had been her plan all along, in fall 1886, Susan put Fannie aboard the Kentucky Central bound for the foothills of the Appalachian Mountains. Hours later, Fannie stepped down from the train car and into her future at Berea College, soon to be enrolled as a bachelor of arts student in the classical course. Perhaps Fannie walked the long block to the campus cluster of mostly redbrick buildings while clutching her bags. Ahead of her were dizzying years of study: astronomy, geography, botany, logic, rhetoric, English literature, chemistry, physics, political science, moral philosophy, geology, mental philosophy, evidences of Christianity, science of government, zoology, and mineralogy. Berea promised "careful training" in Greek and Latin, weekly Bible classes, and regular faculty lectures on "morals and manners" and "true manhood" along with "popular and scientific subjects."

Fannie chose Berea for its demanding curriculum. Soon she was also a part of its social experiment. Since 1865, the school had educated formerly enslaved people like Fannie alongside Kentucky's so-called mountain whites. By the 1880s, the school's nearly four hundred students were almost evenly divided between Black and white young people who had arrived from as far as California to the west and New Jersey to the east. Most were enrolled in the primary, secondary, and grammar courses, while Fannie was one of three in her classics department. Berea students suffered under unwelcome scrutiny, charged with "forcing social equality against nature." Its leaders did not flinch and instead affirmed that all students "recite in the same classes, belong to the same literary societies, sing in the same choir, play in the same brass band, room in the same buildings, and eat at the same tables," though no rules required that they "associate with any that are not agreeable to them." At Allegheny, Fannie had been an outlier. At Berea, she was among the many students who permitted Kentucky to play its part in bringing about "true national progress."

Fannie grew bold at Berea; her faculty encouraged it. At her 1888 graduation, President Edward Henry Fairchild held her up as exceptional and not only because, before Fannie, all the school's women graduates had been white. Commencement ceremonies were, in those years, grand affairs. Thousands arrived by special trains, in wagons and carriages, and on horseback. Guests and graduates alike sported their finest clothes. Fannie's class gathered in the campus tabernacle—every one of its two thousand seats occupied, with many more spectators set up outside. The program began with music—the choir singing "Give unto the Lord." In between were speeches and essays along with more music and singing. Fannie was among the speakers and recited an essay, "Our Centograph."

Three advanced-degree diplomas were awarded, including that of Fannie's AB.

President Fairchild, recognizable for his full beard and receding hairline, was over seventy and in declining health when he stepped up to pay tribute to the graduates. He carried himself like the minister and abolitionist he had been before taking the helm at Berea. After some general remarks, he spoke directly to Fannie. Fairchild admired her intellect: "I had you in classes . . . and, in all my experience of teaching for thirty-eight years, I have never had a better student than you." Where might her outstanding mind take her? Fairchild believed that doors would open for Fannie "everywhere": "Remember that you are admitted to the circle of all those who have attained the title of Bachelor of Arts, and you will everywhere be welcomed within that circle by all." The president continued, saying out loud what many of those gathered quietly thought. Fannie would also confront barriers set in her way by, as Fairchild put it, "a very few who are blinded by an ungodly prejudice." Fannie never forgot that the racism thrust in her way was "ungodly," meaning it was not to be respected. And more than once, Fannie defied it altogether.

—

Fannie set out from Berea, degree in hand, to discover how far it might take her. Immediately she ran up against one version of the ungodly: Kentucky's segregated public school system. She began teaching in the growing hamlet of Somerset, nestled in the southeastern county of Pulaski, among a population of under 1,000 people that by 1890, with the arrival of the railroad, swelled to over 2,600. Fannie was among the migrants who filled the town's boardinghouses and tenements. The school system divided young people starkly between parallel sets of classrooms, just six schoolhouses for Black children versus 126 for whites. During a session that ran somewhere between three and five months, Fannie challenged the minds of the boys and girls who were the youngest of Somerset's Black residents.

Fannie's first months were not only occupied with teaching. She also indulged her fondness for entertainment and, on a January evening in 1889, headed down Main Street along the city's strip of shops and offices. She eyed Owens Opera House, which sat right at the center of town, facing the public square on one side and the county courthouse on the other. The evening's program featured a "free Indian show," lectures on the history, culture, and medicines of Native Americans. While admission was free, the troupe earned its dollars selling ointments, pills, and other remedies. Fannie approached the doors and then entered the hall, surveyed the auditorium, and spied a seat to her liking in the section designated for white patrons only. Undeterred, Fannie took a seat there on the aisle. She was inviting a confrontation.

I imagine Fannie there, borrowing a few clues from the single photo I have of her from those years. She posed in a portrait studio, and her posture was the embodiment of dignity: back erect, shoulders straight, neck long, chin steady. Fannie's eyes were fixed off to the left, contemplating a future that she was already devising for herself. She was not posed stiffly at all, even if her high-collared dress, embellished with fine lace, let

Fannie Miller Williams

on that she was wearing her best. Instead, her countenance was relaxed and her eyes betrayed the hint of a smile.

It was no secret that theater operators patrolled the color line, even if state law did not yet require that they do so. In Danville, the local opera house seated white patrons on the first floor and "coons" in the gallery, as a local newspaper put it. At Owens's, an usher noticed Fannie and, as she later explained, "went to her in a gruff manner and ordered her to move." The two faced off, with Fannie ignoring him and holding firmly to her seat. A local marshal arrived and repeated the usher's order. Fannie shot back, asking "why she was not allowed to sit where

170

she was as she did not think she was harming anyone by sitting there." The marshal repeated that she was to move to the "colored" section. Fannie denounced him in "strong terms," though she never stooped to "indecent or profane language."

Fannie must have been startled when the confrontation got physical. The marshal "caught her roughly by the arm and led her to the door." Police charged Fannie with disorderly conduct and then arrested her. It was a scandal. In Somerset, papers vied over how to tell the story, and not only because it was sensational. The story gave editors an opportunity to illustrate how they regarded the color line and those, like Fannie, who defied it. The *Republican* described Fannie as quiet, polite, and reasonably indignant. In contrast, the *Reporter* labeled her uninvited, loud, and disorderly. In her hometown, Danville, the local *Advocate* reprinted both versions of the story and then declared itself neutral: "It is the invariable rule of the *Advocate* to do justice to everyone, regardless of color or condition in life." The story was bigger than Fannie: It made evident how a new Jim Crow etiquette was remaking life for everyone in Kentucky. It was also personal: A guilty finding might jeopardize her future as a teacher. Friends counseled caution, advising Fannie to pay the fine and court costs to settle things, which she did. Still, she insisted on her version of the facts: Blame lay with the usher and the marshal, whose harshness had provoked her outrage.

Fannie felt entitled to her preferred seat, even if it was in the theater's white section. But on what basis? At first, I felt sure that she was leveling an open protest against the separation of Black from white patrons. But the better I got to know Fannie, the more I suspected that she had something else in mind.

Perhaps she was not directly protesting but instead trying to work around the rules. Perhaps that night, Fannie was dipping her toes into forbidden waters, discovering how far her skin, her demeanor, and her AB degree from Berea might take her. Could she pass? Fannie bluffed the usher and then the marshal, only to be exposed as the exemplary colored woman that she was.

Fannie and her reputation survived the confrontation in Somerset. A few weeks later, she attended a Berea reunion, where throngs packed the college chapel, a gothic-style wooden structure that seated five hundred. Everyone searched the crowd for familiar faces. Some may have already been anticipating the dinner to follow, but most were happy to first hear the speeches. The program was crowded: a welcome by President Fairchild, a response from a class representative, one poem, letters from absent members, songs, and a benediction. Alumni officers for the coming year were elected, Fannie among them. The *Berea College Reporter* later apologized for providing only a "brief account" but also made space for the whole of Fannie's remarks. From the podium, surely dressed in her best—simple but refined—she asked the crowd where her Berea degree might take her and how to get there.

When Fannie had taken a theater seat reserved for white women, her reunion speech showed me, she had been testing a philosophy promoted at Berea: "The great idea of the brotherhood of man." Fannie might have been thwarted in Somerset but when she got to the podium, she urged Berea's leaders to maintain their commitment to educating "our brothers of the mountain region" alongside those who had known slavery's "deplorable" condition. She'd seen signs of the fight that lay ahead: "Alumni and friends, you are wanted. You are needed. The battle is fierce and long. The harvest is plenteous but laborers are few. The demand is, Go ye forth to the battle; march ye upon the field."

Fannie posed a question to the crowd, but she might just as well have been asking it of herself: "Are we ready? We were gathered for a few short years within these walls. No pains were spared in unfolding to us the benefits of an education and in impressing upon us the importance of fitting ourselves for the combats of life, for life's struggles and duties." Fannie believed that all people were "one family" and that "god is the Father of all [and] made [of] one blood all nations." I understood that there before her Berea family, Fannie resolved to challenge "ungodly prejudice." How far she'd go to do that, I wasn't sure.

—

Fannie's mother, Susan, continued to steer her oldest daughter's path. For a long time, she'd been imagining Fannie's future as a part of the burgeoning women's era, with a first-rate education, middle-class tastes, and ambitions that included making a family and also remaking the world. In Danville, some people might have compared Fannie's accomplishments to those of Ormond Beatty's daughter, Pattie. Susan had watched Pattie be educated, wed, and set up in her own household with style. For Fannie, Susan wanted even more. And Fannie was already on her way; with her Berea degrees—the AB in 1888 and later an honorary AM in 1904—she outpaced Pattie.

Susan also hoped that Fannie would marry well, to a man who'd enhance her daughter's distinction. The Professor was

THE TROUBLE OF COLOR

an apt candidate. Their compatibility was rooted in shared beginnings. Both Fannie and The Professor were born in the midst of war and on the cusp of slavery's abolition. Both were raised by women who fueled their aspirations. Later in life, The Professor told of how his mother, though she had died when he was sixteen, had given him "her own sense of perfection, sense of humor, and strength of resolve." Fannie surely admired this, as did Susan.

It was around 1890 when The Professor came to Danville and met his prospective mother-in-law. He was brimming with ambition. The Professor might have talked with Susan about a return to Berea, where he hoped to be one of its few Black faculty members. He may have shared his bigger city dreams that eventually took him and Fannie to Louisville, Covington, and St. Louis, Missouri. He already had a fine reputation as head of Kentucky's colored teachers association and promised to accomplish more of the same.

The Professor and Fannie planned a February 1891 wedding, and the preliminaries were right out of the era's most exacting etiquette books. A newspaper notice announced the impending ceremony on the heels of having sent out "handsomely engraved invitations." Guests were invited to attend the "marriage of Fannie Bell Miller, sister of the polite barber, E.C. Miller, and Frank L. Williams, Thursday evening, February 19th at 5:30 o'clock, in this city." The notice's bourgeois air echoed the mood of Fannie's time in the Danville social-club circle. Her marriage was the next chapter in a trajectory that Susan encouraged.

What no etiquette book explained was the matter of Fannie's name. In a notice meant for all of Danville to see, she was

"Fannie Bell Miller," a young woman with ties to the Bell clan. But Fannie was not destined to be that family's supplicant, as her mother and other former slaves had been. Ormond Beatty was gone, dead after a "brief illness" that he had endured "with manly fortitude and Christian resignation." Fannie made a definitive break. Following her marriage, she forever went by the name Mrs. Frank L. Williams. As a middle-class married woman, Fannie placed herself beyond the reach of Martha Fry Bell and Ormond Beatty, even in memory.

Fannie did not sever her ties to Beatty's daughter, Pattie. But she did reset their terms. Both were married women who had descended from those in the Bells' slaveholding household. Who were they to one another? A fascinating object among Ormond Beatty's papers contains a hint. It is Pattie's address book: a slim, small-format folio bound with a red ribbon. The cover illustration is an art nouveau rendering of three red roses, its colors still rich. The book was gently used and likely kept tucked in a writing-table drawer. During the early twentieth century, Pattie used it to collect memories and keep track of family and friends.

Pattie's address book provides a glimpse into her inner world. She noted the everyday order in her household: the cook, the seamstress. In the section marked "Addresses," she mapped out her social connections to classmates, friends, and family living as far away as New York City to the east and Sacramento to the west. Fannie is there, listed as Mrs. Frank Williams at her St. Louis address: 3973 W. Bell Place. (I cannot help but note that the Bell name managed to find Fannie in Missouri.) Fannie was among those with whom Pattie shared

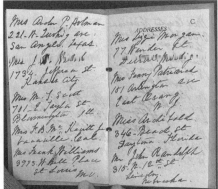

Pattie Beatty Quisenberry address book with entry for Mr. Frank Williams (Fannie Miller Williams)

polite correspondence, holiday greetings, and notes of concern. Gone is young Fannie, marked with the Bell name and owned by Pattie's father. She had become, Pattie acknowledged, the respectable Mrs. Williams of St. Louis.

There was more to the ties between Fannie and Pattie. The editors of the *Kentucky Advocate* appeared to think they were family. In 1931, the paper published a social note about the two: That summer, Pattie was scheduled to host cousins at her Danville home, including, "of St. Louis, Mo., Mrs. Frank Williams." It was a strikingly plain statement. But when I took a closer look, it became clear that the paper had muddled the details. Pattie's visiting cousin was not "Mrs. Frank Williams." It was not Fannie. It was another woman, Pattie's cousin "Mrs. Frank Phillips," who planned to visit Danville that summer.

What sort of evidence is a slip of the pen? What should I make of a local newspaperman who mistook Mrs. Phillips for Mrs. Williams and then took Mrs. Williams to be cousin to

Pattie? It may have been an error to report that Fannie planned to visit Pattie that summer. But to say the two were cousins was closer to truth. Aunt Sweets recalled a friend once teasing her, "Everybody else in Kentucky knows who you're related to." The "everybody" included the editors of the *Advocate*, who let what they knew inadvertently slip. Whether shared in whispers, by innuendo, or through an editor's blunder, Fannie and Pattie, everyone knew, were kin.

—

When Fannie passed for white, it was sometimes sport. It pleased and even amused her to trick the eyes of theater ushers, department-store clerks, and train conductors. Despite their policing of the color line, Fannie evaded them, notching victories for the "brotherhood of man" in which she so strongly believed. By the time she began passing in downtown St. Louis, it was the 1930s. Books like Nella Larsen's 1929 *Passing* and films like John Stahl's 1934 *Imitation of Life* promoted the view that slipping from one side of the line to the other was ill-fated: The fair-skinned mulatto was still a tragic figure. Fannie's local paper, the Black-owned *St. Louis Argus*, added that passing was dangerous, with those who were found out at best discredited and at worst on the receiving end of mob violence.

My Uncle Fuzz confessed to me that Fannie had danced along the color line. The memory was from his teen years when his parents sent Fuzz to live in St. Louis with Fannie and The Professor. He'd benefit, they hoped, from better schools and the better discipline that only grandparents who were also educators could provide. The Professor turned out to be very strict, harsh and impatient with his grandson's fragility. In contrast, Fannie sympathized with Fuzz and stepped up to tutor him after school, especially on the ins and outs of Latin grammar.

Fuzz also remembered Fannie as a difficult woman, especially when it came to color. About his grandmother, he explained in a 2011 interview, "She was able to pass and did pass in St. Louis." He didn't reflect on what drove Fannie. Instead, Fuzz regretted that she'd injured others, his mother, Musie, in particular: "My mother was the darkest of [Fannie's] children. My mother was about my color . . . she's high yellow, we would say. But she couldn't go where my grandmother went. And my mother knew that. And she let me know how much she had been hurt by that." Like his mother, Fuzz could not go everywhere with Fannie. That also hurt.

Fannie was difficult but she was not exceptional, especially in pre–Civil Rights St. Louis. One Washington University sociologist observed that passing was ordinary in Fannie's time. Downtown department stores employed "colored female clerks" whom store managers believed to be white. "There are a few negro women of very light color, who are working in the finest stores of the city. They are efficient saleswomen, and as a consequence are steadily employed throughout the year," he reported. Black folk in St. Louis recalled similar scenes that affirmed the social scientist's findings. Passing was a secret undetected by department-store operators but well-known among Black residents.

Oral histories attest to how commonplace passing was in Fannie's adopted hometown. Pearl McFarland Shanks, as a schoolgirl in the 1930s, saw her teacher waiting in line to enter the whites-only Fox Theater: "We didn't speak to her, but we knew she was passing for white. She looked at us and we looked at her, and we left. . . . We would never think of calling out to our teacher. . . . When I saw my teacher at school, it was never mentioned." This attitude extended to Shanks's schoolmates: "I knew someone at school who was very, very fair—she looked white. When we graduated, I would see her working in certain places where you knew they didn't hire black people. It's okay with me if that's the way she could get a job up in the big office. . . . You don't hold that judgment about them sometimes passing for white, the ones that really look white."

Gabrielle Wilson accompanied her grandmother into the same whites-only theater, the Fox, though it felt risky: "My grandmother took me to the movies before they were integrated. When she took me to the Fox, I remember being told to wait in the car, and she went and bought the tickets. She came back to the car, took my hand and we walked right in." In a large city, anonymity permitted occasional crossing over: "I remember sometimes people asked me if I was Spanish or Italian or whatever." It also divided loved ones: "We didn't pass as an entire family. . . . I went with my grandmother on occasion, and the places we went it seemed we were certainly welcome to go. My father and his parents were darker and couldn't have passed."

Pearl Shanks empathized with women for whom winning a job led them to pass; this was the material meaning of color. The difference between, in her terms, "dark," "light," and looking "white" mattered when it came to work and sociability. Anyone who sized up the women employed in St. Louis department stores, like Famous-Barr, knew so: "The Famous Barr girls . . . —all of the very, very fair girls— ran that elevator where the businessmen were . . . the stock girls were dark, about my color." Gabrielle Wilson knew the downtown St. Louis scene that Pearl described. Still, being "light-skinned," she felt, provoked doubts about whether she belonged in Black St. Louis at all. Her color was "a detriment," Gabrielle felt. It stung when she was bitingly called "cute." The epithet "yellow bitch" wounded.

Fannie's passing hurt Musie and Fuzz. It also chastened me. I knew I was like her. Wasn't I someone who—in a theater, in a department store, or on a train—tricked watchful eyes and evaded the color line? I remember how my father taught me, as a youngster, that when it came to family, I must never pass. He knew how to play with his color, especially when traveling on the rails. Many times he'd slipped unnoticed into a whites-only car and shared Fannie's sense that doing so was good sport. My father also had limits. He never passed when with his mother. He never left her alone on board a train, never lured her into a whites-only establishment. His first obligation, he explained, was to her dignity. He set his own desires aside and shielded his mother from conductors, clerks, and ushers. His message to me: I must not be like Fannie.

—

When his children and grandchildren called Fannie's husband The Professor, it suited him: He was a learned man, like his wife a Berea College graduate, with the bearing of a principal.

Across decades, he led high schools in Covington and Louisville in Kentucky and then did the same with unmatched influence in St. Louis. People recognized him: bespectacled, wearing a three-piece suit, and increasingly rotund as the years went by. The Professor spoke in a baritone that rolled out in paragraphs rather than sentences. Conversations with him left some—like his three daughters—believing their potential was limitless, while my Uncle Fuzz remembered The Professor as stern and aloof. All of this was true.

Frank's family dubbed him "The Professor" as an honorific to compensate for the loss he'd suffered when, even though he was one of its most accomplished alumni, Berea never invited him to join its faculty. A 1904 state law imposed segregation in public education, and Black people were slated to be banished from the school. The Professor was devasted by the rejection of the state legislature, a failed appeal to the US Supreme Court, and then the acquiescence of Berea's president to demands that the school segregate. By 1908, his hopes for a faculty post had been crushed. That fall, he took a new job as principal of St. Louis's Sumner High School. To be thereafter known as "The Professor" was a nod to what could have and should have been.

In their household, The Professor never questioned that Fannie would enjoy her own domain. He walked the walk when it came to endorsing his wife's ambitions. Like him, Fannie managed money and led civic organizations; she was the only one of the two to hold national office. She traveled independently for pleasure and purpose. In nearly all things, The Professor agreed that Fannie should enjoy free rein, and she steered her own course. Still, the color line ran between them.

In downtown St. Louis, Fannie chose to pass, but The Professor never accompanied her on those excursions.

Department stores did not interest The Professor much. But race, and the meaning of his skin, did. Science fascinated him, and he believed that others felt the same. On the pages of the Black-owned *St. Louis Argus* throughout the 1940s and 1950s, he regularly published an opinion column titled Lest We Forget. Those essays, written in a voice that pronounced rather than persuaded, covered topics from political parties and the vote to thrift, education, community building, the dignity of work, and church politics.

The Professor stepped down from the public schools, though not wholly ready to retire. In 1944, eighty and still with a sharp mind, he began to write for the *Argus* from his office in the Enright Avenue home that he and Fannie had shared since the 1920s. His round, casual script—achieved with a fountain pen dipped in ink—filled sheet after sheet. The *Argus* team transferred these pages to typeset columns, and The Professor's words rolled off the press. This way, he remained a presence in the lives of his former students, along with many other readers, in Black St. Louis. His voice boomed off the page—learned, unwavering, and committed to uplift, respectability, and thrift. All he'd learned during years in front of classrooms, board meetings, and teachers' conferences he funneled into the written word.

He never named it as such, but the still lingering theory of mulatto degeneracy troubled The Professor. Were so-called hybrid people inferior in a biological sense? Were they destined for debasement and finally extinction? Unlike Fannie, The

Professor knew little about his family origins. Still, he counted himself among those whose skin—pale with a sallow tinge—told a story of lines having been crossed, even if its details were lost to time. To make better sense of this, he eventually turned to newer ideas about race, ones fueled by an awareness that racism had undergirded Germany's genocidal Nazi regime. The Professor again became a student and discovered new reasons to reject old ideas.

When a pamphlet, *The Race of Mankind*, arrived on his desk, the war in Europe was raging. It was spring 1944, and D-Day was still, unbeknownst to The Professor, weeks off. It was not too soon, however, for Americans to take in lessons from the war crimes that were ravaging the lives of Jews and the others categorized as "degenerates" during Hitler's years in power. Was there a "superior race," one that ranked above all others in a global human order? The Professor heard how this question, one manifestly being answered by Germany's vision, also resonated for Black Americans. He studied the conclusions offered by two distinguished women anthropologists, Ruth Benedict and Gene Weltfish. They not only debunked Hitler's theory but also denied that any race was superior to others. They looked at humankind across the globe and concluded that race reflected only the geographic distance between human populations. It had no social relevance.

This Benedict-Weltfish primer proved useful just a few months later. The *Argus* reported on a conference of white Southern Methodists who conferred on the "race problem." Their leading ministers decried the force of "outside influence" on the region, meaning the influence of northern intellectuals.

They were determined to discourage the mixing of human races and still believed that difference was somehow in the blood. The Professor knew this theory had already been discredited by anthropologists.

He took special exception to the Methodists' suggestion that those who opposed segregation also encouraged people of differing races to mix their blood. The very idea was nonsense: "All mankind of today are of 'blood mixture.'" Policing the color line was futile. On his skin, The Professor's hybridity was evident, reflected in his color, hair, and features. But to be mixed was the norm, not the exception, he explained. There were no pure people, and it was an error to suggest otherwise. This made Fannie's passing more like a parlor trick than a sign of her distinctness. Skin was not evidence of deeply rooted differences; it was merely a reminder that all humans were derived from more than one race.

The Professor got to the heart of what it meant for people to be mixed or hybrid when reviewing the 1950 meeting of the United Nations Educational, Scientific and Cultural Organization (UNESCO). Were people like him and Fannie distinctly inferior, defective, or otherwise deserving of separate treatment? The Professor confronted a theory that had trailed his family and others like it for at least a century. He challenged those who suggested that "human hybrids show undesirable traits, physical or mental defects, or other bad biological effects."

The UNESCO meeting, The Professor learned, had brought together a distinguished team from around the world. Two US representatives participated, including sociologist E. Franklin

Frazier. A senior member of the Howard University faculty, Frazier was also a past president of the American Sociological Association and a widely recognized expert on the history and culture of Black Americans. He arrived at the UNESCO deliberations on the heels of releasing his 1949 study, *The Negro in the United States*. The UNESCO team narrowed the meaning of race: "The biological fact of race and the myth of 'race' should be distinguished. . . . The biological differences between ethnic groups should be disregarded from the standpoint of social acceptance and social action." As Benedict and Weltfish had explained in their 1944 pamphlet, UNESCO concluded that racial differences did not determine the social and cultural capacities of humans.

As I read The Professor's column, I held my breath and scanned quickly to discover whether he would speak of himself—would speak to me. He did, emphatically: The UNESCO group outright rejected mulatto degeneracy and found no evidence that race mixture produced "bad results" in biological terms. "Race mixture" had been "going on from earliest times," they explained, and so-called human hybrids did not possess "undesirable traits, both physically and mentally, physical disharmonies and mental degeneracies." The Professor's column echoed a conclusion reached by the scientists in Paris: "There is no biological justification for prohibiting intermarriages between persons of different ethnic groups." The resulting children were as healthy as any.

The Professor's conclusion lifted me up. It also let me down. He anticipated the children of people like my parents who, willfully and happily, crossed the color line. He anticipated me.

He also may have been looking backward to our family history. It was a reminder that while violence produced some unions and choice produced others, the children of those unions were distinguishable only by superficial differences. Still, a chill ran down my back. The Professor warned that hybrid families risked "a certain social and economic hazard." The 1957 wedding of my mother to my father—The Professor's grandson—would teach our family how hazardous, in postwar America, such unions could still be.

—

The sales floors of downtown department stores might seem like a curious place to search out a family history. Still, I am sure that Fannie's story was, in part, written there. She not only stepped clear over the color line to try a fashionable perfume, model a new hat, or consider the latest hem length or sleeve cut. She also introduced her daughters to a way of discovering who they were in a nation still moving toward integrated public spaces. Her daughter Sweets carried herself like a white woman on some days. She followed in her mother's footsteps, tricking the eyes of clerks and dressing-room attendants. Musie did not. She could not. Still, the two sisters had both claimed department stores as their terrain by the 1960s. Musie and Sweets arrived each year in New York City. They came to shop.

I watched them. I was still a child, not yet a teen, when my parents first dressed me and my siblings in our best, loaded us into the car, navigated the Long Island Expressway and the Midtown Tunnel, and finally parked on a Manhattan side street. Soon we were climbing the red-carpeted steps of the Plaza Hotel, welcomed by men in livery who tipped their hats and held the doors wide. We cut across the lobby—a cavern of marble and gilt—and entered the Palm Court, where, once seated, I tried to maintain my best manners. I squirmed a good bit at a table set with white linen and too many forks. I was a million miles from the pizza parlor and diner counter stools I knew well. Still, as guests of Musie and Sweets, we were welcome.

They made time for tea with us, Musie's grandchildren, but the visit was foremost a reunion for the sisters. Fashion brought them to town. They had appointments at preferred department stores—B. Altman or Saks Fifth Avenue. In-house shoppers anticipated their needs as women required to dress their parts: Sweets for the political scene in Washington and Musie for the politics of campus and of church in Greensboro. They tried on clothes and sipped coffee or tea. Clerks addressed them by proper, polite names—Miss Williams and Mrs. Jones. They charged all purchases to house accounts. If they stood out at all, no one mentioned it. And if they did, Musie knew what to do. Fannie had taught her that when faced with rudeness, she should simply go elsewhere. There would always be some-place where the clerks were gracious, Fannie had reassured her daughters.

When I was old enough to shop for myself, Musie passed Fannie's wisdom down to me. During summer visits to Greensboro, she handed me the keys to her blue Chevy along with her tin department-store charge cards. I steered to a sub-urban mall—the old downtown locations had long before

closed—and wandered among the racks. I tried on outfits, admired myself in three-way mirrors, and hoped that I
appeared a bit more grown than I had the year before.

I was never at ease, even though the clerks mostly ignored
me until I approached the register, ready to check out. I could
not shake the sense that I was passing, and it was a dilemma
from which I could not extricate myself. In the same circumstances, Fannie may well have considered my dilemma to be
sport. She was having fun with the sales personnel. Musie, on
the other hand, likely never knew how it felt to be overlooked.
I gathered my purchases, wrapped in tissue paper and slipped
into a shopping bag. Back in the car, I hurried to Musie's house.
There we all knew who I was and that we were the same.

I worried that when Aunt Sweets gifted me a bit of Fannie's
jewelry, she thought I favored her mother. Sweets thought that
Fannie and I wore the same skin, light and bright. She believed
that our skin was an amulet that bestowed good fortune and
protection against evil. Perhaps this had been true for Fannie,
who used her skin in ways that pleased her and foiled others
in department stores. The same has not been true for me. Our
common skin, on many days, brings on only trouble. When I
see it coming, I reach for Fannie's earring-turned-pendant. I
fasten its clasp around my neck, adjust it at my collarbone, rub
my fingers across its smooth gold, and feel my skin catch on the
sharp facets of its diamond. In that way, I remind myself: It is
not my skin that protects me. It is Fannie.

SEVEN

Color

Just what is the state of the mulatto nation?
—REBECCA WALKER, *MIXED*

M Y GRANDMOTHER MUSIE WAS NINETY-THREE WHEN SHE
died. She lived so long that scholars called on her to help
them document the past. A descendant of enslaved people—
including her mother, Fannie, and her grandmother Susan—
close to the end of the twentieth century, Musie was regarded
by some researchers as an artifact of sorts. Some of them wrote
to her. Others visited her home in Greensboro, North Carolina, carrying notebooks and tape recorders. Everyone asked
her for stories. They were sure that she'd teach them lessons
about living a life that began with her birth in 1890s Danville,
Kentucky, and ended nine decades later in 1980s Greensboro.

Everyone had questions for her about color—where it came
from, what it meant, and how she navigated the line. More
than once, an interviewer prompted Musie to recount her earliest troubles. Susan, she recalled, had taught her how to maneu-
ver around it. When the school year ended, her grandmother

arrived at Musie's Covington, Kentucky, home to take her to Danville for the summer. Susan had a scheme that would let them avoid riding in the train's segregated car. They would not leave directly from Covington; state law required that when they traveled in Kentucky, they do so in a separate coach. However, if they began their trip to Danville in Ohio, they were regarded as interstate travelers and exempt from Kentucky's rules. Susan gathered up Musie, along with the girl's valise and a cold lunch for two, and headed across the river to Cincinnati. Musie watched as Susan bought the first-class tickets she preferred and then wrangled with conductors who tried to deny them their seats. Susan understood the twists and turns of the color line and made certain they traveled unbothered by its rough edges.

Still a teen, Musie left for college and learned to navigate on her own. At the University of Cincinnati, a professor showed her how the color line worked there. He could not bar her altogether and so surrounded Musie with empty chairs. No white students would be required to sit next to her. Still, she explained, when she needed to confer or share the reading with a classmate, the two simply shifted their seats. At a University of Chicago summer session, she met with frank rudeness even from students. Most would not answer simple questions like "Where is the library?" or "Do you have the time?" This was how Musie learned that a good number of white southerners took extra credits at Chicago in June and July.

Musie herself didn't share every story. It was my Uncle Fuzz who told me about one of his mother's most enduring lessons. Her mother, Fannie, could pass, while Musie could not. Still,

Musie (Susie Pearl Williams), University
of Cincinnati yearbook, 1913

Musie was "high yellow," as my Uncle Fuzz put it. In our family, people noticed these finer gradations of color and of hair and
features. These might signal who we were to each other and to
the world. Long before 1982, when writer Alice Walker coined
the term *colorism*, Musie understood its meaning.

—

In the 1920s, Musie was a young wife and mother when a
friend, the anthropologist Caroline Bond Day, invited her
to join a study. Neither anticipated where their collaboration
would take them. Day planned to better understand race by
evaluating hair along with bodies, skulls, and blood quantum.
As a graduate student at Harvard University, Day turned to
methods endorsed by her teachers. Aiming to avenge people like her and Musie, those whom anthropologists termed
"hybrids," Day set out to disprove the theory of mulatto

degeneracy. Mixed people were not at all inferior, in her view, and she chose to study families that were enduring, accomplished, and even distinguished. Renowned scholar W. E. B. Du Bois was among her informants. So was my grandmother.

Day wrote to Musie at home in Greensboro, where she was newly settled. She managed her four children while also rolling up her sleeves at Bennett College, where her husband was the new president. She recruited students, processed paperwork, and entertained supporters. At Day's direction, Musie sent to Harvard two hair samples, one from her own head and another from that of her oldest: ten-year-old Junior. Perhaps she used her own pair of shears, or maybe she reached into her sewing basket for the sharpest scissors she owned. When the samples arrived at Harvard—along with a cache of family

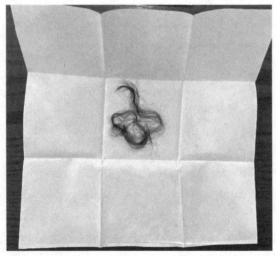

Musie (Susie Williams Jones), hair sample, Caroline Bond Day Papers

Color

photographs—Day placed them in small plastic bags and folded acid-free paper. She preserved single strands between small rectangular plates of glass.

Day charted Musie's family tree on a large poster-board sheet with hair and photos arranged along generational lines. She then added calculations. Each family member was assigned a formula that represented their percentage of Negro versus white ancestry. Day wrote under Musie's high school graduation portrait, "Sue Williams Jones. N 3/8, W 5/8." Day figured that of Musie's eight great-grandparents, three had been Negroes (N 3/8) and five white people (W 5/8.) These figures confused me enough that I went back to my version of our family tree. But nothing exactly lined up. I knew too little about Musie's ancestors to judge Day's calculations. But I did not disagree with her overall conclusion: Musie was a hybrid person.

Hair preoccupied Day. Curls, locks, and strands held keys to human difference. She understood her field's well-known taxonomies. Form: straight, low waves, deep waves, curly, frizzly, and woolly. Texture: coarse, medium, and fine. She noted the streamlined "Davenport" scheme: curly, straight, wavy, and kinky. Day's distinct scheme was ambitious: frizzly-curly; slight frizzliness; harder, crisper frizzly; soft frizzly-curly; temporary frizzliness; soft frizzly; frizzly brown; low waves; narrow wave; deep waved; open curl; marked curliness; crinkly-curly; smooth; silky; almost straight; straighter; very straight; straight mongoloid hair; extremely curved; lie flat; kink up; close spiral; low haired; naturally intermediate; bushiness; soft, silky, also frizzly around the edges.

193

On a work trip to Harvard, I took myself to see Musie's hair. I was already uneasy as I climbed the front steps of the Peabody Museum of Archaeology and Ethnology. Inside the nineteenth-century redbrick building, the rooms were cramped and the stairwells dark and narrow. The corridors and gallery spaces teemed with artifacts of the human past. There I met the custodian in charge of Musie's hair, an osteologist: a young woman in a white lab coat who told me she'd trained at the University of Michigan. "I taught there for many years," I shared, trying to build some rapport. "My work concerns human remains," she offered and then handed me my own white jacket and cotton gloves.

My thoughts ricocheted—"human remains"? I thought of Musie's hair as more like a memento in a lover's locket or a mother's keepsake marked "first haircut," not an artifact. On the outside, I held a dispassionate pose not wanting to give my feelings away. But inside, my stomach flip-flopped. I knew my grandmother's hair better than any scientist in a lab coat. As a girl, I'd kept Musie company as she'd readied for bed. Out of her dress and in a cotton slip, she'd reach behind her head to take down the twist she wore during the day. Methodically, she'd remove the bobby pins, hair falling down her shoulders and then along her back. Musie brushed with deliberate care— one hundred strokes each night with soft, natural bristles. I sat silent, sharing an intimate ritual.

The osteologist was gentle, even respectful as she handed me a small white envelope. In it was a creased sheet of thick acid-free paper. My hands trembled as I undid the tiny puzzle: There it was, a lock of Musie's hair: a long, many-stranded curl, closer in texture to mine than I remembered. My tears burned. I dared not speak, worried that I might sob. With watchful eyes at my back, I stared, took photos, and posed as if on a scientific mission. Really I was just a granddaughter aching for time with Musie. The urge to take the hair home welled up in me. That wasn't possible. But if Harvard would let me, I thought, I'd happily remain there to watch over my grandmother. I knew what was expected of me, so I gently folded the packet, set it down, said my thanks, and walked out into the afternoon sun. That night, back in my hotel room, I scrolled through my photos and then turned one of Musie's hair into the background image on my phone.

In 1932, Caroline Bond Day published her findings in "A Study of Some Negro-White Families in the United States." Recruiting subjects had been difficult: "Individuals have a family history much of which has been shrouded in the mystery and humiliation of illegitimacy." Few were eager to surface "ancestral skeletons," an allusion to descent from slaveholders as well as slaves. Some held back to protect relations who were passing, while others modestly declined in order to avoid unwanted attention. None of this kept Day from concluding that in anthropological terms, there were no significant differences between hybrid versus pure people. Accomplishment abounded across her subjects. Day's faculty supervisor lamented her small sample size but went ahead to further debunk mulatto degeneracy: "I cannot see that these data afford any comfort to those who contend that miscegenation between Negroes and Whites produces anthropologically inferior types."

Musie may have found Day's conclusions affirming. My grandmother did not suffer from a sense of inferiority. But she knew how science saw people like her and would have appreciated any study that reduced her hybridity to irrelevance. I felt much the same until I followed Day's footnote trail. There I discovered that she had built her ideas upon studies written by German men: agents of colonialism and proponents of eugenics. In 1913, medical doctor Eugen Fischer had published *Die Rehobother Bastards und das Bastardierungsproblem Beim Menschen*, or *The Rehoboth Bastards and the Problem of Bastardization in Human Beings*, his study of Namibia's mixed people, inheritors of colonialism's sexual exploitation. In 1927, physician Ernst Rodenwaldt had released *Die Mestizen auf Kisar*, or *The Mestizos of Kisar*, set in the Dutch East Indies. These studies, Day believed, legitimated her own and served as her launchpad. What she could not foresee was that, equipped with their brand of race science, both Fischer and Rodenwaldt would go on to promote the separation and even the extermination of people during the Nazi regime.

Race science cut two ways in Day's time, making it risky. On the one hand, it could be used to challenge systems of racial hierarchies. No race was superior to another in this view. Hybrid people were as sound as any. On the other hand, Day's research affirmed that race was a legitimate and true facet of human difference. That idea, which researchers like Day used to promote human equality, could be picked up by others for far more pernicious purposes. Musie, for her part, when she joined Day's study was thinking less about the dangers of race science and more about friendship. She placed great confidence in Day, trusting that the budding anthropologist would uncover important insights by studying family history. Musie's only surviving letter to her friend brims with warmth, from the salutation, "My dear Carrie," to the sign-off, "Love to you."

Musie believed in Day so much that she shared loved ones' photographs, samples of hair, and stories about her family past. She believed in her friend so much that she recruited The Bishop, her brother-in-law, to Day's study. But while Musie was open and confident, The Bishop held back. Musie explained that The Bishop would not complete a family questionnaire or share his hair. Day's questions were "very personal," he said, and my grandmother wrote to her friend with regrets. The Bishop "felt reluctant" to reveal his side of the story. He believed in God and politics. He believed in the people he came from. But The Bishop did not believe in race science.

—

In my mind, my grandparents were for a long time fixed figures, like characters. This might have pleased them; it certainly pleased me. They were exemplars of a legendary generation, born free and destined for distinction. In a 1903 essay, W. E. B. Du Bois dubbed them the "Talented Tenth": an elite cadre of college-educated leaders who devoted their best to institution building and the progress of Black Americans. As a child, I stood in the warmth of their glow. At nine, I was small, skinny, and shy. Before we headed to Greensboro's coliseum, Musie dressed me in my best: a Carolina blue dress and matching sweater. We sat up front at a round table for eight. The master of ceremonies announced Grandy as a recipient of Greensboro's

Wiley Award for Excellence in Public Education, posthumous recognition of his service as the city's first Black school board member. Music gave me an encouraging look as I walked up front and clutched the framed citation while the audience applauded. That day, I learned the feeling of pride.

My grandparents were, I thought, above reproach. Then I read sociologist E. Franklin Frazier's 1957 book, *The Black Bourgeoisie*. It was already the 1990s. I was in New York City and back at school, getting a graduate degree in history. A professor assigned Frazier, and on a spring morning, I left my Upper West Side apartment and headed out for a day of classes. I dropped *The Black Bourgeoisie* into my bag and headed to the bus stop. I'd get a jump on the day's reading during the ride uptown.

I bounced in a rear seat as the bus lurched and belched, eventually pulling out Frazier's paperback. Its gold cover with bold type boasted, "The book that brought the shock of self-revelation to middle class Negroes in America." *Uh-oh*, I thought. My throat tightened as I read, "The black bourgeoisie has developed a deep-seated inferiority complex. In order to compensate [it] created in its isolation what might be described as a world of make-believe in which it attempts to escape the disdain of whites and fulfill its wish for status in American life." Frazier was out to bury rather than admire my grandparents. I flipped the pages until I found his take on historically Black colleges like Bennett. It was equally unforgiving: "Teachers d students alike are agreed that money and conspicuous consumption are more important than knowledge or the enjoyment of books and art and music."

I arrived at class, squeezed into a small wooden desk, and sat tight-lipped. My professor parroted Frazier, his voice rising as he repeated choice passages. Light skin was not a sign of elite status. Instead, it exposed a defective character. Frazier's words hit me where it hurt: "The hollowness of the black bourgeoisie's pretended 'racial pride' is revealed in the value which it places upon a white or light complexion." Frazier blamed this flaw on long-ago ancestors: "The Negroes who were free before the Civil War, or those who had enjoyed the advantages of having served in the house of their masters." Frazier's blow landed, and he reduced families like mine to caricatures. My professor bellowed, and the class roared. Everyone appeared to be in on Frazier's joke except me. I embodied it.

I hadn't seen Frazier coming. Had my grandparents? From time to time, they'd shared an orbit with him. In 1926, when word reached Frazier that Grandy would be the next president of Bennett College, he sent a note of congratulations. Both were working in Atlanta then—young and striving to fulfill the promise of The Talented—Frazier at Morehouse College and Grandy at the Commission on Interracial Cooperation. Grandy replied in a letter I found among Frazier's papers, "Thank you for your kind note. . . . When you come through Greensboro make Bennett College your headquarters," signed with his bold, round signature—"David D. Jones." Already Grandy was thinking like the institution builder he became. Friendships with men like Frazier were essential to his strategy.

Their connection grew to be more than polite. In 1945, both Grandy and Frazier signed a public letter published by the National Federation for Constitutional Liberties. They were among those who endorsed the War Department's refusal to ban communists from army commissions. In the same moment, both were members of the Council on African Affairs. These affiliations fueled charges against Frazier by the House Committee on Un-American Activities. They led the FBI to track my grandfather's "subversive" associations. Uncowed, the two publicly affirmed their ties. Grandy invited Frazier to speak at Bennett's Sunday-afternoon vespers that fall. His talk on "the Sociological approach to community study" kicked off the semester. In the months that followed, students also heard from Morehouse College president Benjamin Mays, Director of the Council on African Affairs Max Yergen, and head of the Penn School Howard Kester.

Bennett welcomed Frazier like the honored guest he was. At 4:00 p.m., students filed into Pfeiffer Chapel, dressed in their best. A reporter for the *Belle Ringer*, a student newspaper, took notes. Afterward, Grandy and Musie welcomed Frazier at home, where the front rooms were filled with books, art, and a baby grand piano. Musie was likely at her most gracious, serving coffee in her grandmother Susan's cups of delicate gold-rimmed, hand-painted Haviland china. This was Musie's way of welcoming Frazier. She drew him into a conversation that centered on his work and then encouraged students to do the same. The scene was intended to please Frazier, but *Black Bourgeoisie* hints at how it may have been the type of gathering that only unsettled him.

Frazier did not see Musie's home as she did. When she passed him a cup of coffee poured into French china, he saw pretension, while she saw women's hands that cared for guests and invited new friendships. Where the sociologist saw cheap mimicry, Musie saw her own grandmother putting slavery in her past. Frazier saw a "high-yellow" woman putting on airs, while Musie saw on her skin a sign of what the women before her had endured. Musie asked after Frazier's family, while he asked nothing about hers, assuming he already knew who she came from. Frazier believed that my grandmother was all wrong, but really he did not know her at all.

When Musie died, her three surviving children—including my father—divvied up her possessions. Her house was owned by the college, but whatever covered her shelves and stuffed her drawers, hung in her closets and on her walls, they sorted through. Aunt Tuppy lovingly tucked Musie's ashes into a suitcase, destined to rest next to Grandy in a Boston columbarium. A moving company shipped paper cartons north to New York. Among them were eight boxes filled with Haviland china and marked for delivery at my father's suburban duplex.

This was how Susan's china passed from Musie to me. I carted it home: plates for dinner, salad, and dessert; bowls; platters; three terrines; a gravy boat; and a cake stand. There are a dozen coffee cups with matching saucers—the very cups that Musie had passed to E. Franklin Frazier. I cleared my dining table and gingerly unwrapped, one by one, objects long before protected by newspaper turned dusty and yellowed. The beauty was in the pattern's details: small pink flowers on green leafy stalks, clustered at ten, two, and six o'clock on the plates. The maker called the pattern "Apple Blossom." Faded gold leaf–trimmed rims and handles reminded me that they had survived generations of use. Coming across a salad plate snapped in two, I slowed, then carefully assembled stacks of a service for twelve.

My memories of Musie flooded back. At breakfasts and suppers, receptions, and meetings, she presided as the hostess of Bennett College and her family home. She stored her china in a dark, narrow pantry off the breakfast room in cabinets that stretched from floor to ceiling. As a girl, I tugged on the lamp cord and then peeked inside; the doors slightly groaned. I stood still, craned my neck upward, and marveled at dishes we touched only during very special meals. Even today, holding the Haviland cups connects me to Musie and to Susan. Musie explained, "I have my grandmother's cups and saucers. They are old Haviland. . . . During our summers in Danville, one of the things Grandmother did always was to entertain her club of friends." Each time she used them, Musie was reenacting a family ritual.

Musie likely read *Black Bourgeoisie*. The shelves of her library were filled with books by widely read Black authors. Surely she read reviews like "Unhappy Worlds" by Saunders Redding, a scholar remembered as the first Black professor in the Ivy League. Redding admired Frazier's evidence, derived from "individual cases" rather than sociological statistics. He underscored how Frazier had observed "status" and vapid "middle-class" ways among The Talented. Frazier had also uncovered "pain" and "unhappiness," Redding explained. Musie had experienced those feelings during her life. Like Redding, she saw them not as a reflection of her character flaws. Instead, her pain and unhappiness were, as Redding put it, due to how "American culture" had committed its "greatest crimes against black humanity." Rather than blaming The Talented for the ravages of racism, as Frazier had, Musie blamed a nation that had blocked Black Americans' "avenues to social and economic development . . . elemental justice," and "free thought and speech."

Musie encouraged me to read many of the scholarly greats on her shelves—John Blassingame, W. E. B. Du Bois, John Hope Franklin—but not Frazier. I wondered if she'd kept from me how he'd seen her life as a slavish imitation of white values. He'd mocked the drapes, linens and sheets, and handcrafted wallpaper that made her home an oasis. He'd ridiculed her taste for carefully tailored dresses, elegantly modest jewelry, carefully stylish hats, and a subtle splash of Chanel No. 5. Frazier claimed that her skin was a badge of near shame. When she died in 1984, Musie left me to encounter Frazier without her. He rendered our family's pride a twisted fantasy, and still, I cannot help but think that between the lines of *Black Bourgeoisie*, I can also see his pain.

Frazier tried to trap our family in a double bind of class and color. Musie never gave in and remained stoic. Frazier judged her life to be a cheap imitation of that lived by white elites. What did she think? I have pored through her letters, read each line of every interview. I've gazed at each surviving portrait and waded through snapshots of her home. I've scavenged my own memories, jarring them with old newspaper reports. I've let my heart and my gut do the thinking for me. I am certain that Musie never deferred to the assessment of Frazier, even though he was a credentialed, reputation-wielding, book-publishing scholar. Who did she think she was? Her unshakable demeanor said it all.

Musie lived another thirty years after Grandy's death in 1956. The politics of the next generation drew her out of mourning. When in 1960 Bennett students organized a voter registration drive—Operation Door Knock—Musie was there with support, advice, and encouragement. She would have welcomed another chance to host Frazier in her home. She would have pointed out the Driskell oil painting that hung above her living-room mantel, invited him to settle comfortably in her upholstered midcentury modern armchairs, and, with her grandmother's Haviland cups and saucers, served him steaming coffee along with a plate of sweet cookies. She would have inquired about his family, admired his latest publication, and learned how he saw the questions of the day, especially Civil Rights. She would have made certain that Professor Frazier was glad he came. And she'd never have let on how she felt.

—

As a girl, I knew Nurse Trammel's touch nearly as well as that of my grandmother. I remember her smile, her pressed uniform, and her orderly infirmary. She was one of the few people I knew who could openly disagree with Musie and get away with it. The two were companions in my young mind. The summer I turned four, I ran a fever so high that I saw imaginary boats sailing across Musie's upstairs landing. The two were there, taking turns applying cool cloths to my forehead, offering a pan each time I retched, and holding cups of chipped ice to my chapped lips. I knew Nurse Trammel as Alsacious—a moniker bestowed by my older, New York cousins who chose nicknames from their French lessons. Perhaps it was a play on Alsace-Lorraine? On the Bennett campus, she was always Nurse Trammel.

By the time Alsacious cooled my fever in my grandmother's deep porcelain tub, she'd been tending babies alongside Musie for two generations. My Uncle Fuzz recounted what his mother had told him: Alsacious was there in 1928 when he was born at home. She was barely a young woman, just sixteen, not yet a nurse in a certified sense. Alsacious must have applied whatever she'd learned back home in Alabama in that birthing room. She'd seen a lot of us Joneses grow up by the time she sat close to me, whispering lullabies in my child's ears as we waited out the worst.

She came to Greensboro from her family's farm in Five Points, across the Georgia border in central Alabama. Montgomery to the southwest was the nearest city, though Atlanta to the north wasn't much farther away. But these places were little more than dots on the map, far from her daily life. Five Points was a small, rural crossroads put on the map by the East Alabama Railway, which opened a depot there in 1887. Today the place boasts of having been connected to the electric power grid in 1925, when Alsacious was a teen.

Her father was a farmer, and my memories match the official evidence of their growing, landowning family. Today the county still has the names of Alsacious and her brother on a deed to sixty-six acres that face County Road 160. She took me there when I was eight or nine, driving her wide, American-made sedan south from Greensboro. Alsacious was at the wheel, while I took up the passenger seat, barely tall enough to see over the dashboard, my bare thighs sticking and unsticking to the padded pleather seats. I felt special when Alsacious introduced me to her people and did my best to behave. One afternoon, someone placed me atop a horse, set the reins in my hands, and left that creature to trot me into a berry patch swarming with bees. Blackberries. I waited until a kind soul— one of Alsacious's nephews—extracted us.

Alsacious left for Greensboro in what I'm sure was, to her parents, a chance for their eldest daughter to enjoy a life beyond the farm. In Five Corners, Alsacious's mother had a growing brood: four girls and five boys by the time Alsacious was ten. At the same moment, Musie and Grandy arrived at Bennett with a campus to build but also a household to run, including the matter of soon-to-be-four children. I don't know what sort of bargain her parents struck with my grandparents. Perhaps it

Alsacious (Alsie Trammel), back row, last on the right, Bennett College High School Class, 1932

was as simple as labor in exchange for food, shelter, and other necessaries. Alsacious, it seems, rewrote the terms. It took time, but eventually she was enrolled at Bennett, attending the high school department. In summer 1932—she was twenty—Alsacious donned all white and a string of pearls and stood with the twenty-one other young women who also received diplomas. In another five years, she earned her place among the school's college graduates, a proud member of the class of 1937.

When my Uncle Fuzz recalled those years, he was adamant that Alsacious was like a sister to him. He meant to say that she was not a mammy figure, even though she had a hand in raising him and his siblings. By terming her his sister, he meant to distinguish Alsacious from the many workers who had managed his family's campus life: laundresses, groundskeepers, mechanics, and cooks. *Sister* was an honorific intended to raise Alsacious to a status that approximated his own. I can imagine her face had Alsacious heard this story. She'd cock her left eyebrow up—listening, but with a critical ear. She'd grin a half smile, giving away her amusement. Her arms would be crossed at her chest, signaling her skepticism. She'd hold back her words for a time. But likely she would be thinking that Fuzz and Musie's other children were not like siblings at all. They were more like kids next door for whom Alsacious babysat from time to time.

More than once, my Uncle Fuzz told me about how he had confided in Musie that Alsacious had been like a sister to him. Musie rejected this, shutting him down with an insistence that he never again say such a thing. Fuzz was ashamed, though not because his mother could openly scold him even as a grown

man. He was ashamed to learn that his mother denied any kinship with Alsacious. For Musie, he learned, that was unthinkable. My grandmother ordered her world by blood and also
by class and color. Alsacious, a deep-brown-skinned girl from
rural Alabama, might be many things to Musie's family, but
kin was not one of them.

Fuzz did have a sister: Tuppy. She attended Bennett for a
time alongside Alsacious, but little about their experiences was
the same. Tuppy was obliged to attend Bennett as an endorse-
ment of the school her father led. This required that she give
up her dream of college up north. Her parents compensated
their daughter by gifting her a precollege year abroad, learning French language and culture in Grenoble. After graduation
from Bennett, Tuppy went on to medical school. Her father, a
muscular ally with connections across higher education, aided
her every step of the way. Alsacious had no such help. She
managed her own destiny and endured hardships that Tuppy
never knew, such as working to pay fees and tuition.

Alsacious finished her bachelor studies two years ahead
of Tuppy. That spring, Bennett's school paper boasted about
its young women graduates, three-fourths of whom were
bound for teaching. Not Alsacious. She was reported to be
"privately employed" in New York, the only member of her
class mentioned in those terms. A daughter of one of Greensboro's most prosperous families had married a man from New
Jersey. Alsacious joined the two in New York and in 1940
managed their house in Manhattan, reported on the census as
"Maid." My sketchy memory says that at this moment, Musie
and Alsacious fell out, or perhaps it was their falling-out that

led Alsacious to leave Greensboro. This may have been her best way forward, but when Alsacious compared her fate to that of Tuppy or the members of her college class, the differences were apparent.

In 1942, Alsacious returned to Bennett, determined to reset the terms of her affiliation. She enlisted in the US Cadet Nurse Corps. By 1947, she'd earned her BS in nursing from New Orleans's Dillard University. At Bennett, her domain was no longer Musie's home. It was instead Kent Hall, where she appeared most days in a crisp white uniform, topped by a Flossie nurse's cap. She single-handedly built up Bennett's infirmary, which today bears her name. She was newly baptized Nurse Trammel. During summers, when regular school-year duties lightened, Alsacious spent afternoons in Musie's home. There she taught me how to care for ripening peaches, outfitted me in handcrafted dresses, sent a chuckle my way when my grandmother got stern, and let me have the run of the infirmary on Sunday afternoons. I never tired of handling tongue depressors and stethoscopes, the instruments of her profession.

What Fuzz meant to say when he called Alsacious his sister was that he loved her. And she, in her way, loved him back. I am certain of this, if only because I felt the deep affection that ran from her to me. But we were not her family. When she retired, Alsacious did not remain at Bennett or linger long in Greensboro. Instead, she headed out to spend the rest of her years in Atlanta, where her brother had already set up their new household. The two planned to live together for the first time since their childhoods in Alabama. While she had been a caretaker, a nurse, and even a friend, Alsacious had always been someone else's sister. For her, family had always meant her people from back in Five Points.

———

Musie lived a public life. Civic projects drew her out of widowhood: the founding of a new YMCA, the construction of a new hospital, and the opening of a full-service public library for Black Greensboro. Voter registration through Bennett's Operation Door Knock was for her important and thrilling. Still, her family life remained private. Dr. Merze Tate, a historian on assignment for Harvard's Schlesinger Library, entered this preserve in 1977. A taxi dropped Dr. Tate at Musie's home on Greensboro's east side, and she headed up the front steps onto the porch. The August-afternoon sun was high and hot and the shade a welcome place for waiting. Pushing the doorbell, Dr. Tate waited. Musie opened the screen door and welcomed her guest into the dappled living-room light.

Dr. Tate—tall, even stately—was dressed for the occasion and expected that Musie would be too. Musie would have chosen a dress, silk or a light wool blend, with short sleeves and a belt at the waist. Her cocktail watch sat on her wrist and her wedding ring on her left hand. A brooch or pendant finished off her look. Dr. Tate carried with her a notebook, cassette-tape recorder, and familiarity with Musie and Bennett College: In the 1930s, Dr. Tate had headed the school's history and social science department. Their meetup was a reunion.

Dr. Tate was best known as a diplomatic historian and member of the Howard University faculty. But when the Schlesinger

Library, dedicated to women's history, proposed collecting Black women's oral histories, Tate signed on. The goal was to remedy the absence of sources about women of Musie's generation. Among those included were luminaries such as activist Dorothy Height, artist Lois Mailou Jones, icon Rosa Parks, and writer Dorothy West. Dr. Tate also interviewed Musie's sister, Aunt Sweets. The library included over seventy individuals who illustrated how Black women, Musie among them, had shaped the first half of the twentieth century.

The two women—acquainted for forty years—sat beside one another at Musie's dining table. Dr. Tate described the scene: "A period early American, one might say, home, early American furniture in the dining area where we are, and attractive furnishings throughout the home." In my mind's eye, I can see the room: polished furniture, floral wallpaper, long drapes, rush-seated chairs, and Chinese vases perched on a low, broad chest filled with linens and silver. I hear the two fumbling with the technology. Then Dr. Tate's voice comes through, setting the mood with a bit of nostalgia: "It is a pleasure for me to be here today. I have memories of receptions held here when I was teaching at Bennett in the 1930s, and indeed it is a great joy to spend this afternoon and part of tomorrow recording Mrs. Susie Jones for the black history of our distinguished women."

"Mrs. Jones, it might be well if we would start with your roots, since roots are now so important in people's lives." Dr. Tate began with a reference to the book and television miniseries *Roots*. Over that afternoon, Musie recounted her family story from time with her grandmother Susan in Danville to her upbringing in Kentucky and on through her many years in

Greensboro. The next morning, Dr. Tate returned. Anticipating their conversation, Musie had spread out family portraits—especially those of her grandchildren—on the table. The same photos ordinarily decorated the walls of Musie's small downstairs den. It wasn't very long before Dr. Tate focused on me and my siblings. She probed, "Now these three [photos] I've kept together because they are in color and they belong in the same family." They were our school portraits taken ten years earlier.

I'd been in the fourth grade. Today I've nearly forgotten the gap between my front teeth that, over time, narrowed. But the pink, sleeveless, empire-waist dress with a bow and fuzzy white polka dots is still familiar. I can almost feel how the crinoline-like underskirt crunched when I sat down and scratched at my thighs when I walked. Across the foreheads of my younger brother and sister, I recognize my mother's shaky scissor work, done with her only pair—heavy and dull—resulting in bangs that never lined up. We three resembled each other, though we were not a matched set. I think I see the same look in our eyes.

Dr. Tate wanted to ask Musie about color, specifically the meaning of our color. It was a relevant question. The two sat together only ten years after the US Supreme Court had given interracial marriages constitutional protection. North Carolina's antimiscegenation laws, which dated back to 1715, were no longer valid. Still, how to think about the children of those unions was unclear. Dr. Tate fixed her attention on our photos, and Musie grew uneasy. She had always worried not about who we were but instead about who we *thought* we were. Our skin carried a hint of yellow that turned warm shades of bronze and brown only after a summer in the sun. Our hair—mine and my brother's with a gentle wave, my sister's bone straight—was wash-and-go. Our life in a nearly all-white suburban enclave was shaping us in ways that were more than skin deep. After all, we were learning from school friends to eat cream-cheese-and-jelly sandwiches, dance to the Osmond Brothers, and idol-ize Nancy Drew, while at home our father spun Miles Davis and Motown, hurried us to the television to catch Bill Cosby on *I Spy*, and served up scrapple and grits as Sunday-morning fare. Musie knew that our generation was growing up amidst a mash-up of color, class, and new doors that appeared nearly wide open.

Musie, in contrast, never changed. I didn't notice how she aged and every summer her home was just as we'd left it, down to the toys and trinkets I'd stashed in a bedside table. She was our tutor, planting lessons deep in our psyches and even spring-ing an occasional quiz. I was eight on a steamy summer after-noon when we lay on mats in Musie's darkened dining room. There were six or eight of us in total: my brother, my sister, and I plus a few neighborhood friends. The awnings were up and the curtains drawn. Musie and Nurse Trammell sat side by side, shushing as we settled in. On most days, they told a story. But on this one, there was a test. "Children, we have a question," Musie began. I perked up. "Who here is a Negro?" my grandmother queried in a warm but serious tone. She and Nurse Trammell watched for our responses. "Who here is a Negro? Raise your hands," Nurse Trammell nudged. This was a version of the "Who do you think you are?" question, but it came wrapped in kindness and concern.

I was eager to please and prided myself on being a good student. Still, I hesitated and sneaked a look around the room. Perhaps my hand went up only after our neighbors, the deep-brown-skinned Miller boys whom I so admired, raised theirs. Maybe I was confident, thrusting my hand in the air without another thought: I knew that when the word *Negro* was used, it included my father and me. Recounting the story much later, my grandmother explained that my hand went up first. Only then did my younger siblings raise theirs. Neither Musie nor Nurse Trammel took note of how the other children—all brown and beige—responded. The test was just for us.

Her concerns and our confusion were not subjects that Musie intended to speak about with Dr. Tate. The mood between them grew awkward as Musie felt pressed to explain our looks. She paused for a beat and then said, "Yes, these are Paul's children." She dutifully introduced us as the offspring of her middle son. "Oh yes. They're very interesting," Dr. Tate observed, using a deceptively vague term. My grandmother kept her composure and said nothing, refusing to answer the question that *interesting* suggested. We were, to Dr. Tate's eyes, interesting as in curious, as in strange, as in nearly inexplicable. Dr. Tate did not have the right words for how we looked, and my grandmother did not offer any.

Dr. Tate tried another approach, this time commenting on my sister's photo: "She has almost blondish hair and light brown-bluish eyes." This was nearly a lie. As many times as I've looked at my sister's school photo, I've never seen what Dr. Tate described. I can only think that her words were less a literal account than a query—or even a provocation. She

Martha S. Jones,
circa 1967

Paul M. Jones, Jr.,
circa 1967

Laura F. Jones,
circa 1967

meant that we were descendants of the Jones clan, but not only that. She saw in our faces, Dr. Tate meant to say, evidence of our parents' illicit union. We were too light, too mixed, too much of something that neither Musie nor my father possessed. When she called my sister "blonde with light eyes," Dr. Tate's curiosity overrode her regard for my grandmother's privacy.

She wanted Musie to go on the record about color, about our color and what it meant. Was Dr. Tate among those who believed that my siblings and I were regrettably "monstrous" creatures, as did those who defended antimiscegenation laws? Did she subscribe to the view that lightness, narrow features, and limp hair were tickets to relative advantage? Perhaps she was just unsure about what words to use when it came to us. Dr. Tate asked a final question, this one about our mother, again referring to my sister's photo: "What is her mother, do you have a picture of her mother?"

Listening to their exchange, I can almost hear Musie stiffen. She'd been raised not to speak about color. But for both women, applying a label to my mother was easier than assigning one to us, her children. Musie indicated that she kept a photo of my mother in her sitting room and then offered a curtly frank reply: "Their mother is white American." Musie had reached her limit. She admonished Dr. Tate, reminding the younger woman where the boundaries lay: "You must remember, situations have so much to deal with these kinds of things and so we just don't label them too much." I can see Musie. Seated straight-backed in a dining chair, wrists gently resting on the edge of her oak table for eight. Her warm smile gone, replaced by stern, straight lips. Her voice, usually lyrical and lilting, dropped down two octaves almost to gravel.

While they sat on opposite sides of an interview that day, Musie and Dr. Tate shared an important quality. Neither had the right words—polite words—for us. My grandmother did not believe in labels; she did not countenance them. Dr. Tate had none of her own. Long past were days when a common, respectable lexicon included terms like *mulatto* or *quadroon*. By 1977, those words carried pejorative connotations derived from slavery and eugenic science. They were slurs. The two old acquaintances arrived at a stalemate, without words even as the tape turned and captured all that was said between them. With more polite expressions, such as *mixed-race* and *biracial*, still out on a distant horizon, silence was all they had.

———

It was 1993, nearly ten years after Musie's death, when I finally returned to Greensboro. I took a vacation from my job as a lawyer and traveled alone. I boarded at New York Penn

Station, impressed with my bold independence. As the miles dragged on along the stop-and-start route, an odd worry surfaced: Was it wise, safe even, to travel in North Carolina alone? It was an old concern, one I'd inherited from Musie. One she'd inherited from Susan. *Take care not to travel alone.*

I stepped down onto the platform in Rocky Mount, North Carolina, and immediately began to size up my surroundings. I chose chain hotels, hoping that corporate protocols encouraged the equal treatment of all guests. I scoped out local restaurants, preferring those with Black or Brown diners already seated. If they were served, I would be too. I hurried through my itinerary: a quick walk along the oceanfront, a brief peek into a local crafts studio, and snapshots of roadside historical markers. After five days on the road, I arrived in Greensboro and breathed a bit easier. It felt almost like home.

I checked into a motel on the highway, kicked off my shoes, and opened the local paper. A review of a new Italian restaurant caught my eye. I'd mark my return to Musie's hometown with dinner out. I spread a map across the passenger seat, drove west to a strip mall on the other side of town, and parked. "Table for one." The place teemed; obviously others had read the same review. But I was quickly seated near the kitchen and soon sipped a glass of red wine with my book open in front of me: Alice Walker's *Possessing the Secret of Joy*. I felt confident and even proud to have returned to Greensboro on my own. The next day, I'd visit the Bennett College campus.

After another look at the menu, I ordered fettuccine alfredo, which arrived in a large bowl, steaming hot. I tuned out the bustle around me—waitstaff, bussers, and customers headed to the restrooms in back. The best way to ward off anxiety was to bury myself deep in Alice Walker. I dreaded the prospect of being mistaken for who or what I was not. I worried that the host's graciousness was premised on his assumption that I was white. I sat with an open book by a Black author, hoping to clue him in to the realization that I was not. What I hoped for most was that no one much cared.

Unbidden, my waitress approached, standing over my right shoulder. I couldn't make her out and simply felt her presence. And then: "Can I ask you a question?" She spoke with a slight accent that was not southern. "Yes," I replied while wishing I could say no. I fixed my eyes in front of me while she continued, "What race are you?" My eyes lowered, I scanned the room for whoever was coming to eject me—or worse. I looked up at my waitress, who smiled, bright and all teeth. I could not reconcile what I saw with the warning bells ringing in my ears.

Did someone say "Danger!" or was that just a voice inside my head? Where was the nearest exit? Did I have my car keys? If I left quickly but without paying, wouldn't I compound my troubles? There was nothing to do but manage an answer. I rifled my mind and finally spoke back. To this day, I don't remember what I said. Whatever it was, I hoped it would settle any confusion, allay any concerns, and buy enough time to pay the check and get safely back to my car. I hoped I'd live to regret having traveled to North Carolina alone.

I was still looking up at the waitress as my brain fog began to lift. She was, I could see plainly, a brown-skinned woman with bone-straight black hair. She was Filipina and, when she asked my race, was acting alone. My waitress wasn't there to out me or to police the color line. She was curious, while the rest of the restaurant buzzed just as it had when I first walked in. I maintained my best poker face, just long enough for her to move on to the next table. What, I wondered, was she going to ask them? I returned to my fettuccini; the pasta trembled as I lifted a forkful to my mouth.

I'd not managed to pass, I realized. Instead, I'd been exposed for the ambiguous-looking person that I was. Later that night, back in my motel room, I breathed easier. Still, before turning off the lights, I pondered a long time and then slid an enormous chest of drawers in front of the door.

EIGHT

Integration

My boy, you are by blood, by appearance, by education, and by tastes a white man. Now, why do you want to throw your life away amidst the poverty and ignorance, in the hopeless struggle, of the black people of the United States?

—James Weldon Johnson,
The Autobiography of an Ex-Colored Man

M Y FATHER'S EARLIEST MEMORIES REVOLVED AROUND THE Bennett College campus. He'd been born in Atlanta. But just months later, he, his siblings, and their parents, Grandy and Musie, were on their way to Greensboro, North Carolina. It was late in 1926 when they loaded up all they had in trunks and crates destined for Grandy's hometown. The place their family knew best was Warnersville. But Musie focused on getting her brood settled into a new home, the president's house at Bennett College—two stories, three porches, a basement, attic, and two baths. It sat on a gentle hill that looked out across campus. From infant buggy rides to wobbly toddler steps and on through fast-paced boyhood races, Paul crossed the long, elegant walkways and alley shortcuts of the college like a person truly at home.

For his family, Bennett was also a fishbowl. His parents expected to be watched. Whether headed across campus or across town, they carefully chose their garments, hairstyles, and gait. They learned how to manage everyday encounters with students and more formal visits from parents, trustees, and donors. As Bennett's first couple, they greeted, made small talk, and listened to concerns. They embodied responsible stewardship. My father and his siblings—Junior, Tuppy, and Fuzz—enhanced Bennett's charm; their grooming and good manners let visitors know that Grandy and Musie would also care for students. When the children ran errands, completed chores, and even got slightly underfoot, they promoted Bennett as a family affair.

Paul M. Jones and siblings Tuppy, Junior, and Fuzz

Paul and Fuzz

This fishbowl atmosphere included being photographed. His parents trained Paul to be seen, often posing before a camera. He nestled between the knees of his big brother at six or seven, serious-faced in tailored shorts, a collared shirt, jacket, socks, and polished shoes. He posed side by side with his younger brother, Fuzz, the two in matching short pants and jackets, smiling from ear to ear. He already dressed smart, a habit he maintained over a lifetime. Paul's portraits in those days were staged, while at live events, his cracks showed. Musie recalled including him at a formal dinner, seated next to her. Bored, Paul dipped his spoon in the gravy and wrote CAT and DOG on the tablecloth, then wrapped his napkin around his head. Musie recalled how he then whispered, "Mama, I'm doing fine, am I not?" This scene reminds me that at home, expectations of Paul were high, and as a boy, he innocently defied them. It is a glimpse of a man I knew to be stern at the dinner table as a trusting and playfully sweet child.

—

By the time Paul was eleven, it was clear that his difficulties went beyond occasional dining-table hijinks. He could not read or write at grade level. His older siblings were already launched: His brother Junior at Phillips Andover, a New England prep school. His sister, Tuppy, recently returned from a study year in Grenoble, France, enrolled at Bennett. His parents' attention turned to Paul, whose learning troubles they did not understand. Experts, they hoped, would turn things around. In summer 1937, Grandy headed to New York's Columbia University to take graduate courses. He brought

Paul along and enrolled the boy at the Teachers College Summer Demonstration School.

Teachers College—a towering complex constructed of dark red bricks and brownstone trim—was like no place Paul knew. He craned his neck upward and took in its gables, dormers, and lantern towers. Details like ornate masonry, sloped roofs, an elaborate cupola, and a clock tower added to the grandeur. Inside, an experiment in progressive education was underway. A team of professionals set aside rote lessons, grades, and prizes and adopted experiential learning. With teachers as facilitators, children were encouraged to discover their own talents and motivations. This meant that Teachers College was, for Paul, in one respect very much like Bennett: It was also a fishbowl. Paul and his sixth grade classmates studied while graduate students of education—teachers in training—looked on.

For Paul, a lot was new at Teachers College, and he spent most days on his own. Grandy was busy with his studies. Paul arrived each morning at the Demonstration School and did as his father advised: He put his best face forward. Paul's classmates included local children along with others from as far away as Washington and Colorado, Alabama and Texas. Together they explored, hands-on, flood control and soil erosion, map design, bookbinding, and art making with clay, wood, and paint. Their bodies moved in sync while the group sang, swam, and danced. His teacher, Hazel Carey, summed up her impressions: Paul was "friendly and helpful," was "well-liked," and "worked well and faithfully," with an attitude that was "so good." He adapted well to the social challenges of a new school in an unfamiliar city.

In academic terms, Paul struggled. Teachers College was a fresh start, far from his disappointing performances in Greensboro. In New York, no one called him by his family nickname: Stooge. In their letters to one another, Grandy and Junior, Paul's oldest brother, referred to him that way. Encountering this, I wanted to think that "Stooge" might have had an affectionate or playful connotation. But everything I learned about the term convinced me that it was chastising and cruel. At home, Paul was known as Stooge: an inferior type, the butt of jokes, and someone not dumb but not bright and far too easily won over.

His teacher may not have known the depths of Paul's history. Still, it pained her to report to his parents that he "was severely handicapped by a serious reading weakness." Paul's written English was also deficient. My grandparents might have worried that Ms. Carey, a white New Englander trained at Columbia, saw Paul through prejudiced eyes. But they did not. Instead, they agreed and took her advice to heart: "See that [Paul] receive competent coaching both in and out of school." His summer at Columbia was fateful. Paul and his parents spent the next decade searching for educators who could resolve his learning problems. When I arrived at Columbia decades later to study history, I walked in my father's uneven footsteps. As had been true for him, my time there changed the course of my life.

—

When his parents sat down to plan what was next for Paul, all signs pointed to Columbus, Ohio. There he could receive an excellent education at the Ohio State University Laboratory

School, one of the country's most highly regarded progressive learning environments. In Columbus, Paul would also have family. He would live with The Bishop, Grandy's older brother, who was in Ohio on assignment for the Methodist Church. His parents sent Paul off with a promise: He would be in good hands with The Bishop. The older man had long before cared for his wayward brother, Grandy. Now he would similarly look after his nephew Paul, Grandy's son. Paul unpacked at his uncle's two-story dark-brick Bronzeville home and quickly fell in with his cousins. His notes home were cheerful. He thanked his mother for sending a Christmas box and reassured her, "[I] still love you very, very much." Paul was learning how to put on his best face long-distance.

He crossed town on his way to the Lab School, which sat on a northwest corner of the Ohio State campus. If Paul sometimes rode the city's crowded streetcars, he felt the tensions that gathered when Black and white riders were thrown together. As he took his place at school, his new classmates had questions. "When he first came the children asked him whether he was Spanish because of his dark olive skin," one teacher reported. Paul's reply was, as she told it, direct: "No, I'm a southern negro." He was learning what it meant to be misapprehended.

Paul often talked over his difficulties with adults. If he told The Bishop that schoolmates had misread him, the older man would have shared a story of his own. As a young husband, The Bishop had attended a fair with his wife and their friends. Arriving at the Ferris wheel, in a gallant gesture, he let the group board ahead of him. As he then stepped forward to hop into the cab, the attendant whispered, "Take the next car, sir; don't crowd in with those niggers." The Bishop replied, "Humph. I'm a nigger myself." Paul came from people who expected to be misread but never allowed such encounters to ruffle their feathers.

Paul's presence introduced a "racial question" at the Lab School, a teacher reported. Running through his classroom were new concerns: Could Black and white students learn together or become friends? The same teacher reported that it was Paul, with "sincerity and friendliness," who "reduced [the racial question] to a matter of no importance." Paul was twelve, and my own back aches a bit at reading how he bore the burden of integrating the Lab School. Everyone there lived and worked in a city, Columbus, where segregated housing patterns ensured the segregation of public schools. Paul bravely faced the challenge. "My school is coming along just fine," he assured his parents. When a teacher invited him to serve on a panel that would discuss race relations, he dutifully agreed. Paul had introduced a question and then was asked to answer it.

—

As he entered his teens, Paul strained under The Bishop's strict rules. He felt sure it was time to move on, leading him and Grandy to plan a change. Paul set his sights on the Mount Hermon School, and Grandy wrote the headmaster to request a place for his "second boy, Paul." They arrived at Hermon for a visit in mid-March, bundled up against the early-spring cold. The campus was near the Connecticut River, just five miles south of where Massachusetts meets New Hampshire. Even before Paul and Grandy arrived, the staff had assembled a file that is today preserved in the school's archives. On Grandy's letter of introduction, someone had marked in red pencil "negro." The word jumps off the page like a slur, especially when compared to Grandy's formally typeset query. Seeing this, I grew uneasy about what awaited Paul.

I imagine that he was awed by Hermon's beauty. The school was nestled just to the east of the Berkshire Mountains. Charming cottages lined the main road, the headmaster's house sat on a bluff, and all around, the air was freshly crisp. Behind the scenes, things were less bucolic. Paul and Grandy met with the head of admissions, Gordon Pyper. He was not an imposing man, about five years Grandy's junior, slim, with blue eyes. He was a Hermon graduate, class of 1928, and served as a spokesperson and gatekeeper.

Paul and the rest of his family were subjected to Pyper's scrutiny. He reported that Grandy was "a delightful person" and "friend and classmate of Pres. Wriston of Brown [University]." In other words, Grandy was connected in higher-education circles. His older children were enrolled at Wesleyan University and Boston University Medical School. As for Paul, Pyper judged him to be "14, large, just a fair student." This struck me as mistaken. Paul was not very tall; at fourteen and even as an adult, he was no taller than Pyper, who was five foot eight. It wasn't likely that Pyper meant to say Paul was overweight. His teachers at the Lab School approvingly noted his "good structural and muscular makeup [and] splendid physique." From the start, Mount Hermon saw Paul through peculiar glasses.

It took him hours seated at a table in Columbus to write a formal letter of application. Hermon required that it be in

Paul's hand. He chose his words carefully and wrote in print rather than cursive. The effect was deliberate but awkward. Paul randomly mixed capital and lowercase letters. His sentences veered up to the right, at odds with the margins. He clearly went back to make corrections and squeezed in dropped letters and whole words. My husband, an expert in the history of reading and writing, took a look at my father's letter and then turned to me at our table in the Hermon archives. "Dyslexia," he pronounced. That diagnosis and the light it shed on Paul's challenges as a reader and writer were not yet known when he applied to Hermon. Only a small number of educators in the 1930s recognized pupils who suffered from what was then termed "word blindness." Paul's deficits were chalked up to laziness.

Grandy completed Paul's application form from his office in Greensboro. There he encountered Hermon's questions about color. Where question six asked for the applicant's NATIONALITY, Grandy inserted the phrase AMERICAN NEGRO. Question seven called for the applicant's COLOR. Grandy left the line blank. This may have been an oversight. But given the care he took with the form, Grandy was more likely making a point. Perhaps he elevated the significance of the category AMERICAN NEGRO when he noted it as a NATIONALITY rather than a COLOR. He couldn't know that someone at Hermon had crudely marked his initial letter with "negro." Still, he knew these loaded questions demanded that he push back with deliberate self-regard.

Paul arrived at Hermon more on his own than ever, with the so-called racial problems that had begun at the Lab School

trailing him. One instructor noted Paul's poor academic performance and added, "He also seems to have more than average
difficulty in resolving his racial problems. He is a very lonely
boy." He was lonely, at least at first, confessing to his mother,
"Saturday was parents day here at school. I was feeling pretty
low because so many other parents of other kids were [here]."
Musie and Grandy were in the midst of a fundraising campaign
and could not get away. His loneliness took over as the campus
filled with families who came by train and by car. Classmates
sat surrounded by their broods and clans. Parents carried gifts,
special meals, and warmth that only those who've known a
boy all his years can offer. Paul was rescued by Gladys Duncan,
who traveled to Hermon from Washington, DC, to spend the
day with her son, Charlie. Paul reassured his parents, "Charlie['s] mother was up so it was fairly nice."

That afternoon launched Paul's lifelong friendship with
Charlie. They were an odd pair: Charlie would be class salu-
tatorian, while Paul fought to stay academically afloat. Charlie was at ease on Hermon's campus, while Paul struggled to
fit in. One thing they shared: Both had fathers occupied by
demanding careers. Grandy was building Bennett, while Charlie's father, Todd Duncan, was riding the wave of a performing
career, known to audiences for originating the role of Porgy in
the Gershwin opera *Porgy and Bess*. The two shared one more
thing: Both were among a handful of Hermon students who
labeled themselves Negro.

Paul latched on to Charlie, who was one version of everything he admired. Charlie's father visited Hermon, and whether
he performed or simply shook hands, Paul later glowed to his

brother, "Todd Duncan was up here. He was a big success." As for Charlie, Paul sat in the campus chapel as his friend delivered an afternoon speech, then gushed in a letter home, "Charles spoke here Sunday. One boy said to me, 'I have been here three years and it is the best speech I have heard in that chapel.' . . . They really like him." Paul's pride beams off the page.

Dad took us on annual visits with Charlie in the 1960s and '70s. We were on our way to visit Musie in Greensboro and broke up the 550-mile road trip with a stopover at the Duncans' Washington, DC, home. The kids headed to the basement or the yard, while Dad and Charlie talked sports, debated politics, and traded gossip. By then Charlie was the distinguished man his parents had hoped Hermon would make of him, embodying all the promise of the Civil Rights generation. He was a Harvard Law grad, NAACP legal defense team veteran, assistant US attorney, professor and then dean of Howard Law School. He stepped out most days in tailored suits, gold-rimmed glasses, and shoes shined to a mirrorlike finish, with monograms on his briefcase, wallet, and handkerchiefs. Charlie remained, as our regular visits to his home demonstrated, among my father's dearest friends.

I'd always assumed that the strong feelings between my father and Charlie were mutual. Then I read interviews that Charlie gave later in life and had to think again. He remembered Dad, though without naming him, when he recounted his time at Hermon: Charlie had "made one lasting friendship in preparatory school." That friend, I'm sure, was Paul. When he recalled being Black at Hermon, Charlie told another story.

He'd been the only one: "When I got to Mount Hermon, it was all white, I was the only black person around." Hermon's yearbooks make plain that Charlie misremembered the campus in those years. Among his classmates were a half-dozen other Black students. He'd left them and my father out of the story. I understood that Charlie may have felt alone at Hermon; he was an outstanding, even exceptional student. Still, I'm sure that this version of Charlie's story would have disappointed my father. Charlie's company, at Hermon and in the years that followed, had done so much to cure Paul's loneliness. He'd have hoped to in turn help Charlie feel less alone.

Charlie may have come by his confusion honestly. During his years at Hermon, it wasn't always clear who was Black and who was not. A case in point was his ski-team buddy Albert Chandler Johnston, Jr. Like Charlie, Paul considered Albert a friend despite what many Hermonites judged to be their apparent differences. This started with their applications. Where Grandy left Paul's COLOR blank, Albert's parents described him with one word: *white*. The two boys also hailed from differing parts of the country. Albert had grown up in New England, while my father was from the South. They excelled at very different sports. Paul lettered in football and basketball, while Albert stood out as captain of the ski team.

Their biggest difference concerned color. Both young men could pass, but only Albert did so during his years at Hermon. Midway through his studies, on a visit home, Albert's parents privately revealed to their son that they and he were colored. He returned to campus, where Hermon students policed the color line. It was not easy for Albert to keep their secret within the family. He later recounted how classmates suspected he was not who he said he was. Some attempted to out Albert, like a roommate who accused him, "What are you? A kike or a Greek or what? Well, I bet you've got some nigger in you."

Albert's mother, like Mrs. Duncan, extended special kindnesses to Paul. His parents were consumed with fundraising and the construction of new facilities at Bennett. It was Mrs. Johnston who brought Paul news. He wrote to Grandy and Musie with gratitude for "Al['s] mother," who kept him abreast of goings-on at Bennett. She'd brought him a news clipping that featured the dedication of the new Pfeiffer Chapel there in 1941. "I saw a picture of the chapel," he wrote excitedly to Musie. Paul was a boy far from home whose parents rarely made the trip to Hermon, and Mrs. Johnston's attention helped ease his isolation. If Paul suspected that Albert and his mother were, like him, not white, he quietly kept their confidences.

Albert graduated with his family secret intact. Only later, in spring 1947, did he share it, first with filmmaker Louis de Rochemont and then with *Reader's Digest* magazine. In June 1949, de Rochemont released his film *Lost Boundaries*, reenacting for the big screen a saga that began during Albert's years at Hermon. Albert sent Paul a Christmas card that December; it is saved among Paul's letters. It was likely the last time the two were in touch.

Like Charlie, Albert taught my father lessons about whom he admired and whom he might aspire to be. There was Charlie, the stellar student destined for distinguished leadership. The exceptional young Black man. There was Albert, who lived his early years on the other side of the color line. All their lives were shaped by immersion in overwhelmingly white worlds, often far from family and the familiar. Charlie taught my father that boys like him might grow up to be big men on campus and in the world. They might also, as Albert's example showed, become white.

—

Paul was anxious during his last months at Hermon. World War II was well underway, and he was eager to join the Allied forces. His eighteenth birthday arrived in May 1944, and Paul immediately registered for the draft. A Selective Service clerk sized him up: "Negro. 5' 7½ inches. 165 pounds. Eyes brown. Hair brown. Complexion dark." He returned to Greensboro that June, waiting to be called up. Then the war effort turned. The D-Day invasion at Normandy was followed by the liberation of Paris. The conflict in Europe appeared to be ending. Paul's future grew less certain. He waited, at home with his parents for the first long stretch since he'd left for Columbus seven years before. Grandy grew increasingly uneasy.

His father kept Paul busy on the Bennett campus with what Grandy termed "menial jobs"—waxing floors and collecting endowment pledges. I imagine that the latter involved going door-to-door to receive monthly promises. Paul remained cheerful while his father fretted in letters to his oldest son, Junior, who was stationed in Italy. They still referred to Paul as Stooge even though at Hermon, he had adopted a new nickname, Jonesie. His father wrote to Junior, "[Paul] is a handsome brute, but does not seem conscious of it." This label was new—and double-edged. Deeming Paul handsome, as in pleasant to the eye, might be generous. But *brute* reduced Paul to little more than a crude, stupid, and barely human creature.

His father doubted Paul. This helped me understand why my father so valued the chance to serve in the military. The army rated him 1A, wholly fit for duty. In October, he was finally summoned to Fort Bragg, less than one hundred miles away to the southeast, in Fayetteville. He made the journey to preinduction with boys from Greensboro, some of whom he'd long known. Examiners appointed Paul leader of his contingent: "Special confidence being placed in the integrity and ability of Paul Maurice Jones," the notice read. Grandy, looking right at Paul, could not understand his son. Together they waited for Paul's full induction: "I don't know how torn up he is on the inside about [the wait], but he remains an outward happy-go-lucky spirit," Grandy wrote to Junior. Paul, so different in ability and temperament from his father and brother, was a mystery to them.

Where Grandy saw confusion, I could not help but see Paul's emerging strengths. I hoped that my father's confidence was growing. Grandy repeated for Junior some of what he was observing. Among the crowds of men at Fort Bragg, Paul had been struck by "the number of people who could not read or write and . . . the number who were rejected for physical reasons." Despite his low marks and learning difficulties, when measured against men who'd spent their youth in local schools or in fields or factories, Paul stood out as well educated. Paul also possessed a growing emotional intelligence. Grandy reported, "Paul has a great concern about people, [the] poor conditions of our people weigh on him considerably."

His turn at boot camp finally arrived, and Paul headed west to the Great Lakes and Camp Robert Smalls. I can't say how, but he eventually landed among the many Black enlistees in FDR's segregated navy. Months of ups and downs followed, and Paul grew mercurial. He started out elated, writing to his parents, "It is your sailor friend again. I am fine, and still in love with it." Remarkably, he was reunited with Charlie Duncan: "Charlie and I have been put in the same company. So it looks like we will go to boot camp together. Aren't we lucky. We are boiling over with joy." Eventually they became a team: company clerk and assistant clerk.

Those happier times did not last. After only a few weeks, Charlie headed out for officer training at Dartmouth, where he was already an enrolled student. Paul tried to keep up with his friend but instead stumbled. First, he tried a V-12 test that was the entrée to the Naval College Training Program. "I think I passed it O.K.," he shared with his mother's sister, Aunt Reecie. His "scores were very low," and Paul grew indignant when he was recommended for duty as a pharmacist's mate, a carpenter's mate, or at sea. He did not qualify for college or the officer track and was instead offered a chance to teach "illiterates," servicemen who could not read or write. Paul declined. Perhaps, for a young man with serious learning difficulties, the assignment was too close for comfort.

He also encountered racism head-on at Camp Robert Smalls. Paul fumed, "We have a new company command and no one likes [him.] He is white and calls the fellows Boy." Then his letters home grew cryptic. Paul relied upon a sailor friend, also from Greensboro, to visit his parents and tell them "everything." Perhaps his officer's racism grew more intense. Maybe it was accompanied by physical abuse. Whatever troubled him at Camp Robert Smalls, Paul did not risk putting it on paper.

With the war in Europe ended, uncertainty clouded life in the navy. Paul's post imposed too few demands and allowed for a great deal of free time. He battled boredom by heading to Chicago, about forty miles down the Lake Michigan coast. There his Aunt Reecie provided meals and a place to sleep when he wasn't crashing at the USO. The parties were long and exhausting, but he met "Chicago's lovely young ladies" at AKA sorority formals. Paul regularly asked his parents for money in those months, but it wasn't until early summer that he confessed to "gambling rather heavily." He had lost "quite a bit." Over the course of a few months, Paul's mind changed by 180 degrees. The young man who had loved his first weeks in the navy wrote home, "Boy, I tell you the first chance I get to get out. . . ."

His transfer from the Great Lakes to New York's Staten Island might have given Paul a fresh chance. The sprawling facilities at Tompkinsville brought him closer to family and friends who lived up and down the seaboard: North Carolina, Washington, DC, New York, and Boston were a direct train ride away. He served aboard YHT-7, a scow that carted goods between ship and shore, while he occupied leave time with regular trips to Manhattan. "I am enjoying myself here very much," he wrote to his parents. Paul loved seeing old friends, many of them students at North Carolina's historically Black colleges: "Smith, Shaw, A&T, Bennett and N.C. State."

The best of Paul's former self sometimes surfaced. At Hermon, he'd been recognized as among the sharpest dressers. Paul wrote to his Aunt Sweets, angling for a new wardrobe: "In the Navy I am try[ing] to be the well dress[ed] man. I wish to buy myself a couple of items which will help me to be the well dress[ed] navy man now that I am going to be station[ed] on this side for a couple of years, I hope." He implored Sweets to, along with other family members, support a $55 fund that would let him show up to parties looking clean and sharp. I recognized this man, someone always concerned with being well-dressed.

For my father, clothes were a second skin, which for him meant sporting Brooks Brothers suits, oxford shirts, and leather loafers buffed to a blinding shine. He appreciated the pleasures of texture, movement, fit, color, and pattern. He expressed himself in ties and socks, cuffs and styled lapels. In his closet always hung a tuxedo for evening soirees and tennis whites for the court. When I landed my first lawyering job, I followed Dad's lead and bought two pinstriped suits off the rack at Syms, a bargain department store. At the eye shop, I picked out a pair of black horn-rimmed glasses. Our sartorial choices mattered, he taught me. With them, we might best encourage others to see us as we hoped to be seen.

Paul approached a breaking point. When another sailor stole his wallet, it was the last straw. Paul raged, which only landed him "in trouble," disciplined before a captain's mast and punished with a ten-day restriction. The navy felt like a dead end, and Paul wanted out: "I am going to begin working on a discharge somehow or another and if I can't get an honorable, I will just have to take a dishonorable and like it." Having fallen short of his ambitions, Paul lamented his limited future: "Here I . . . spent 7 weeks trying to develop leadership going to petty officer school, yet damn it, it looks like I'll never even be a petty officer. Seaman second [class] now and more than likely always."

Musie and Grandy increasingly worried about Paul's state of mind. Reading his letters from this period, I understand why. Even looking back from the distance of many years, I am terrified for him. He appeared to be spiraling downward. One tortured paragraph captured his mood: "Things are going well with me," he wrote to his parents. And then "I am getting crazier each day in this damn Navy." His use of profanity was uncharacteristic. "I hope there will be something worthwhile left in me when I get out. I have my doubts about the whole thing." Paul could not imagine a worthwhile future for himself: "Maybe I will be good for selling newspapers on some corner, and I have my doubts about that. . . . I was built to be a flop and I guess I will always be flopping and messing up."

With his parents back in North Carolina, nearby family members rallied around Paul. First was his older sister in Boston, Tuppy, a physician completing her postgraduate training in psychiatry. She arranged for Paul to see a New York analyst, Edith Taglicht Schmidt, who later became known for her view of boys and men as emotionally more vulnerable than girls and women. Paul admitted to Dr. Schmidt that he wanted nothing more than to leave the navy. She endorsed this, writing to Musie and Grandy, "I am a little worried about him. . . . I feel he needs a change very badly." Her concern was plain, but Paul remained

THE TROUBLE OF COLOR

bound to the navy. She assessed him as "depressed," but Grandy remained unable to see that the source of Paul's troubles was illness rather than attitude. He replied to Paul's doctor with no more than an acknowledgment that his son was "rebellious."

In spring 1946, Paul's honorable discharge date neared, and Aunt Sweets briefly took him in at her Washington, DC, flat. Looking to reestablish his bearings, Paul looked up the mother of his Mount Hermon friend Charlie Duncan. She let him know that Charlie's graduation from Dartmouth was coming up, and Paul seized on the occasion: "Seeing how I have Thursday and Friday off, I am going." It was the start of a transient period, and Paul became untethered. The next fall, he enrolled at Ohio State, where he didn't last the year. This time, it was his mother, rather than Grandy, who stepped in. She wrote directly to the dean: "Mr. Jones and I are greatly concerned about Paul. He has not made a very satisfactory adjustment since he has been out of the service." Paul turned up for a time in Detroit, working in a cousin's drugstore chain. Next was Boston, where Paul settled down for a moment, comforted by the closeness of his sister, Tuppy.

He tried college again, this time at Boston University, where he lived with six hundred young men recently discharged from the service, only twenty-five Black students among them. His sister arranged for Paul to see a new psychiatrist, whose assessment was bleak. The doctor expressed regrets to Grandy and Musie: "I'm afraid there is nothing that family can do for [Paul] now." I knew how his family, especially its women—his sister, his aunts, his Detroit cousin, and his mother—had done all they knew how to stabilize Paul. They never stopped loving him. Still, Paul's psychiatrist may have been right. Nothing his family might try seemed to matter.

In winter 1950, Paul landed a job moving stock in a New York City department store. His Aunt Sweets coached him in those months, step-by-step, via regular letters. He replied with daily reports that chronicled his hunt for better work. They went back and forth about making a budget. Her most reassuring advice: "All things take time." Paul lived a rootless existence. His home was a West Side YMCA. He had occasional visits with his siblings, but he was no longer part of their social set. That holiday season, he was alone and living hand to mouth. Paul sat down to let Musie and Grandy know how he was faring. It was Christmas Eve, and his mood was sober and humble: "More than anyone, you two have lived my sorrows and joys. . . . God bless you both."

—

On Christmas Day 1954, my father tried to end his life. He stood on a subway platform and then threw himself in front of a moving train. He was twenty-eight years old and living alone in a cheap New York City hotel. His attempt failed. Police officers gathered him up out of the city's bowels and handed his bruised person over to the keepers of Bellevue Hospital's locked ward. Among New Yorkers, *Bellevue* is synonymous with *crazy*, and to be admitted there was to be branded as among the city's most disturbed—that's saying a lot in a town with plenty of madness to go around.

Paul discovered that Christmas can be a deeply lonely season in New York. The streets bustled with people who peered into holiday windows, vendors who sold fir trees, Santa Clauses who rang bells for charity, and carolers who shared their songs on street corners and church steps. Even everyday folk appeared fully in the spirit: they hauled gift-wrapped boxes; carted oversized turkeys; sported their snazziest, fresh-pressed party clothes; and hurried to the next cheer-filled affair. Holed up in a tiny hotel room, as Paul was, New York's holiday chaos only heightened his isolation and underscored his despair. That year, my father succumbed to troubles for which even he had no name.

Paul came to believe that he'd cheated death. He told me the story when I was seven or eight. It was a summer evening, and he was onto his second J&B and soda. Glassy-eyed, he sat in a folding chair on our tiny front stoop and beckoned me to join him. Reluctantly, I did. Perched on his lap, close enough to smell the alcohol on his breath, I listened while my father recounted how he'd tried to end it all on one lonely Christmas. It was his second encounter with fate, he explained. The first had occurred when, as a student at Hermon, he'd been aboard the Congressional Limited, headed from Washington to New York Penn Station. "My seat was in car 8," my father whispered. Then he marveled, "I decided to head two cars back to find a snack." At that moment, just outside Philadelphia, the train came off the rails. "All of the dead were in cars seven and eight," news reports later explained. My father was uninjured but knew that many of his seatmates had not been so fortunate. Grandy heard the news and immediately wrote to the headmaster at Hermon: Paul "was not hurt physically but we are anxious to know if he suffered any nervous shock." There on our front stoop, the tone of his voice and the look in his eyes let me, his daughter, know that he had.

In the dark, surrounded by the sounds of crickets singing, trash cans being hauled to the curb, and a neighbor's television carrying across the night air, my father told me stories, hoping I'd understand him. He was not the father he aspired to be or the best of husbands, either. Maybe if I understood where he'd been, what he'd endured, how more than once he'd come close to not being there at all, I would forgive him. He hoped I'd pardon him for the things he had not done and those he would never do in the years to come. He asked me to share his burdens, shoulder them when he could not. He needed a companion rather than a child.

I learned the complete details of my father's suicide attempt years later from letters written by Grandy. They were neatly arranged in folders, set out on my table in the Amistad Research Center reading room. My grandfather, whose confusion had kept him at a distance from Paul, finally sprang into action. His letters pleaded, implored, and expended every ounce of his political capital in a campaign to get Paul the best treatment available. Paul's sister, Tuppy, by then a fully credentialed psychiatrist, advised her father. When Paul finally was admitted to the FDR Veterans Hospital in Montrose, New York, Grandy's desperate fear gave way to gratitude.

I don't know much about my father's time as a psychiatric inpatient. The Veterans Administration long ago routinely destroyed his file. I do know that his doctor was among the era's best, a professor of social psychiatry at Cornell University Medical College who also consulted for the

Veterans Administration. His specialty, psychosomatic medicine, assumed that interactions between biological, psychological, and social factors regulated the balance between health and disease. He treated scores of veterans who, like Paul, struggled after returning to civilian life. My father's team included a psychiatric social worker and a clinical psychologist who believed that family, work, and community were essential to the "adjustment" of civilian veterans. Thankfully, by the latter months of 1955, Paul was better. The hospital sent him back to New York.

—

Paul quickly landed a job as a mail-room supervisor and then worked his way up to office manager. By the next January, in 1956, one year after his admission to Bellevue, he was living at the Lenox Hill Neighborhood House in Yorkville on Manhattan's east side. Founded in 1894 to support European immigrants, like Chicago's Hull House and Lower Manhattan's Henry Street Settlement, Lenox Hill supported health-care access, employment, and tenants' rights. Its headquarters were set up in a 1928 building that included a swimming pool, gymnasiums, a theater, a rooftop playground, a kitchen, offices, and small single bedrooms for staff affiliates. In the evenings, Paul was responsible for supervising a local youth group—the Imperials. My grandmother saved copies of his detailed reports, which reveal Paul to have been a thoughtfully mature young man in charge of, rather than among, the troubled.

Later that month, Grandy died. He was sixty-eight and did not survive what had been a three-year-long battle with bladder cancer. Those years had taken him to New York and to Boston for treatments; Tuppy managed his care, advised by Junior's wife, who was an oncologist. Still, Grandy died on the Bennett College campus, in the home that he and Musie had shared since their arrival there in 1926. At his funeral, Bennett's Pfeiffer Chapel was filled beyond capacity, its benches lined with family, faculty, friends, students, trustees, staff, dignitaries, and alumnae. The campus was by then in the hands of Dr. Willa Player, who had taken Bennett's helm when Grandy's condition had worsened. His closest friend, Morehouse College President Benjamin Mays, delivered a stirring eulogy. The Bishop, a man ordinarily eager to hold forth from the pulpit, sat stoically silent as others paid tribute to his baby brother. Newspapers remembered Grandy as "a shoemaker's son" who had built "one of the South's most beautiful colleges." As I reconstructed these events, I was grateful that the tragedy of my father's suicide attempt, followed by the good fortune of his psychiatric treatment, had allowed Grandy and Paul to truly reconcile.

Paul briefly returned to Greensboro for the installation of Grandy's ashes in the altar of Bennett's chapel. Shortly afterward, he formally thanked the campus community: "I must somehow express my most sincere thanks to the many of you who contributed so much in making Dad's funeral a memorable occasion." In his family, where Paul had often felt like an outlier, he was finding his place. Though grief filled, he honored his father's memory with graceful devotion. He wrapped his arms around his mother and became her confidant. His regular letters to her included reminders about his father's wisdom: "You are your own agent" and advice about finances:

"You're not poor. Therefore, you can get away from Greens-boro any time." He became her pillar: "You don't have to do anyone['s] bidding. So you make your own plans as you see fit and only if you want to."

The next December, almost two years after his suicide attempt, Musie expressed her deep gratitude to Paul. The change in him was not only remarkable but ensured that his mother survived: "My days have been easier because of your constant attention which stems from love and imagination." Had anyone before ever deemed Paul constant? Now his mother, who knew Paul's struggles as well as anyone, saw him as just that. Your father "told me few things about the future," Musie wrote. "One was to keep myself looking nice. The other was that Paul is going to be alright." She gave voice to a precious promise, a fragile hope. I sat holding her note in my hands decades later and trembled as within me, my own hopes for him surfaced.

I can't say that my father's focused calm was due to my moth-er's influence, but I do know that at the very moment that he blossomed into a mature young man, he was also courting her: Sue Yager, the granddaughter of German, Austrian, and Irish immigrants. The two were a study in contrasts. She was from Buffalo, New York—a place of steel and prisons. A working-class high school valedictorian for whom social mobility meant working in offices rather than factories. He was from Greens-boro, North Carolina, a place of tobacco and later Civil Rights sit-ins, born into the Black elite. In 1956, both worked and roomed at Lenox Hill. In his first stable home after years as a transient, Paul worked in an office by day and managed the

Imperials at night. Sue took shorthand, typed, and filed in the executive offices. Together they found their adult bearings.

Somehow they both felt at home. Paul fit in with a house staff that mixed Americans with European immigrants, laborers with university-trained elites, and transients with local community workers. His years—in prep school, the navy, and drifting from place to place—prepared him. For Sue, the Lenox Hill neighborhood dwarfed her east Buffalo enclave. But she was surrounded by familiar types: white, working-class immigrant families who were not very different from her own. Paul didn't mind being the only one in the Lenox Hill community: It mirrored his time at the Lab School and Hermon. As for Sue, her growing closeness to Paul allowed her to feel a little less provincial, even a bit worldly. She loved to recall the effect of my father's charms on her and how he charmed everyone while playing bridge with the older ladies or ironing his shirts on Saturday mornings as opera wafted from his transistor radio.

Once they decided to wed, Paul's regular letters to his mother, Musie, chronicled the strife that his proposal to Sue invited. She returned to Buffalo and broke the news to her clan: She was going to marry a man who was neither German nor Catholic. Nor was he white. Sue's family balked, and Paul explained to Musie, "[Sue] told them what she was going to do. However you can well [i]magine that none of this has set well." One of my mother's aunts warned that Sue was on the brink of cutting off those closest to her. She was. Musie, by contrast, encouraged the two. When Paul advised her about their tight budget, she sent him the small diamond engagement ring and matching gold band she had worn as a young bride. In those days, she wore a second platinum set with a larger stone that Grandy had later gifted her. His mother touched Paul deeply with the magnitude of her gesture: "You knew I had wanted to get Sue a ring . . . once [I] got it on her finger she was thrilled!"

In New York, their confidantes included a supportive "young priest," and more than once, my father quoted him: "No matter what you do [Sue's family] won't [ac]cept it until it happens." Attitudes about interracial marriage were changing slowly, even within the Catholic Church. The Council of Bishops condemned antimiscegenation laws because they prevented priests from marrying a Catholic of one race to a Catholic of another. Nothing was new, however, in Paul's home state of North Carolina. As they had since 1715, lawmakers there continued to bar marriages across the color line. Paul and Sue were reassured to know that New York law allowed them to take a license whenever they were ready.

Passion bound Paul and Sue joyfully to one another. In the face of their critics, they not only stood together but also held one another up. I knew them later in their lives, when differences of faith and color, along with strained finances and a string of infidelities, had led to chronic conflict. After acrimonious years, they separated in the early 1970s. But in the months leading up to their marriage, even battered by her family's racism, my parents permitted love to propel them forward. They briefly considered giving up. It pained Paul, but he offered Sue a chance to delay their plans. She, he explained to Musie, "has ruled this out." Sue assured him that her mind was made up.

They wed on Saturday, June 29, before a Catholic priest who assumed that children would come along. He had Paul commit—in writing—to raising us as Catholics. My father remained a Methodist, but in 1957, just his promise was enough to straighten the crooked line of faith that separated him and Sue. Only a few photos of that day have survived. I know that my mother was beautiful in an ensemble that said "Audrey Hepburn." Musie and her sister, Sweets, made sure the arrangements were just right. This meant festive, but no alcohol or dancing. My New York cousins, still girls, dressed up and hung around the cake table. My mother made sure I would remember one last detail: Of her Buffalo family, only her brother attended. His face was sad and stern, as if he were at a funeral rather than a wedding.

My parents set up in a West 104th Street walk-up. One week shy of their first anniversary, I was born and soon baptized a Catholic just across Broadway at the Church of the Ascension. It

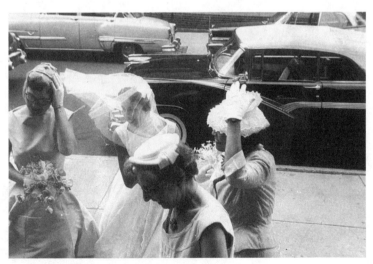

Sue (Suzanne Yager Jones), wedding portrait, 1957

was a broad white-stone Romanesque building with an ornate interior courtesy of the early-twentieth-century immigrant craftsmen who early on worshipped within. I can't know for certain what the mood was in 1958. Today the parish's website urges, "No matter your age, race, gender, or sexual orientation, there is a place for you at Ascension Church." It must have been, at least on my day, that Ascension welcomed us. My parents stood at the font along with my godparents as the priest anointed my head, baptizing me Martha Suzanne. My first name honored my mother's German American aunt, Martha. My middle name, Suzanne, in its various derivations ran from Susan in Danville to Musie in Greensboro, through my mother, Suzanne, from Buffalo, and finally down to me. In conformance with church law, I was made into a Catholic, but nothing in that law defined who I was along America's color line.

—

In 1962, my parents moved our family from a small Central Harlem apartment to a Long Island tract house. I was four. They had in mind a garden, barbecues, and better public schools. But what they soon met up with was redlining, restrictive covenants, and other discordant vestiges of Jim Crow. They sent me away that summer, to Musie in Greensboro, leaving them more time for their toddler son, my mother's July due date, and a grueling search for a new home. Shut out more than once in Westchester, they headed to Long Island, a small town with an under-sixty-minute commute to Manhattan: Port Washington.

Some might associate the place with its waterfront mansions (one owned by John Jacob Astor's descendants) or its sand-mining operations, which are said to have paved most of Manhattan over the course of a century. The town's affordable cookie-cutter houses, constructed after World War II, drew my parents there. They set their sights on 64 Wakefield Avenue: a cape, battleship gray inside and out, postage-stamp front yard, two dogwoods and a mimosa. Three bedrooms, one bath, a combo washer-dryer, and a back garden that spilled onto a country-club golf course, one that barred people like us from membership. There are two stories about how they pulled off the purchase despite neighbors who opposed their moving in. I documented one in the county deed books. The sellers were South Africans, ending a temporary stay in the United States, who did not subscribe to America's Jim Crow thinking. That system eerily resembled what they knew at home.

I grew up believing that only non-Americans might recognize and even welcome us as a family. I heard another story more recently from a former babysitter. His mother was a white artist living nearby. He recalled that she posed as a prospective buyer, secured a contract, and then transferred it to my parents. True or not, these stories let me know that for our family, landing in Port Washington was no simple matter. The ugly past and a fraught present collided as my parents put together a small inheritance from Grandy with a GI Bill mortgage and created a place we called home.

My parents were immediately lonely, isolated in an all-white cul-de-sac. My mother turned to writing poetry, reflecting on how, after the movers left them to sit amidst unopened boxes and unarranged furniture, unease engulfed them. They did not regret having left behind the rattle and bang of Manhattan's streets for the ice-cream-truck bells and lawn mowers of a tree-lined dead end. But they did grow weary of neighbors who peppered their days with snubs and slights that sometimes escalated into menacing phone calls and bomb threats. Many of the tiny houses that lined South Salem's winding streets bustled with sociability. But no one invited my parents to cocktail parties or cookouts. It was a cold start to a new life.

Little by little, Paul's charm and Sue's wits won them friends. The first were members of the local Community Relations Council, advocates of housing integration. Soon there arrived at our house artists, priests, teachers, and social workers. My parents set down their rose-colored glasses and discovered that poverty and racism also made the town run. Social justice became their shared commitment. By day, they worked in offices. On nights and weekends, they organized for civil rights, against the Vietnam War, to end poverty, and to build affordable housing. My father became chair of the Community Action Council board, while my mother ran the office. Our dinner-table talk was of expanding public transportation, standing up a credit union, stocking a food co-op, and supplying a health clinic. In Port Washington, my parents dove into the good fight.

—

What was evident at home, we never said out loud: Dad lived a divided existence. With us, he was impatient and volatile. He spent most nights drinking Scotch and soda until he couldn't. He stocked his liquor cabinet with bottles that clinked each time he lifted the antique top—I can still hear the sound today.

The tinkle of ice cubes in a highball glass followed. Company came by less and less often, and when crowds showed up, it simply meant he wasn't drinking alone. During the day, he was sober and made the commute between home and Manhattan on the Long Island Railroad. A bite of supper and he'd head out to chair a meeting, present a proposal, conspire about the next protest, or grace a fundraiser for the latest good cause.

I knew him as two-faced. At home, Dad wrestled with demons by drinking them away. In public, he was a civic leader whom teachers, friends' parents, and even some neighbors admired for the changes he made in our town. He earned a place among local civic leaders and eventually hatched a plan: He would run for school board. Dad assembled a team, sat for headshots, wrote a position statement, laid out flyers, answered questions from a nonpartisan commission, and took to walking downtown while shaking a lot of hands. He drafted me and my siblings to pass out leaflets to commuters during the evening rush. As they dashed from humming train coaches to exhaust-spewing station wagons and sedans, we shoved leaflets into their hands.

As the campaign wore on, I kept my distance. But I never stopped eavesdropping. Frequently my father picked up the phone to update Musie on his progress. She knew that my father's ambitions were owed in part to Grandy's service as Greensboro's first Black school board member. Within our family, this was common knowledge, but Dad never spoke publicly of his father's accomplishments. Instead, he began to construct fictions about himself. When I read in our local newspaper that Dad was a graduate of Boston University,

I knew that was untrue. I also recognized the tale. Dad had spread the same falsehood two years earlier after his election as head of the Community Action Council. Under pressure to achieve and even excel, my father knew that claiming a bachelor's degree, rather than a failed semester or two, made for a stronger candidate profile.

Dad invited strangers to take a good look at him. I know that they did not see what I did. He posed with carefully groomed

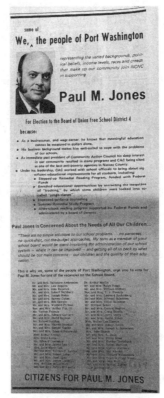

Paul M. Jones, school board
campaign ad, 1971

lamb-chop sideburns that gave his features a dramatic edge. He circulated his face on flyers, posters, and newspaper ads. He stopped strangers on Main Street, extended a hand, and pitched his platform. One supporter wrote in a letter to the editor, "He knows the problems, and more important, the feelings, of the poor and the idle class, the unemployed and the commuter, the blacks and the whites." My father's team made sure that voters understood that experience had given him insight and empathy. But they never told anyone what to make of him.

Our local paper rarely labeled people by race. It was a 1970s color-blind approach to journalism. The editors instead let photographs do the talking. If they wanted to emphasize that a news subject was Black, they published a portrait alongside the text. Black and Brown faces—grainy on the page—appeared regularly. We knew that the heads of the county human rights commission and NAACP branch were Black because the photos told us so. What did people see when they looked at Dad? Only once, in 1969, did the paper note him as Black: Ours was "the first black family to move into a previously all white neighborhood in Port Washington." But that revelation appears to have been forgotten. By 1979, when a local reporter published a history of Dad's most active years, he named another family altogether as Port Washington's first. Our family's story—we really were the first—was erased. Dad, I am sure, let that happen.

I steered clear of my father's public life, anxious that I could not anticipate which story he would tell. I left him to navigate that world without me. At the same time, I was busy navigating my own world at a new junior high school. It must have been my friend Lauren who told her friends that while I might not look Black, I was. During the first week, I spied her at the other end of a dim, narrow hallway, talking with a crew of girls I did not know. As I approached, Lauren looked up at me and then down at her shoes. All the energy emanated instead from Nadine. A head taller and two years older than me, she glared in my direction and sneered, "What do we have here?" and then "Empty your pockets." Before I knew it, my hands were turning the pockets of my blue jeans inside out. My lunch money spilled across the linoleum tiles. As Nadine scooped it up, a bell rang. The hall filled with students, and I slipped away.

The hallways of our junior high school teemed with lots of teenaged angst. It took a few more encounters with Nadine before I understood why I vexed her. Nadine thought that when walking around in my skin, I was putting on airs. I was pretending to be or even masquerading as someone I was not. I was just another brown-skinned girl who had learned to trick the eyes of others. Nadine dressed me down with her words, rifled my pockets and my shoes for coins, and aimed to expose me for who I was, for who she knew me to be. My own confusion only fueled Nadine's contempt for me, and I had no idea how to settle our misunderstanding. I was an easy target. So was my father. I pictured him in the newspaper, at a candidate forum, and up and down Main Street, and I was afraid. When they came to shake him down, expose him for who he was, would he be ready? Who did he think he was, anyway?

—

"Copy that, Black Kojak." I was driving across town to see Dad, having borrowed his car—a green Ford Pinto—for the day. It was the exact same model Pinto that was later recalled because its gas tank exploded on impact. For a teen, it worked: sporty, low to the ground with bucket seats, a gearshift that mimicked a manual, and an eight-track player. Dad had modified the car to suit his latest passion, the CB radio. Adopted from long-haul truckers, the setup was a transmitter with a handheld mic—press with your thumb to speak. CBs let drivers use shorthand to track traffic, scope out rest stops, and chatter about weather, road conditions, and speed traps ahead.

Dad loved being behind the wheel—always at ease. He leaned back, left hand steering, right arm flung over the adjacent seat. Passing, weaving, merging smooth as butter. He eyeballed truckers, admired their road habits. He believed that eighteen-wheeler drivers were smarter and safer than most others. Hungry, he took his breaks at truck stops, where federal rules barred Jim Crow, grabbed a stool at the counter, and ordered the trucker's special. They also knew the best places to eat, he was sure.

When in the '70s CB radios became a fad, Dad outfitted his cars and had the house rigged up. The living room base station squawked and hissed when he surfed its channels, mostly picking up idle chatter. A nearby shop outfitted his cars, hardware bolted under the dashboard, a long, flexible chrome tentacle atop the roof that caught the airwaves. His radios weren't elegant, but they seemed a tad futuristic, permitting us to connect in real time, via voice, while on the move. Dad advised that we each needed a handle, a unique name so that we'd recognize one another over scratchy frequencies. I have no recollection of what I chose but will never forget Dad wryly announcing his:

Black Kojak. A twist on a television character—a cool, handsome, bald detective played by the Greek actor Telly Savalas. Kojak dressed to the nines and nearly always had a Tootsie Pop in his mouth, fiddling with it like a cigarette or toothpick. He growled, "Who loves you, baby?"

I loved this Dad, the one with a sense of humor. After losing his school board election, he'd withdrawn from activism. He'd been trounced. He'd also pulled away from our family and, with little ceremony, moved in with his lover and her children across town. He shed his cookie-cutter business suits for leisure suits, boots, and loud print shirts. He slipped a ring on his left pinkie finger, bought an electric razor, and started each day by shaving his head clean. If you told me he'd buffed it, I'd have believed you. He replaced his lamb-chop sideburns with a goatee he wore the rest of his life.

One way to get closer to Dad was to follow him down the road to his passions. Alongside CB radios, he loved his fish tanks. Forty and fifty gallons, some long and low, others narrow and tall. He brought home clear plastic bags filled with angelfish and Oscars, swordtails and neon tetras, zebra fish and guppies. He filled weekends with innovations in equipment and experiments on which fish lived peacefully with others. He enlisted us to clean tanks, change filters, and keep up feeding schedules. For my bedroom, across town at my mother's house, Dad taught me to set up a ten-gallon aquarium with my own small school of Oscars.

While Dad was indulging in pricey hobbies like CB radios and exotic fish, at my mother's house, we were barely getting by. Dad never made a child-support payment in those years, and Mom quietly kept tab of each missed check—$125 a month. But if I even hinted that Dad might spend his cash more wisely, I risked his cutting me off. Instead, I indulged in the pleasures of calculating the reach of a CB signal or arranging the aesthetics of angelfish. I tucked away what troubled me.

I loved Black Kojak. Yes, I badly wanted him to help Mom buy oil for the furnace, gas for the car, meat for the dinner table, and occasional school supplies. But I settled for a dad who was nearly as hip as TV's wildly popular star. And our dad–cum–'70s cool cat exceeded the swagger of the Savalas personality. After all, he was Black. Briefly in those years, Dad wore Blackness like a singular pleasure, a stylish accessory, a quality that put others to shame.

"Copy that, Black Kojak," I radioed Dad from the driver's seat of the Pinto. We didn't have a lot to talk about on my short drives across town: a fender bender, a slight jam, or a sighting of the police cruiser that stalked the corner of Shore Road and Manhasset Avenue. What mattered was that I had Dad's attention, shared his joy, and matched his passion. These were precious scenes: Dad barking, bluffing, and bs-ing over the shortwave. And then they were gone. The era of the CB faded, and the invention of the portable phone loomed. Dad uninstalled his radios, retired his handle, and shelved his Blackness. I almost never saw him wear it again.

———

For twenty-five years, my father lived a commuter's life. His days began and ended like those of the thousands of New Yorkers who trekked between the city and the suburbs. Men and women pulled on business gear—suits and ties, skirts and pumps—outfits that marked them as members of a striving white-collar class. Each morning, Dad headed to the railroad station, found his spot on the open-air platform, jockeyed for a seat, and rode the fifty minutes it took to get from Port Washington to Manhattan. Riders then disappeared into a labyrinth of narrow, dark passageways that led to subway lines. Each morning, Dad was one among the streaming horde as he grabbed an uptown-bound train.

As a girl, I learned my father's routine by accompanying him to work from time to time. Long before I was old enough to earn a paycheck and prior to the establishment of "take your daughter to work" day, my father believed I should understand what it meant to make a living. Someday, he was sure, I'd be like him and like my mother and work nine-to-five in a Manhattan high-rise. As a boy, he'd learned how to carry responsibilities on the Bennett campus. My training ground was his office on the Upper West Side. I was always excited on those days. As we made our way, my father kept me close, but not too close. He encouraged me to be confident when I rode commuter trains, hailed taxis, and jumped on and off subway cars.

I also learned my father's habits. On the Long Island Railroad, he had a favorite car: second from the rear, where smoking was allowed. He also preferred a four-seat arrangement. Many days, someone in a nearby quartet would reach between their seat and the wall and fish out an old cardboard placard stashed there. On a table constructed with their knees and that sheet of posterboard, a poker game ensued. Dad was an anxious loser by day and preferred to gamble at a neighbor's poker table late at night. The evening ride home was bawdier. Dad grabbed a drink in the bar car or from the barman who pushed a cart along the platform. Riders sipped beer in wet, gleaming bottles and gulped cocktails poured into tall waxed paper cups. The demands of the workday fell away. Ties were loosened, and pumps were exchanged for sneakers. I stayed quiet, watched, and learned my father's version of what it meant to unwind.

I was in his office to learn its etiquette. My father was a stern instructor who expected me to watch and get things right. He tested my skills and gradually let me shuttle papers between cubicles, collate and staple copies, and occasionally answer a phone: "Good morning, St. John's Associates. How may I direct your call?" He was most concerned that I remain polite and respectful of everyone, whatever their position. On one visit, I referred to his woman colleague as "Greenie," the nickname my father used. He snapped and then spoke in a voice that was low and flat: "Never. Do. That. Again." "Apologize to Mrs. Green," he directed, and I did, red with shame. In the hierarchy of his office, children like me ranked at the bottom of the pecking order. I've never forgotten Mrs. Green and the respect due to people like her.

Only later, on a holiday break from college, did I finally make the same commute on my own. Dad got me a job selling tickets at the Metropolitan Museum of Art, where he worked behind the scenes. We rode the same train most mornings, but I sat at a distance from him. Up ahead, I watched as Dad held court with his commuter buddies; among them were young women for whom Wall Street's doors were just opening. I wasn't surprised to see him put on a bit of charm for them. But when he got winks and smiles in return, I felt like a voyeur. Lilting voices sang out, "Have a great day, Paul," and "See you tonight, Paul," as the train doors slid open. "Watch the gap," an automated voice reminded as we spilled out into the station. I breathed easier only after Dad and I lost one another in the crush of subway riders.

Two years later, I'd dropped out of college and moved in with my father full time. Set up in the basement, I spent many months lost and depressed before I finally landed an office job: answering phones and handling mail. Once again, Dad and I made the same commute. Neither of us was a morning person—"The Joneses love to sleep," we'd say. So, with wet hair and coffee or toast in hand, we'd jump into his car and ride to the railroad station. Then one day, when Dad's car was in the shop, we rode along with his friends. He and I squeezed into the cramped back seat. The driver was a man I did not know; the woman riding shotgun also worked at the Met.

I was tuned out when the three began their morning back-and-forth. I'd no interest in their musings about sports, politics, and gossip. My eyes had begun to close when the driver made an unmistakably racist, anti-Black comment. He targeted professional athletes, likely basketball players. He didn't use the N-word; didn't need to. He made his point without it. I startled and my mind raced: Didn't this man know who we were? Dad and I locked eyes in the rearview mirror.

Here we go, I thought. *Let's see Dad handle this*. And then . . . nothing. My father did not utter a word. Instead, his eyes darted in a way that said he was going to let the remark go.

He looked toward his friends in the front seat. I kept my eyes on my knees. At the station minutes later, I twisted out of the car, skipped a polite "Thanks for the ride," and did not look back. I hurried down the platform, as far as possible from the spot where I knew Dad and his friends would board. I took a seat and pressed my face against the window, numb. Riders squeezed on. Some stood until the aisles were full. The conductor's voice filled my head: "Plandome, Manhasset, Great Neck, Little Neck, next stop Penn Station." Dad, I imagined, was laughing it up with friends, as he did most mornings. At home that night, I said nothing. We both knew that my father had failed to defend me. He had failed to defend us. His humiliating silence rang in my ears.

Years later, in another New York City museum, I took myself to see the work of artist Adrian Piper. At the gallery entrance sat a small stack of 2-by-3½-inch yellow-brown cards. I idly picked one up, thinking it a keepsake. Rather than a souvenir, it was a soul saver. Piper had, I learned, presented the same "calling card" to offenders like my father's foulmouthed friend: "I am black. I am sure you did not realize this when you made/laughed at/agreed with that racist remark in the past. . . . I regret any discomfort my presence is causing you, just as I am sure you regret the discomfort your racism is causing me." Piper's card let me know that in that car, I'd not been alone. Adrian Piper, I understood, had been with me all along.

I reflected on what I knew about the life my father had made. He married a second time, a Jewish American woman whose children he loved as if they were his own. They all adored him in return. He lived in an ethnic enclave, mostly surrounded by

Italian Americans whose skin resembled his shade of olive. He frequented the same bars and restaurants they did and enjoyed the friendships he made there. On the train, at the corner store, in the nail salon and barber shop, he was met with warm greetings. In my father's life, the color line faded; faint and most days easy for him and those around him to overlook. His contentment came from being known simply as Paul.

My father's bargain would not be mine. It demanded a silence I could not maintain. It required a self-denial I could not endure. I made myself a promise. My body might mystify. It often confused. It would sometimes provoke. It was sure to anger some and amuse others. Still, I would follow Adrian Piper and learn to flip the script. Like James Baldwin, I would nurture my capacity for love of self and discover a radical tenderness for others. I would never forget that I was not alone. Nearly all of us have been injured in encounters with the jagged color line—my father included. I would learn to love him as he was, and I would leave him behind.

CONCLUSION

Love

My story would be very different if love had not forced me to attempt to deal with myself. It began to pry open for me the trap of color.

—JAMES BALDWIN, *NO NAME IN THE STREET*

Mom,

I will never forget the evening we looked together at my birth certificate—you, a mother so-called white and, me, her daughter not quite. It was rare for us, together, to face the color line. Most days, it was something we avoided so consistently that anyone listening in would have assumed that between us ran an unspoken understanding. But we'd never arrived at an accord. Instead, noise filled the space between us. I think of it as white noise, and the play on words lets me smile. Mostly, static filled the distance between us, where discordant questions thrived on things unsaid.

Do you remember how, at nineteen, I hatched plans to study abroad? You neither objected nor encouraged. I knew my wish to spend the fall in Copenhagen, Denmark, didn't

wholly register for you. I was breaking with the terms of your
upbringing in east Buffalo, where nobody had suggested that
you attend college, much less board a transatlantic flight to
study Scandinavian-style social welfare. I had so many questions about who I'd be when I got off the plane after leaving New York and, via Reykjavik, landing in Europe and the
unknown. Who might I become so far from you and Daddy?
But we kept it light, mostly chatting about my host family,
adapting to local ways, and the possibility of a bargain-rate rail
pass that would be my gateway to Europe.

I knew you had come on board for my adventure when
eventually you invited me to go shopping, and not only for
the practical things. Your eyes twinkled as you explained that
I must have a beautiful coat and stylish travel bag. I think you
were channeling what you'd read in the *New York Times* travel
section, which you did every week after finishing the cross-
word puzzle—in pen. It was no secret that we didn't live on a
travel-section budget. So, as you often did, you scoped out the
right Manhattan discount district, where we persuaded whole-
salers, working out of dingy bins in cramped storefronts, to
part with a single faux-shearling coat and a small brown leather
duffel. I still carry that bag today.

You were imagining my version of the European grand
tour while I completed the paperwork. I had watched as you
had applied for your first passport not many years before.
You and a friend had briefly headed off to visit France and
Italy. We'd been left, three teens, pretty much on our own.
Still, I admired you for breaking with expectations and getting far from our stifling suburb. It was my turn, and I got

down on my hands and knees at the back of your bedroom closet, where our family strongbox was tucked into a dark corner. A steel fireproof keep-safe with a cheap lock that was never latched, the key lost years before. There you set aside mortgages, insurance policies, divorce papers, and birth certificates.

I lifted the box, which was heavier than I remembered, set it on your bed, and slipped out its manila folders and business envelopes. My birth certificate was there, folded into well-worn thirds, a reverse copy with a black background and white print on shiny heavy paper. I ran my fingers across the raised health department seal. Carefully I flattened it out and scanned the details: my birthdate—June 22—and where I'd been delivered—St. Clare's. I recognized you and Dad, my parents—names, ages, and places of birth. Daddy, the Atlanta-born southerner, eight years your senior, and you, born and raised in Buffalo.

I looked again, and the word *white* stopped me cold. Well, not at first. Finding that word below your name made sense. I knew your mother, Mae, had come from Irish people, while your father, Frank, had been born into a clan of Germans, nineteenth-century immigrants. In my mind, your whiteness figured like a fact, not a social construction, and finding it on my birth certificate was no surprise. But Daddy marked as white? My heart raced as I frantically scanned the paper. Was this *my* birth certificate? There was my name and date of birth. I flipped the paper over, held it closer to my face. Yes, below his name in the blank for COLOR OR RACE was typed the word *white*. Someone nineteen years before had made a terrible mistake. Daddy, as we both knew, was not, by birth-certificate terms, white at all.

I stared out the window, paralyzed. I knew I needed that birth certificate and passport if I was going to Denmark. No matter how hard I wished it, this misunderstanding about Daddy's race—and mine—would not simply go away. I sat on the edge of your bed, running through likely scenarios. Would officials scrutinize my form and the supporting documents? Would they scrutinize me? What if I was denied that all-important ID or was charged with perpetuating a falsehood? I don't know how long I'd been sitting there when I heard your car pull into the driveway. Even before you came through the front door, as usual a bit crumpled after your commute from Manhattan, I was standing there waiting. I let my story about the strong-box and my troubling birth certificate spill out. The question "What should I do?" hung for a moment between us.

You set your newspaper and tote bag on the dining table and then slipped off your shoes. Together we headed into your bedroom, where the offending birth certificate still rested on the flowered spread. You sat down, and through the window behind you, the lush green of your summer garden shimmered in the early-evening light. The house was quiet. I put my birth certificate into your hand, insistent. You reset the mood by staying cool.

You then shared a story about the day of my birth: a Sunday, just before noon, hours of labor but not too many, and a happy delivery. Every year as far back as I could remember, you'd started my birthday—at my bedside and later on the phone—with this tale. But there was more, you continued:

Daddy hadn't been present for my birth. I sat up straight, and my furrowed brow revealed my puzzlement. You reassured me: This was typical. Sitting as we were in the 1970s, when fathers coached labor, caught babies, and cut umbilical cords, we had forgotten that in the 1950s, fathers sat in waiting rooms, paced linoleum corridors, or smoked cigarettes out on the curb. That's what Daddy, you chuckled, was doing in front of St. Clare's Hospital on West Fifty-First Street with his buddy Bobby while I was being born.

Soon I was smiling too. Your storytelling banished the threatening images of gruff passport officers from my mind. In their place surfaced visions of Daddy and Bobby, as young men, bs-ing, something I'd seen them do countless times: on our sofa, on a beach blanket, on a long car ride, and while watching a game. While I was being born, they squatted on the curb, in shorts with their bare knees up by their shoulders, mouthing Marlboros as yellow Checker cabs whizzed by. They kept one eye on the door for someone bringing news, all the while witnessing a parade of doctors, nurses, and the Franciscan sisters who ran the place, outfitted in full habits. They passed time fueling hopes for a better Giants football season and hardly noticed the everyday denizens of Hell's Kitchen who happened by.

Upstairs on the labor and delivery ward, for a time it was just us, you explained. Daddy arrived later—coming up on the elevator and required to wash up—only after I'd been delivered, swaddled, and tucked into a plastic bassinet. Your obstetrician never met him, did not know who or what Daddy was, you seemed to say. That same doctor, when completing my birth certificate, didn't hear Daddy's colloquial drawl or observe the flare of his nose. Did not shake his strong, light-brown hand. The man who delivered me, you said with a matter-of-fact shrug, looked at you, looked at me, and recorded us all as white.

It was many, many years later the next time I took a close look at my birth certificate; you and Daddy were both gone, and I was piecing together our family story. A fresh copy arrived by mail, and I carefully slid my finger along the envelope flap and unfolded the certified record. I knew that I'd find you and Daddy both marked as white. What caught my attention was the name of your doctor: Vaughn C. Mason. I'd heard it before and could almost hear your voice, distant but unmistakable: "Dr. Mason this . . . and Dr. Mason that . . ." Mason was more to you than a strange physician who'd happened into that delivery room. He was *your* doctor.

I popped open my laptop and scoured newspaper databases for "Vaughn C. Mason." He wasn't difficult to find. In fact, his traces were in just the places where you'd once known him: Dr. Mason, with privileges at St. Clare's, where he'd delivered me. Then on the staff at Sydenham Hospital, where he'd attended the births of my siblings, Paul and Laura. Dr. Mason, with an office on Amsterdam Avenue at 152nd Street in Harlem's fabled Sugar Hill. The same Dr. Mason who, in 1961, became head of the all-Black National Medical Association, the professional organization born out of the "exigencies of the American environment," as a founder put it. Dr. Mason, who'd come of age when much of medicine, and its professional societies, was segregated. Dr. Mason, who was a leader among Black doctors. He had fought for professional and health equity: national health insurance, desegregated hospitals and medical schools.

I drew in a deep breath, trying to make sense of what I'd discovered: Your obstetrician, Dr. Mason, was the Black physician who had marked my father as white on that birth certificate. It occurred to me that Aunt Jane—your sister-in-law—was herself a New York physician and a colleague to Dr. Mason through service to the National Medical Association. Hadn't she been the one to give you, newly expectant, medical advice and then recommend Dr. Mason? The connection was becoming clear. On the summer day I was born, Dr. Mason knew us. He knew precisely who you, Daddy, and I were.

My cousin, Aunt Jane's daughter, didn't remember Dr. Mason, but she did remember her mother's advice about filling in forms and checking boxes, like on birth certificates, census returns, and job applications: "When asked for your race, simply leave the space blank." My aunt suspected that such data might be used against us, "to round us up," my cousin explained. I remembered legal scholar Derrick Bell's parable of the space traders. Aliens came to earth and offered the United States wealth, energy, and a clean environment in exchange for Black Americans. The country took the deal and gave Black people up to beings who took them to the unknown. When it came time to determine who was Black, and thus subject to the bargain, birth certificates were the answer. I'd worried mostly about what my birth certificate said about me, but for others, it led to concerns about how the data it generated might do us in altogether.

I don't know how well you got to know Dr. Mason during months of prenatal visits. Maybe he was one of those Black physicians who believed that there was something sinister about reducing children to mere categories. Doctors like him knew well how pernicious thinking about race had rationalized the genocide of Jews and other so-called degenerates in Europe and fueled Black inequality at home. In Dr. Mason's time, there was even a small cadre of Black doctors who, when completing birth certificates became part of their regular duties, substituted the word *human* for terms like *Negro* or *colored*. Did you suspect, as I do now, that Dr. Mason had been intentional, rather than careless or even presumptuous, when he completed my birth certificate? He was making a statement when he marked Daddy as white, though I cannot say for certain what it was.

I remember a time, at age seven or eight, when I got it into my mind to change my name. Martha, I felt sure, was too old-fashioned for a schoolgirl. I wanted to be called Kathy, like the older girls on our block. You played along, even allowing me to sign homework and letters with "Kathy" for a time. I persisted, and you promised that when I turned eighteen, you would support my name change and even come up with the court fees. Over time the name Martha grew on me. I wish I could ask you now about changing my race. If I'd asked you to help change my birth certificate, would you have said yes?

Dr. Mason was wrong, but he was also right. For reasons lost to us, he reported that you and Daddy were white, and by implication I was too. That was an error. But in making that mistake, he was also correct. I was destined to be misapprehended, misunderstood, and mislabeled. Dr. Mason wrote a very early chapter in my story and wove me into our family saga. Between us—mother and daughter—I knew you'd say that it never mattered what my birth certificate said. You didn't care whether it named me Martha or Kathy. It changed nothing when Dr. Mason labeled me white instead of Black. You'd never set out to tell me who I was. You'd never instructed me about who I should become. In your eyes, I was destined for a future that defied the limits of any boxes I might encounter.

—

Dad,

You understand, I hope, why my story about your death begins with that day in 1954 when you put yourself in front of a moving subway car. We know you survived—you became my father four years later, in 1958. Still, the troubles that lifted you up off the platform and down onto the tracks never wholly left you. I knew you only as well as a daughter can know her father, as a witness to the decades that followed. I was not yet fifty when you died in 2004, and our years together were a long coda during which you, and I with you, worried about how things would end.

I was there when you confronted mortality in 1968. By then you were the father of three and a man of the suburbs. I was at the home of a friend, nine years old, when our blue square-backed Volkswagen pulled into the circular drive. I saw Paul and Laura sitting in the back, but Mommy was not behind the wheel. Instead, it was her lover. I snarled, "Didn't expect to see you," flopped into the front seat, and slammed the door. "Your mom asked me to collect you," he flatly offered. "Your dad is sick, in the hospital with a heart attack." I tried not to let my feelings show, but inside I was terrified. In a matter of days, you were back at home, but I could see that your heart was broken.

You were tougher than the heart disease that plagued you. We were all caught off guard when it was kidney cancer, undetected until it had engulfed your insides, that took you away for good. For me, your death arrived the instant that my thinking shifted from the unexpected to the inevitable. I was on Martha's Vineyard for a vacation when Laura called unexpectedly to say that you were hospitalized. She tried to sound reassuring—"probably pneumonia"—but I should get to Long Island quickly. I caught the first ferry, a barge, at dawn. Parked amidst cargo and trash, I took a long drag from a tall iced coffee and hoped we were all overreacting.

Four hours later, I was hurrying along the polished corridors of St. Francis Hospital. I dreaded the place, its chemical smell, beeping alarms, and sickness on the faces of people all around. I knew the back way in and avoided a stop for a visitor's pass. We'd been here many times, and I expected to find you propped in a bed, IV lines draped, the TV going, and family keeping you company. As I made the turn toward your room, I saw up ahead a small huddle of familiar figures. It was your wife and children talking with a white coat who explained that it was not pneumonia. I leaned in and heard that you had renal cancer. It had spread to your lungs, which now struggled for air. We'd arrived at the inevitable.

I stood at the foot of your bed, under the TV with my back against a cold, slick cinder-block wall, and remained still as family and nurses shuttled in and out. I flashed back to years earlier when, in the minutes before your second heart bypass, we had sat on the edge of your bed in that same hospital. You'd bravely reassured me that I'd be alright even if you were not. This time, no one told you your prognosis. But I think you knew it was grave. I looked at you across the room and for a moment our eyes locked, and I felt your fear shudder through me. I held your gaze for that long instant, the only comfort I knew how to offer.

Daddy, I'd sat many a vigil in your hospital rooms over the years. Artery blockages. Stroke recovery. Too many pills. Bleeding ulcers. A small lung tumor. Most recently a broken ankle when you'd fumbled on the winter ice. Usually it was just us, your kids and your wife; there was a routine to it. But this time the inevitable brought your baby brother, Fuzz, in from Atlanta. Mommy arrived, and I watched from the corridor as her lips murmured near your ear.

We stayed all that day and into the evening, time marked by the rhythm of nurses taking vitals and the setting of the sun. We took turns breaking for coffee down the hall at the hospital cafeteria: a Formica-covered emporium with a menu scrawled on a chalkboard. The place was run by a man named Freddie at whose counters I'd eaten since junior high school. He took our orders of fried things—eggs, potatoes, grilled cheese—and tall glasses of soda. Back in our half of your small room, I watched your wife make decisions that you all had rehearsed: no to extraordinary measures and yes to hospice.

We gathered at your bed that night, each taking a turn whispering gentle words, all of which ended with an upbeat "See you tomorrow, Dad." I wasn't sure how much you could hear between the monitors beeping, oxygen flowing, and the effects of pain meds. I moved forward, standing very close, just to your left, and reached down to take your hand. Did you hear me when I softly offered, "Good night, Dad. Sleep well." Perhaps you felt my touch. With our fingers interlaced—yours wide and wedged between my smaller ones—and my right hand holding your left, I lifted our grasp toward me, gently leaned down, and for a long moment held my lips to the back of your hand.

I hope you also felt what then came over me: forgiveness. Years before, the color line had divided us. I'd managed its sharp edges without you. Without gloves. Without wire cutters. Without heavy boots to protect my tender feet when I misstepped or when others stepped on me. So often I'd wondered what you knew or what you might have taught me about how to remain unscathed. But there by your bed, all that was in an instant gone. My chest warmed with an unfamiliar feeling: a daughter's love, unfettered, radiant, total. This must have been what I'd felt in those first hours after being born, when I first felt you close by my hospital bassinet. I had always adored you just that way.

Dr. Mason may have been mixed up about us, but I was not. With my lips pressed to your flesh, along with the inevitability of your loss, Daddy, I experienced what I'd thought was impossible—unconditional love for you. It was a moment so grace filled that, were I writing fiction, I might end our story here: Long-estranged daughter reconciles with father at death-bed. Readers might appreciate a poignant reconciliation. But as you know, our reckoning was not quite over.

When the phone rang early the next morning, a tiny knot of dread in my chest warned me not to pick up. I did and heard Laura's voice: "It's Dad. He's gone." I grabbed an overnight bag, jumped behind the wheel of my Jetta, and headed back to you. Your death set rituals in motion. Your wife put the arrangements in our hands—your children—and we worked out a wake, cere-mony, and burial, all through a local funeral parlor. For my part, I composed an obituary, found a minister, and wrote a eulogy. For a few hours, I ventured out alone and let a local shop owner outfit me in a black pantsuit and two silk blouses. I also let her soothe me with kind words and then sat alone under the glare of the fitting-room lights. Sadness consumed me.

A call came from the funeral director. He'd be sending your body to the crematorium in the morning: Did we want a last viewing of the casket? Your wife was certain she did not; she'd said her goodbyes. We kids piled into a car and took the ten-minute drive to town, where the mortician led us to his basement. The room was dark with low ceilings, like some-place Hollywood would have staged. He pointed to a plain box, telling us that in it was you. We stood silent. I recited a short prayer to myself, the "Our Father," which I still recalled from catechism class. We hugged and even joked a bit. Then time was up, and we squeezed into an adjacent office to go over the funeral details.

I can read upside down. It's an old lawyer's trick that I don't use very often. On that night, it served me well. My eyes wandered across the undertaker's desk while he previewed the next days in detail. Its surface was cluttered with paperwork, a receipt book with real carbon paper, and a stack of promotional calendars with an ad for the funeral home. Then I lit on an official-looking document—unwrinkled, as if it had just been completed. It was a death certificate. Yours. I half listened with my ears, willing my eyes to focus. On top was your name, date and time of death, and a small box checked "Male." OF HISPANIC ORIGIN? No. Then question 10: "DECEDENT'S RACE: CHECK ONE OR MORE RACES TO INDICATE WHAT THE DECEDENT CONSIDERED HIMSELF OR HERSELF TO BE." With a typed "XX," someone had marked box A for "White/Caucasian." The mortician droned on, so no one heard my heart sink or the moan that escaped my lips. I felt the whole of your seventy-eight years and my forty-seven combined land on me and stood very still in front of the man who had, with his hunt and peck on a tiny electric typewriter, squeezed every aching, curious, humorous, accidental, cruel, and even convenient misapprehension of our lives into the check of a box.

The next day, we buried you, the man who'd made me Black, as white. And like that, I let you go. After all, what can I say about the color of love?

AFTERWORD

How I Know
What I Know

Does history believe in itself even as it happens?
—HILTON ALS, *THE WOMEN*

M Y FIRST VISIT TO A "REAL" ARCHIVE—REAL AS IN A BRICK-
and-mortar site with a professional staff and formal
rules—was to the Amistad Research Center in New Orleans. I
still worked as a lawyer in those days and went hunting for family history on holidays and weekends. I dragged my sister along
for a "vacation," with the promise that we'd do the things tour-
ists do: from barhopping in the French Quarter to early-morning
beignets at Cafe du Monde and a dinner at Dooky Chase. I also
insisted that we start each day in the Amistad. We boarded the
St. Charles Avenue streetcar, and my mind turned to the clack,
clack, lurch of wheels on metal during the long trek from the
Central Business District to Uptown.

Just off the avenue on the campus of Tulane University, the
Amistad was for generations one of the few US repositories that

collected materials from the African American past. It makes sense, then, that when my grandfather's older brother, known in these pages as The Bishop, made plans to preserve his letters and other papers, he turned to the Amistad. He felt identified with the place because he'd spent his early career and raised a young family in New Orleans and then later returned to retire at nearby Gulfside, Mississippi. I discovered The Bishop there, cataloged alongside writer Chester Himes, musician W. C. Handy, actress Fredi Washington, artist Hale Woodruff, and members of the Morial political dynasty. I felt sure that these were the people with whom The Bishop would be delighted to spend an archival eternity.

It fell to my grandmother Musie to eventually find a permanent home for the papers of my grandfather, known to us as Grandy. She also chose the Amistad in a gesture both practical and poetic. Grandy too was cataloged among many early-twentieth-century people of consequence. He was also near his beloved older brother, The Bishop. They had been tight companions in life, and it made sense that they remained so in the perpetuity of memory. It had been hard for Musie to part with Grandy's papers, as I recall, and she tried to remove materials that she deemed private before posting the boxes to New Orleans. I knew this and couldn't help but feel that I was prying when I opened folder after folder. Just as she'd feared, I discovered manila files labeled "personal" and faced, for example, the raw details of my father's 1954 suicide attempt.

One Amistad staff member took an interest in me from the first moment I appeared at her desk. I handed in my call slips, and when, fifteen minutes later, I returned to pick up the first box of Grandy's papers, she stopped me. "You're a Jones, aren't you?" Surprised, I blankly replied, "Yes, I am." "I knew it," she exclaimed. I must have looked puzzled, so she continued, "I had one look at you and knew you were a Jones. I'd recognize a Jones anywhere." She was someone who had known The Bishop's family and, I assumed, was pleased by her powers of recognition. Me, I was pleased to be recognized. After all, I was there on a hunt for family history. *Amazing*, I thought. *Here in New Orleans, folks are familiar with my people, and they recognize me.*

The day continued, with me back and forth, trading one box for the next and working through Grandy's letters. In those days, I wore my hair long—down to the middle of my back. That afternoon, as I passed her desk, the same staff member was in the midst of training a new student worker. She was using her teacher's voice as she instructed the young person, who stood silent, nodding. She turned to me: "Stop a minute." I did. "I've been telling this young man about the history of color here in New Orleans." I nodded. "I've been telling him that I, with my light brown skin, am too dark by this city's terms." She held out her forearm. *My* skin began to crawl. "I told him that you are not." I began to sweat a little too. "Look at this," she said to the young student and then reached out and took a lock of my hair between her fingers. She raised it up into the air like a specimen. I was Exhibit A. "See, this is what I mean." I stood there, an aspiring storyteller who was also the story.

—

Writing memoir has been a leap for me. In graduate school, my mind was trained to venture back in time. This book, as

I explored five generations of family stories, also required my heart to travel, back and forth and back again. I came to know the past and also feel it. Along the way, I became a believer. I discovered my faith in the capacity of words to help me know myself and the people who made me. I started this book without anyone from whom to seek permission; my elders were gone. All I had was the belief that if I dedicated the best of myself to them, to their memories, and to making sense of their lives, the result would be a tribute worthy of all they were, of all they endured along the color line.

Early in the writing, my editor advised me that *The Trouble of Color* would not have footnotes. It is, after all, a work of literature rather than of history. Tiny end-of-paragraph numbers, long the tools of my trade, would only distract readers. They were, in fact, a crutch. I learned new ways of conveying truths about the past. Yes, there were certainties that lined up with facts and figures. And this book rests upon many of those. Still, to tell our family story required that I incorporate other truths, the types I associated with poetry, fiction, and art. I would have to earn a reader's confidence on the page. Persuasion would come not by appending lists of sources or a copious appendix but instead by the transformation of words into feelings. I set out to blend language with sound, structure, and cadence; to hear, smell, and even see the past through the eyes of my imagination. I hoped that readers would *think* and then discover how to *feel* the ancestors who have shaped us.

Family stories, tucked away in my heart and mind, were my first guide. I learned to listen carefully for tales that were distant, faint, fragmentary, and fraught. When I was growing up, adults let me listen in on their grown-up talk. Nestled in an oversized chair, crouched atop a staircase, or unnoticed at a picnic or barbecue, I heard about characters from our past. I lurked during parties that rocked my parents' suburban living room while Scotch and stories spilled in equal measure. I sat upright at my grandmother's dining table during her luncheons with lady friends, absorbing lessons like how to choose a fork while they sprinkled polite conversation with gossip. Eavesdropping won me insights that no interview would ever surface. My elders understood history—of slavery, racism, and civil rights—and told tales that wove them into the fabric of the epic past. But the history of a family? I came to understand this as a process of tellings and retellings that were unfolding rather than static, always changeable, contradictory and conflictual.

Other stories came to me as unwelcome confessions. Guts sometimes spilled: My father two drinks in confessed with me perched on his knees; my Aunt Sweets rambled on over a scratchy telephone line from St. Louis; my mother's brother mailed missives that brimmed with sardonic wit. Aunts and uncles talked on top of one another at the Thanksgiving table or over dessert and coffee. Distant relations got their grievances out in wedding-reception halls and over cold lunch after a funeral. I learned stoicism in these moments and practiced an impassiveness that helped me manage tough revelations. It is a skill that I rely upon even today. At many moments, I also turned inward. I took to heart the recommendation of memoirist Eileen Simpson and assumed "the position of a person being psychoanalyzed." I lay on my couch and associated freely. I let buried insights surface, overcame fears of the unknown, and learned to be at ease with my fragility. The result is a story that is uniquely mine.

Family members who put their stories on paper—my grandmother Musie, her sister Aunt Sweets, The Bishop, my Uncle Fuzz, and more—were my interlocutors. Each of them carefully chose their published words, crafted to withstand the test of time. They each produced an official version of our saga, and for a long time, I accepted their stories like gospel. Later, in graduate school studying history, I was advised that when writing about them, I should be less worshipful. Here I have approached family storytellers as one part critical reader. I had to keep in mind that their stories were fashioned to reflect the needs of their time, not mine. Still, I remained, despite the risks, two parts an admiring heir. I discovered strength and perceptiveness when I treated my ancestors' stories with the seriousness they deserved.

I waited until the passing of my parents' generation to write these stories down. This was not out of fear or vengeance. Instead, this book emanates from longing. It was my chance to talk again with ancestors, to revive our conversations, and to begin new ones. In each generation, many people in my family strove to write down truths that went far beyond facts and figures. I learned from their ideas. I also argued with their interpretations and rethought their conclusions. I marveled at their contradictions and broke with some of our most often-repeated anecdotes. The stories that, once upon a time, they told birthed me. I, in turn, have birthed the tales told here.

I have always been a pack rat, at work collecting the materials that appear in this book. Filed away in my basement are notes passed to me in seventh grade Spanish class, diaries, letters, greeting cards, and news clippings. My grandmother encouraged just this when I was only a toddler. My mother helped by saving many of her letters. I was just two—we lived in an upper Manhattan walk-up—when my grandmother began to send me keepsakes. An envelope arrived, and in it was a news clipping titled "Bennett Development Is Credit to Jones," a posthumous assessment of my grandfather's work for the college he had headed. My grandmother's cover note anticipated the person I am today: "Dear Martha: This is for your keep sake box." With this, she set me on a path collecting pieces of the past and toward this book.

Others have allowed me to be the keeper of their papers. After Musie preserved many of my father's letters, from his boyhood through the 1960s, I inherited them from him. A dear cousin allowed me, as we closed her mother's home, to keep the letters that my Aunt Tuppy had written to their parents in the same years. My mother saved nearly every letter she received starting in the 1950s, after she'd escaped Buffalo and landed in Manhattan. They are a rich chronicle, told mostly through the long, rambling missives of her older brother. Not long ago, my sister sent me a small box of documents with a note that kindly dubbed me the family historian. Inside was my grandmother's voter registration record, something I'd searched high and low for in official repositories. All along, it had been among our family keepsakes.

My grandfather and his brother—Grandy and The Bishop—produced the sorts of papers that won them space on the storage shelves at the Amistad Center. Most members of our family left very little behind. To discover these more elusive lives, I have looked into documents produced by slaveholders, court clerks, census takers, and pension officials, among others. These records were created to affirm the importance or the efficiency of their creators. My family members were often incidental. Still, in this way, I found hints about my Danville, Kentucky, family in deeds, wedding bonds, and death certificates. Unexpectedly, I also found my family buried in the papers of Ormond Beatty, a local college president who counted them among his assets as enslaved people.

From Beatty's ledgers, I learned how my great-great-great-grandmother Nancy had remained bound to him even after slavery ended. On roughly maintained columns, Beatty marked down the everyday events of her life: wages, debts, loans, purchases, and gifts. It was a sobering honor to spend the many hours it took to sift through Beatty's dry business records looking for signs of Nancy's precious humanity. Most days, even when the work was slow or frustrating, a quiet current of gladness sustained me. Some moments were even joy-filled, such as when I discovered that Nancy had had two sisters—Tinah and Betty. The three had remained together until the end of their lives, despite how slavery had threatened to separate them. Often I have been the very first person—seasoned researcher and searching descendant—to hear their lives coming through paper and ink.

Knowing more has also demanded time to comb through raw documents like Beatty's ledgers. I've also taken the time required to leaf through courthouse folios, city directories, and newspaper runs. When I searched for details about my father's life as a suburban activist, I read a decade's worth of our local weekly, the *Port Washington News*. Only one full run has survived, much of it on fragile paper, and it is safeguarded by the town's librarians. The US census was digitized only after I had spent many Saturdays alongside other family historians at the downtown Manhattan branch of the National Archives. I sat at a microfilm machine, hooked up reel after reel, and slowly filled out our family tree.

I have also taken time to sit with what I've learned. I granted myself patience as I processed new feelings. Some discoveries took me months and even years to fully confront. When a cousin sent me a complaint filed by our great-great-grandmother Isabella against the man who had owned her and fathered her children, I dutifully saved it to a hard drive. Then, though I never forgot it, I left Isabella's message from the past in the cloud and unopened for years. Before I could understand her story, I needed to learn about how enslaved women survived, or did not survive, the abuse they endured. I was fortunate to be guided by the recollections of an enslaved woman who had lived just downriver from Isabella, Harriet Jacobs. Harriet recounted how she managed her own ordeal, threatened by white men's desires, in her book *Incidents in the Life of a Slave Girl*. The company of other storytellers gave me the courage to face the unsettling past and to absorb its force in the present.

To strengthen my own gut sense, to hone my ability to know a truth when I see it, I turned to other storytellers whose truths often go beyond the archival record. My teachers are poets and novelists, essayists and filmmakers. They are artists.

They extend from DaMaris Hill's lyrics in *Breath Better Spent* and Natasha Trethewey's prose in *Memorial Drive* to the women who inhabit Toni Morrison's *The Bluest Eye* and Nella Larsen's *Passing*. I have watched Sarah Jane's on-screen pathos in *Imitation of Life*. Through immersion in visual culture—from the dazzling possibilities of eighteenth-century casta paintings to the boundary-defying performances of Adrian Piper and the terrible veracity of Kara Walker's silhouettes—I discovered how stories move me. I learned to feel through laughter too, induced by the fiction of Mat Johnson and the *We're Mixed, of Course We . . .* TikTok series. I came to know what I know because the archive pointed the way, and then I allowed experience and intuition to guide me along the rest of the journey.

Imagination helped me confront the past, even when the archival trail had gone cold. Often I was not satisfied to simply lament that which I could not know. Instead, I speculated about what might have been. Records like Ormond Beatty's ledgers at first told me little more than how Beatty saw Nancy and how the two interacted. But with them in mind, I shifted my gaze away from details about Beatty's management of capital, goods, and enslaved people and toward Nancy. I tried standing where she once had, near the plot where her house once sat or at the site where she is buried. Beatty's world faded, and Nancy's became vivid. I could nearly see her as she tended a small garden, prepared meals for the grandchildren next door, and nursed her husband, Edmund, as he aged. I could see Nancy, neatly dressed, seated in her daughter Susan's buggy, headed to the downtown photo studio where she sat for the portrait that today hangs above my writing desk.

As the bibliography included here reflects, I am indebted to scores of historians, chroniclers, and other writers about the past. I have re-created lives and a family, but I have also re-created scenes and whole worlds that I could glimpse only because other writers studied them before me. Only a very few of these authors wrote about members of my family or even knew we were silent participants in the stories they told. Still, their work turned on the lights of the past for me. I could place Fannie in downtown Danville or St. Louis and describe Mary and Elijah at home in Little Texas. I was able to visualize Paul at Mount Hermon or on Long Island. I relied on the research of others who before me wrote about these places and others, along with the habits and moods of their inhabitants.

This book is a dialogue with my family. It is also a dialogue with those who write about the past in which my family made its way. My themes—from slavery through emancipation, Jim Crow, and finally Civil Rights—are enduring. They involve some of the richest and most confounding questions that can be asked about the American past. Few historians will find their ideas directly represented in this book. I have recounted stories that are particular, peculiar, and often defy wisdom derived from social, political, or cultural history. Still, I hope my historian readers will discover in these stories fresh explanations of the past. I read their work and appreciate the opportunity to then depart from their thinking.

The Trouble of Color is a meditation on my ancestors. It is an immersion in the stories they once upon a time told and the tales that others crafted about them. It is about the past and how it is present even now. Through recollections, shards of paper, along with hopes, dreams, and fears, I have aimed to recover my family's richest legacy. Each generation told the tales it best knew. Each one told the tales they needed to face troubles and also reach for the promise of their time. I have stepped into that stream and joined a tradition of family storytelling, all along in the company of dear ancestors who keep me company. They have granted permission, encouraged, intervened, and loved me every step of the way. Because of them, I am. Because of them, I know what I know.

Acknowledgments

Thank you to the Library of Congress John W. Kluge Center, the Wissenschaftskolleg zu Berlin, and the Johns Hopkins University Krieger School of Arts and Sciences for supporting the research and writing of *The Trouble of Color*. I am indebted to the Hurston/Wright Foundation and the Newport MFA Workshop for encouraging me to set aside my historian's habits and discover the possibilities of memoir. Annabelle Headley provided research support and critical thinking during a summer research assistantship.

Tanya McKinnon and the team at McKinnon Literary were the first to encourage me to tell the stories I've written down here. Tanya and her daughter Viviana have made sure that I know whom I am writing for and why I write at every step along the way. Brian Distelberg and the team at Basic Books bestowed upon me their confidence as I began this book and then brought a rare mix of compassion and professionalism to seeing it through.

It is my great good fortune to have talented friends and colleagues who have read and commented on drafts. Thank you to Veronica Chambers, Ada Ferrer, Ariela Gross, and Leslie Harris for reading with such care and then challenging me to always aim higher. Thank you also to Stephane Gerson and the participants in the March 2020 Scholars and Their Kin symposium and Kendra Field and the participants in the November 2019 Writing Family, Reconstructing Lives symposium.

It is to my family that I am most indebted. Ancestors have kept me company at every turn, leaving breadcrumbs that have led me to insights. My cousins—the Joneses, the Bonners, the Evanses, the Murphys, and the Millers—have been kind, generous, and feeling companions as I've worked through the ideas expressed here. My husband, Jean Hébrard, would be content if I simply acknowledged that he kept me company in the archives and read many drafts. But what I know is that his unwavering love for me and for everyone who appears in these pages has made this work and my life's work possible. If I have had one reader in mind, it is my brother, Paul. His love for me is a blossom rising out the ashes of our family past. He has trusted me without question and faithfully read these pages despite how they sometimes caused his heart to ache. There is no sister more fortunate than I.

Two years ago now, I mentioned the subject of this book at the close of a talk. I was responding to the question "What are you working on now?" As I stepped down from the podium, I saw a woman approaching from the back of the room. As she got closer, I could see her and myself in her. But what led me to pick up my pace were the tears welling in her eyes. Without an introduction, we embraced. "I see you," I whispered in her ear. This book is indebted to everyone who has been snagged by the color line and then shared their pain, joy, humor, and grief. This book is for all of us.

Berlin, Germany, July 2024

Bibliography

African-American Settlements and Communities in Columbus, Ohio: A Report. Columbus, OH: Columbus Landmarks Foundation, 2014.

Alexander, Adele Logan. *Ambiguous Lives: Free Women of Color in Rural Georgia, 1789–1879.* Fayetteville: University of Arkansas Press, 1991.

Alexander, Adele Logan. *Princess of the Hither Isles: A Black Suffragist's Story from the Jim Crow South.* New Haven, CT: Yale University Press, 2019.

Ards, Angela A. *Words of Witness: Black Women's Autobiography in the Post-"Brown" Era.* Madison: University of Wisconsin Press, 2015.

Austin, Paula C. "How Family History Opens New Archives." *Black Perspectives*, November 18, 2022.

Bardaglio, Peter. *Reconstructing the Household: Families, Sex, and the Law in the Nineteenth-Century South.* Chapel Hill: University of North Carolina Press, 1995.

Bartov, Omer. *Tales from the Borderlands: Making and Unmaking the Galician Past.* New Haven, CT: Yale University Press, 2022.

Bell, David A. "Ego-Histories." *New York Review of Books*, June 22, 2023.

Bell, John Frederick. *Degrees of Equality: Abolitionist Colleges and the Politics of Race.* Baton Rouge: Louisiana State University Press, 2022.

Bell-Scott, Patricia. *The Firebrand and the First Lady: Portrait of a Friendship; Pauli Murray, Eleanor Roosevelt, and the Struggle for Social Justice.* New York: Knopf, 2017.

Berry, Stephen. "Dwelling in the Digital Archive: A Meditation on the Civil War Governors of Kentucky Project." *Register of the Kentucky Historical Society* 117, no. 2 (Spring 2019): 161–178.

Bibliography

Binford, Lewis. "Comments on the 'Souian Problem.' *Ethnohistory* 6, no. 1 (1959): 28–41.

Biondi, Martha. *The Black Revolution on Campus.* Berkeley: University of California Press, 2012.

"Black Archival Practice II." *Black Scholar* 52, no. 4 (Winter 2022), https://www.bu.edu/afam/2022/11/04/now-available-52-4-black-archival-practice-ii/.

Blassingame, John W. "The Recruitment of Colored Troops in Kentucky, Maryland and Missouri, 1863–1865." *Historian* 29 (1967): 533–545.

Block, Sharon. "Lines of Color, Sex, and Service: Comparative Sexual Coercion in Early America." In *Sex, Love, Race: Crossing Boundaries in North American History,* edited by Martha Hodes, 141–163. New York: New York University Press, 1990.

Bouquet, Mary. "Family Trees and Their Affinities: The Visual Imperative of the Genealogical Diagram." *Journal of the Royal Anthropological Institute of London* (March 1996): 43–66.

Bradley, Stefan. *Harlem vs. Columbia University: Black Student Power in the Late 1960s.* Champaign: University of Illinois Press, 2009.

Brawley, James P. *Two Centuries of Methodist Concern: Bondage, Freedom and Education of Black People.* New York: Vantage Press, 1974.

Brimmer, Brandi. *Claiming Union Widowhood: Race, Respectability, and Poverty in the Post-Emancipation South.* Durham, NC: Duke University Press, 2020.

Brooks, James F., ed. *Confounding the Color Line: The Indian-Black Experience in North America.* Lincoln: University of Nebraska Press, 2002.

Brown, Kathleen M. *Good Wives, Nasty Wenches, and Anxious Patriarchs: Gender, Race, and Power in Colonial Virginia.* Chapel Hill: University of North Carolina Press, 1996.

Brown, Richard C. *The Presbyterians: Two Hundred Years in Danville, 1784–1984.* Danville, KY: Presbyterian Church, 1983.

Buckley, Gail Lumet. *The Black Calhouns: From Civil War to Civil Rights with One African American Family.* New York: Grove Atlantic, 2016.

Buckley, Thomas E. "Unfixing Race: Class, Power, and Identity in an Interracial Family." In *Sex, Love, Race: Crossing Boundaries in North American History,* edited by Martha Hodes, 164–190. New York: New York University Press, 1990.

Campt, Tina M. *Image Matters: Archive, Photography, and the African Diaspora in Europe.* Durham, NC: Duke University Press, 2012.

Caro, Robert. *The Power Broker: Robert Moses and the Fall of New York.* New York: Knopf, 1974.

Cecelski, David S. *The Waterman's Song: Slavery and Freedom in Maritime North Carolina.* Chapel Hill: University of North Carolina Press, 2001.

Chafe, William. *Civilities and Civil Rights: Greensboro, North Carolina, and the Black Struggle for Freedom.* Oxford, UK, and New York: Oxford University Press, 1981.

Challis, Debbie. *The Archaeology of Race: The Eugenic Ideas of Francis Galton and Flinder Petrie.* New York: Bloomsbury, 2014.

Charles, Julia S. *That Middle World: Race, Performance, and the Politics of Passing.* Chapel Hill: University of North Carolina Press, 2020.

Clark, Emily. *The Strange History of the American Quadroon.* Chapel Hill: University of North Carolina Press, 2013.

Clark, Emily. "The Tragic Mulatto and Passing." In *Palgrave Handbook of the Southern Gothic,* edited by Susan P. Castillo. London: Palgrave Macmillan, 2016.

Colbert, Soyica Diggs, Robert J. Patterson, and Aida Levy-Hussen, eds. *The Psychic Hold of Slavery: Legacies in American Expressive Culture.* New Brunswick, NJ: Rutgers University Press, 2016.

Cole, Jennifer. "For the Sake of the Songs of the Men Made Free: James Speed and the Emancipationists' Dilemma in Nineteenth-Century Kentucky," *Ohio Valley History* 4, no. 4 (Winter 2004): 27–48.

Collins, Patricia Hill. "It's All in the Family: Intersections of Gender, Race, and Nation." *Hypatia* 13, no. 3 (Summer 1998): 62–82.

Connery, Robert H., and Gerald Benjamin. *Rockefeller of New York: Executive Power in the Statehouse.* Ithaca, NY: Cornell University Press, 1979.

Crafts, Hannah. *The Bondwoman's Narrative,* edited by Henry Louis Gates, Jr. New York: Warner Books, 2002.

Crossland, William August. *Industrial Conditions Among Negroes in St. Louis.* St. Louis, MO: Mendle Printing, 1914.

Crothers, A. Glenn, and Tracy E. K'Meyer. "'I Was Black When It Suited Me; I Was White When It Suited Me': Racial Identity in the Biracial Life of Marguerite Davis Stewart." *Journal of American Ethnic History* 26, no. 4 (Summer 2007): 24–49.

Coulter, Merton E. *The Civil War and Readjustment in Kentucky*. Chapel Hill: University of North Carolina Press, 1926.

Dagbovie, Pero Gaglo. *The Early Black History Movement, Carter G. Woodson, and Lorenzo Johnston Greene*. Gainesville: University of Florida Press, 2007.

Davis, R. P. Stephen, Jr., Patrick C. Livingood, H. Trawick War, and Vincas P. Steponaitis, eds. *Excavating Occaneechi Town: Archaeology of an Eighteenth-Century Indian Village in North Carolina*. Chapel Hill: University of North Carolina Press, 2020.

DeCharez, Jeremy, and Cassie Jin Lin. "'The Faithful Work of Drowning': A Reparative Reading of Ocean Vuong's 'Telemachus,'" *Explicator* 78, no. 2 (2020): 66–70.

Dickens, Roy S., Jr., H. Trawick Ward, and R. P. Stephen Davis, Jr., eds. *The Siouan Project, Seasons I and II*. Chapel Hill: University of North Carolina Research Laboratories of Anthropology, 1987.

Dickey, Bronwen. "She Was Killed by the Police. Why Were Her Bones in a Museum?" *New York Times*, October 19, 2022.

Dunlap, David. *From Abyssinian to Zion: A Guide to Manhattan's Houses of Worship*. New York: Columbia University Press, 2004.

Edwards, Laura. *The People and Their Peace: Legal Culture and the Transformation of Inequality in the Post-Revolutionary South*. Chapel Hill: University of North Carolina Press, 2009.

Elliott, Matthew. "The Inconvenient Ancestor: Slavery and Selective Remembrance on Genealogy Television." *Studies in Popular Culture* 39, no. 2 (Spring 2017): 73–90.

Emberton, Carole. "Searching for Carolina: 'Disciplined Imagination' and the Limits of the Archive." *Register of the Kentucky Historical Society* 117, no. 2 (Spring 2019): 345–356.

Ethridge, Robbie. *From Chicaza to Chickasaw: The European Invasion and the Transformation of the Mississippian World, 1540–1715*. Chapel Hill: University of North Carolina Press, 2010.

Fackler, Calvin Morgan. *Early Days in Danville, Kentucky*. Louisville, KY: Standard Printing, 1941.

Favors, Jelani M. "Race Women: New Negro Politics and the Flowering of Radicalism at Bennett College, 1900–1945." *North Carolina Historical Review* 44, no. 4 (October 2017): 391–430.

Favors, Jelani M. *Shelter in a Time of Storm: How Black Colleges Fostered Generations of Leadership and Activism*. Chapel Hill: University of North Carolina Press, 2019.

Feimster, Crystal N. "Keeping a Disorderly House in Civil War Kentucky." *Register of the Kentucky Historical Society* 117, no. 2 (Spring 2019): 301–322.

Field, Kendra T. "The Privilege of Family History," *American Historical Review* 127, no. 2 (June 2022): 600–633.

Field, Kendra Taira. "Talk One Thing: Writing Family History in an Afro-Native World." *Southern Cultures* 28, no. 3 (Fall 2022): 42–47.

Fielder, Brigitte. *Relative Races: Genealogies of Interracial Kinship in 19th Century America*. Durham, NC: Duke University Press, 2020.

Fienberg, Stephen, and Margo Anderson. *Who Counts? The Politics of Census-Taking in Contemporary America*. New York: Russell Sage Foundation, 1999.

Finkelman, Paul. "Thomas R. R. Cobb and the Law of Negro Slavery." *Roger Williams University Law Review* 5, no. 1 (1999): 75–115.

Fischer, Eugen. *Die Rehobother Bastards und das Bastardierungsproblem beim Menschen: Anthropologische und ethnographiesche Studien am Rehobother Bastardvolk in Deutsch-Südwest-Afrika* (The Rehoboth bastards and the problem of bastardization in human beings: Anthropological and ethnographic studies of the Rehoboth bastard tribe in German Southwest Africa). Jena, Germany: G. Fischer, 1913.

Forbes, Jack D. *Africans and Native Americans: The Language of Race and the Evolution of Red-Black Peoples*. Champaign: University of Illinois Press, 1993.

Ford, Bridget. "Black Spiritual Defiance and the Politics of Slavery in Antebellum Louisville." *Journal of Southern History* 78, no. 1 (February 2012): 69–106.

Frankel, Nora Lee. *Freedom's Women: Black Women and Families in Civil War Era Mississippi*. Bloomington: Indiana University Press, 1999.

Franklin, John Hope. *The Free Negro in North Carolina, 1790–1860*. Chapel Hill: University of North Carolina Press, 1995.

Gaines, Alisa. *Black for a Day: White Fantasies of Race and Empathy*. Chapel Hill: University of North Carolina Press, 2017.

Bibliography

Gascoine, Kelly G. "Counting People of Color: The Jeffries Family of Whitley County, Indiana." *Hoosier Genealogist: Connections* 51, no. 1 (Spring/Summer 2011): 18–23.

Geizer, Bernard Paul. "The Construction of Academic Facilities for the State University of New York: A Performance Evaluation of the State University Construction Fund." PhD diss., New York University, 1974.

Ginzburg, Carlo. "Family Resemblances and Family Trees: Two Cognitive Metaphors." *Critical Inquiry* 30, no. 3 (Spring 2004): 537–556.

Glasker, Wayne. *Black Students in the Ivory Tower: African American Student Activism at the University of Pennsylvania, 1967–1975.* Amherst: University of Massachusetts Press, 2002.

Glazer, Judith S. "Nelson Rockefeller and the Politics of Higher Education in New York State." Albany, NY: Nelson A. Rockefeller Institute of Government, 1989.

Graham, Lawrence Otis. *Our Kind of People: Inside America's Black Upper Class.* New York: HarperCollins, 1999.

Graybeal, Lesley M. "'Too Light to Be Black, Too Dark to Be White.'" *Native South* 5, no. 1 (2012): 95–122.

Graybeal, Lesley Marie. "(Re)constructing and (Re)presenting Heritage: Education and Representation in an American Indian Homeland Preservation Project." PhD diss., University of Georgia, 2011.

Green, Tiffany L., and Tod G. Hamilton. "Beyond Black and White: Color and Mortality in Post-Reconstruction Era North Carolina." *Explorations in Economic History* 50, no. 1 (January 2013): 148–159.

Greenidge, Kerri K. *The Grimkes: The Legacy of Slavery in an American Family.* New York: Liveright, 2023.

Griffin, William W. *African Americans and the Color Line in Ohio, 1915–1930.* Columbus: Ohio State University Press, 2005.

Haeger, John D. *John Jacob Astor: Business and Finance in the Early Republic.* Detroit, MI: Wayne State University Press, 1991.

Hahn, Cynthia. "What Do Reliquaries Do for Relics?" *Numen* 57, no. 3/4 (2010): 284–316.

Harrison, Victoria L. "Man in the Middle: Conway Barbour and the Free Black Experience in Antebellum Louisville." *Ohio Valley History* 10, no. 4 (Winter 2010): 25–45.

Bibliography

Harrold, Stanley. *Border War: Fighting Over Slavery Before the Civil War.* Chapel Hill: University of North Carolina Press, 2010.

Hartman, Saidiya. *Wayward Lives, Beautiful Experiments: Intimate Histories of Social Upheaval.* New York: W. W. Norton, 2019.

Hazel, Forest. "Occaneechi-Saponi Descendants in the North Carolina Piedmont: The Texas Community." *Southern Indian Studies* 40 (October 1991): 1–29.

Hazel, Forest, and Lawrence A. Dunmore III. *A Brief History of the Occaneechi Band of the Saponi Nation.* Burlington, NC: Occaneechi Band of the Saponi Nation, 1995.

Hecimovich, Gregg. *The Life and Times of Hannah Crafts: The True Story of the Bondswoman's Narrative.* New York: Ecco, 2023.

Heckman, Richard Allen, and Betty Jean Hall. "Berea College and the Day Law." *Register of the Kentucky Historical Society* 66, no. 1 (January 1968): 35–52.

Heeb, Bernhard S., and Charles Kabwete-Mulinda. *Human Remains from the Former German Colony of East Africa: Recontextualization and Approaches for Restitution.* Göttingen, Germany: Vandenhoeck & Ruprecht, 2022.

Hill, Ruth Edmonds, ed. *Black Women Oral History Project*, vols. 1–10. Westport, CT: Meckler, 1991.

Hobbs, Allyson. *A Chosen Exile: A History of Racial Passing in American Life.* Cambridge, MA: Harvard University Press, 2014.

Hochschild, Jennifer L., and Brenna Marea Powell. "Racial Reorganization and the United States Census, 1850–1930: Mulattoes, Half-Breeds, Mixed Parentage, Hindoos, and the Mexican Race." *Studies in American Political Development* 22, no. 1 (April 2008): 59–96.

Hollis, Jeanne Simkins, and George C. Simkins III. *Shades of Privilege: Two African-American Families That Helped Transform the Carolinas, and the Nation.* Pennsauken, NJ: BookBaby, 2022.

Holloway, Jonathan Scott. *Jim Crow Wisdom: Memory and Identity in Black America Since 1940.* Chapel Hill: University of North Carolina Press, 2013.

Howard, Victor B. *Black Liberation in Kentucky: Emancipation and Freedom, 1862–1884.* Lexington: University of Kentucky Press, 1983.

Hunter, Tera W. *Bound in Wedlock: Slave and Free Black Marriage in the Nineteenth Century.* Cambridge, MA.: Belknap Press, 2017.

Hyde, Anne Farrar. *Born of Lakes and Plains: Mixed-Descent Peoples and the Making of the American West*. New York: W. W. Norton, 2022.

Jasanoff, Maya. *The Dawn Watch: Joseph Conrad in a Global World*. New York: Penguin, 2017.

Jelks, Randal Maurice. *Benjamin Elijah Mays, Schoolmaster of the Movement: A Biography*. Chapel Hill: University of North Carolina Press, 2012.

Jones, Bernie D. *Fathers of Conscience: Mixed-Race Inheritance in the Antebellum South*. Athens: University of Georgia Press, 2009.

Jones, Mark, and John Wertheimer. "Pinkney and Sarah Ross: The Legal Journey of an Ex-Slave and His Wife on the Carolina Borderlands During Reconstruction." *South Carolina Historical Magazine* 103, no. 4 (October 2002): 325–350.

Joseph, Ralina L. *Transcending Blackness: From the New Millennium Mulatta to the Exceptional Multiracial*. Durham, NC: Duke University Press, 2013.

Kalifa, Dominique. *Vice, Crime, and Poverty*. New York: Columbia University Press, 2019.

Kiesel, Diane. *She Can Bring Us Home: Dorothy Boulding Ferebee, Civil Rights Pioneer*. Sterling, VA: Potomac Books, 2015.

Kirakosian, Katie V., and Alan C. Swedlund. "Glass Cabinets and Little Black Boxes: The Collections of H. H. Wilder and the Curious Case of His Human-Hair Samples." *Historical Archaeology* 53 (2019): 280–294.

Kridel, Craig. "And Gladly Would She Learn: Margaret Willis and the Ohio State University School." In *Founding Mothers and Others: Women Educational Leaders During the Progressive Era*, edited by Alan R. Sadovnik and Susan F. Semel. London: Palgrave, 2022.

Lamore, Eric D., ed. *Reading African American Autobiography: Twenty-First Century Contexts and Criticism*. Madison: University of Wisconsin Press, 2017.

Leonard, Elizabeth D. *Slaves, Slaveholders, and a Kentucky Community's Struggle Toward Freedom*. Lexington: University of Kentucky Press, 2019.

Levine, Robert S. "'That Grim Sphinx': Literary Historicism and Tourgée's *Toinette* Novels." *American Literary History* 34, no. 1 (Spring 2022): 224–236.

Levy, Daniel S. *Manhattan Phoenix: The Great Fire of 1835 and the Emergence of Modern New York*. Oxford, UK, and New York: Oxford University Press, 2022.

Lewis, Linden, Glyne Griffith, and Crespo Kebler, eds. *Color, Hair, and Bone: Race in the 21st Century.* Lewisburg, PA: Bucknell University Press, 2008.

Lewis, Patrick A. "The Democratic Partisan Militia and the Black Peril: The Kentucky Militia, Racial Violence, and the Fifteenth Amendment, 1870–1873." *Civil War History* 56, no. 2 (June 2010): 145–174.

Livesay, Daniel. *Children of Uncertain Fortune: Mixed-Race Jamaicans in Britain and the Atlantic Family, 1733–1833.* Chapel Hill: University of North Carolina Press, 2018.

Lovett, Laura L. "'African and Cherokee by Choice': Race and Resistance Under Legalized Segregation." *American Indian Quarterly* 22, no. 1/2 (Winter–Spring 1998): 203–229.

Lowery, Malinda Maynor. *The Lumbee Indians: An American Struggle.* Chapel Hill: University of North Carolina Press, 2018.

Lucas, Marion B. *A History of Blacks in Kentucky from Slavery to Segregation, 1760–1891.* Frankfort: Kentucky Historical Society, 2003.

Lusane, Clarence. *Hitler's Black Victims: The Historical Experiences of Afro-Germans, European Blacks, Africans, and African Americans in the Nazi Era.* New York: Routledge, 2002.

Madden, T. O., Jr. *We Were Always Free: The Maddens of Culpepper County, Virginia; A 200-Year Family History.* New York: W. W. Norton, 1992.

Maddox, Samantha. *I Am My Own Odysseus: The Margaret Willis Story.* Columbus, OH: AAUS Electronic Publishing, 2001.

Madsen, Axel. *John Jacob Astor: America's First Millionaire.* New York: John Wiley, 2001.

Mann, Curtis. "The African-American Farmers of Chikapin Hill, Sangamon County, Illinois, Part 1." *Historico: The Newsletter of the Sangamon County Historical Society,* September 2008.

Marshall, Anne E. *Creating a Confederate Kentucky: The Lost Cause and Civil War Memory in a Border State.* Chapel Hill: University of North Carolina Press, 2010.

Marshall, Anne E. "Kentucky's Separate Coach Law and African American Response, 1892–1900." *Register of the Kentucky Historical Society* 98, no. 3 (July 2000): 241–259.

Mazower, Mark. *What You Did Not Tell: A Russian Past and the Journey Home.* New York: Other Press, 2017.

McBride, W. Stephen. "Camp Nelson and Kentucky's Civil War Memory." *Historical Archaeology* 47, no. 3 (2013): 69–80.

McDaniel, Karen Cotton. "Local Women: The Public Lives of Black Middle Class Women in Kentucky Before the 'Modern Civil Rights Movement.'" PhD diss., University of Kentucky, 2013.

McGinnis, Andrew M. "Between Enthusiasm and Stoicism: David Rice and Moderate Revivalism in Virginia and Kentucky." *Register of the Kentucky Historical Society* 106, no. 2 (Spring 2008): 165–190.

McKittrick, Katherine. *Demonic Grounds: Black Women and the Cartographies of Struggle*. Minneapolis: University of Minnesota Press, 2006.

Miller, Eben. *Born Along the Color Line: The 1933 Amenia Conference and the Rise of a National Civil Rights Movement*. Oxford, UK, and New York: Oxford University Press, 2012.

Milteer, Warren Eugene, Jr. *North Carolina's Free People of Color, 1715–1885*. Baton Rouge: Louisiana State University Press, 2020.

Moore, Edmund A. "Robert T. Breckinridge and the Slavery Aspect of the Presbyterian Schism of 1837." *Church History* 4, no. 4 (December 1935): 282–294.

Moran, Rachel F. *Interracial Intimacy: The Regulation of Race and Romance*. Chicago: University of Chicago Press, 2001.

Morgan, Francesca. *Nation of Descendants: Politics and the Practice of Genealogy in US History*. Chapel Hill: University of North Carolina Press, 2021.

Murray, Robert. "The Half That Is Never Told: Creating a Useful Past at Centre College." *Ohio Valley History* 21, no. 2 (Summer 2021): 6–21.

Nagel, James. *Race and Culture in New Orleans Stories: Kate Chopin, Grace King, and Alice Dunbar Nelson*. Tuscaloosa: University of Alabama Press, 2014.

Newman, Brooke. *A Dark Inheritance: Blood, Race, and Sex in Colonial Jamaica*. New Haven, CT: Yale University Press, 2018.

Oakley, Christopher A. *Keeping the Circle: American Indian Identity in Eastern North Carolina, 1885–2004*. Lincoln: University of Nebraska Press, 2005.

Orton, Samuel T. "'Word-Blindness' in School Children." *Archives of Neurology and Psychiatry* 14, no. 5 (June 1925): 581–615.

Orton, Samuel T. *Reading, Writing and Speech Problems in Children*. New York: W. W. Norton, 1937.

Otele, Olivette. *African Europeans: An Untold History*. New York: Basic Books, 2021.

Owens, Emily A. *Consent in the Presence of Force: Sexual Violence and Black Women's Survival in Antebellum New Orleans.* Chapel Hill: University of North Carolina Press, 2023.

Painter, Nell Irvin. *Sojourner Truth: A Life, a Symbol.* New York: W. W. Norton, 1996.

Painter, Nell Irvin. "Was Marie White? The Trajectory of a Question in the United States." *Journal of Southern History* 74, no. 1 (February 2008): 3–30.

Paschal, Richard A. *Jim Crow North Carolina: The Legislative Program from 1865 to 1920.* Durham, NC: Carolina Academic Press, 2021.

Pascoe, Peggy. *What Comes Naturally: Miscegenation Law and the Making of Race in America.* Oxford, UK, and New York: Oxford University Press, 2010.

Paull, Bonnie E., and Richard E. Hart. *Lincoln's Springfield Neighborhood.* Charleston, SC: History Press, 2015.

Pearson, Susan J. *The Birth Certificate: An American History.* Chapel Hill: University of North Carolina Press, 2021.

Peck, Robert McCracken. *Specimens of Hair: The Curious Collection of Peter A. Browne.* New York: Blast Books, 2018.

Pennington, Karen L. "Three Presidencies: Academic Leadership in Changing Times; A History of the State University of New York, the College at New Paltz, 1948–1979." PhD diss., State University of New York at Albany, 1994.

Peterson, Carla L. *Black Gotham: A Family History of African Americans in Nineteenth Century New York City.* New Haven, CT: Yale University Press, 2011.

Pols, Hans, and Warwik Anderson. "The Mestizos of Kisar: An Insular Racial Laboratory in the Malay Archipelago." *Journal of Southeast Asian Studies* 49, no. 3 (October 2018): 445–463.

Popkin, Jeremy D. *History, Historians, and Autobiography.* Chicago: University of Chicago Press, 2005.

Porter, Kenneth Wiggins. *John Jacob Astor: Businessman.* Cambridge, MA: Harvard University Press, 1931.

Prasad, Chandra, ed. *Mixed: An Anthology of Short Fiction on the Multiracial Experience.* New York: W. W. Norton, 2006.

Prewitt, Kenneth. *What Is Your Race? The Census and Our Flawed Efforts to Classify Americans.* Princeton, NJ: Princeton University Press, 2013.

Prince, Vida "Sister" Goldman. *That's the Way It Was: Stories of Struggle, Survival, and Self-Respect in Twentieth-Century Black St. Louis.* Charleston, SC: History Press, 2013.

Purdy, Michelle A. *Transforming the Elite: Black Students and the Desegregation of Private Schools.* Chapel Hill: University of North Carolina Press, 2018.

Ramage, James A., and Andrea S. Watkins. *Kentucky Rising: Democracy, Slavery, and Culture from the Early Republic to the Civil War.* Lexington: University of Kentucky Press, 2011.

Redman, Samuel J. *Bone Rooms: From Scientific Racism to Human Prehistory in Museums.* Cambridge, MA: Harvard University Press, 2016.

Regosin, Elizabeth, and Donald Shaffer. *Voices of Emancipation: Understanding Slavery, the Civil War, and Reconstruction Through the U.S. Pension Bureau Files.* New York: New York University Press, 2008.

Rhyne, J. Michael. "'Conduct . . . Inexcusable and Unjustifiable': Bound Children, Battered Freedwomen, and the Limits of Emancipation in Kentucky's Bluegrass Region." *Journal of Social History* 42, no. 2 (Winter 2008): 319–340.

Richter, Amy G. *Home on the Rails: Women, the Railroad, and the Rise of Public Domesticity.* Chapel Hill: University of North Carolina Press, 2005.

Robinson, Lori S. "Bound by Slavery." *Crisis* 112, no. 1 (January/February 2005): 30–35.

Rodenwaldt, Ernst. *Die Mestizen auf Kisar* (The mestizos of Kisar). Batavia: Kolff, 1927.

Romano, Renee C. *Race Mixing: Black-White Marriage in Postwar America.* Cambridge, MA: Harvard University Press, 2003.

Rosen, Hannah. *Terror in the Heart of Freedom: Citizenship, Sexual Violence, and the Meaning of Race in the Postemancipation South.* Chapel Hill: University of North Carolina Press, 2009.

Rosenthal, Caitlin. *Accounting for Slavery: Masters and Management.* Cambridge, MA: Harvard University Press, 2018.

Ross, Thomas E. *American Indians in North Carolina: Geographic Interpretations.* Southern Pines, NC: Karo Hollow Press, 1999.

Rothman, Joshua. *Notorious in the Neighborhood: Sex and Families Across the Color Line in Virginia, 1787–1861.* Chapel Hill: University of North Carolina Press, 2003.

Saunt, Claudio. *Black, White, Indian: Race and the Unmaking of an American Family*. Oxford, UK, and New York: Oxford University Press, 2005.

Savage, Barbara D. *Merze Tate: The Global Odyssey of a Black Woman Scholar*. New Haven, CT: Yale University Press, 2023.

Schor, Paul. *Counting Americans: How the U.S. Census Classified the Nation*. Oxford, UK, and New York: Oxford University Press, 2017.

Schwalm, Leslie. *A Hard Fight for We: Women's Transition from Slavery to Freedom in South Carolina*. Champaign: University of Illinois Press, 1997.

Sears, Richard D. *Camp Nelson, Kentucky: A Civil War History*. Lexington: University Press of Kentucky, 2002.

Sharpe, Christina. *Monstrous Intimacies: Making Post-Slavery Subjects*. Durham, NC: Duke University Press, 2010.

Shaw, Gwendolyn Dubois. *Seeing the Unspeakable: The Art of Kara Walker*. Durham, NC: Duke University Press, 2004.

Shermer, Elizabeth Trandy. "Nelson Rockefeller and the State University of New York's Rapid Rise and Decline." Rockefeller Research Reports online, 2015, https://rockarch.issuelab.org/resources/27918/27918.pdf.

Shodell, Elly, ed. *Particles of the Past: Sandmining on Long Island 1870s–1980s*. Port Washington, NY: Port Washington Public Library, 1985.

Simpson, Eileen. *Reversals: A Personal Account of Victory over Dyslexia*. New York: Washington Square Press, 1979.

Smith, Christi M. *Reparation and Reconciliation: The Rise and Fall of Integrated Higher Education*. Chapel Hill: University of North Carolina Press, 2016.

Smith, Ernest Ashton. *Allegheny, A Century of Education, 1815–1915*. Meadville, PA: Allegheny College History Company, 2005.

Springle, Ray. *In the Land of Jim Crow*. New York: Simon & Schuster, 1949.

Sullivan, John Jeremiah. "Rhiannon Giddens and What Folk Music Means." *New Yorker*, May 13, 2019, https://www.newyorker.com/magazine/2019/05/20/rhiannon-giddens-and-what-folk-music-means.

Tallant, Harold. *Evil Necessity: Slavery and Political Culture in Antebellum Kentucky*. Lexington: University of Kentucky Press, 2003.

Tallbear, Kim. *Native American DNA: Trial Belonging and the False Promise of Genetic Science*. Minneapolis: University of Minnesota Press, 2013.

Taylor, William Harrison, and Peter C. Messer, eds. *Faith and Slavery in the Presbyterian Diaspora*. Bethlehem, PA: Lehigh University Press, 2016.

Bibliography

Traverso, Enzo. *Singular Pasts: The "I" in Historiography*. New York: Columbia University Press, 2023.

Wald, Gayle. *Crossing the Line: Racial Passing in Twentieth-Century U.S. Literature and Culture*. Durham, NC: Duke University Press, 2000.

Walker, Rebecca. *Black, White, Jewish: Autobiography of a Shifting Self*. New York: Riverhead Books, 2001.

Wallenstein, Peter. *Tell the Court I Love My Wife: Race, Marriage, and Law—An American History*. New York: Palgrave Macmillan, 2002.

Ward, H. Trawick, and R. P. Stephen Davis, Jr. "The Evolution of Siouan Communities in Piedmont North Carolina." *Southeastern Archaeology* 10, no. 1 (January 1991): 40–53.

Ward, H. Trawick, and R. P. Stephen Davis, Jr. *Indian Communities on the North Carolina Piedmont, A.D. 1000 to 1700*. Chapel Hill: University of North Carolina Research Laboratories of Anthropology, 1993.

Ward, H. Trawick, and R. P. Stephen Davis, Jr. *Time Before History: The Archaeology of North Carolina*. Chapel Hill: University of North Carolina Press, 1999.

Washington, Margaret. *Sojourner Truth's America*. Champaign: University of Illinois Press, 2009.

Watlington, Patricia. *The Partisan Spirit: Kentucky Politics, 1779–1792*. New York: Atheneum, 1972.

Watson, Alan D. "Sailing Under Steam: The Advent of Steam Navigation in North Carolina to the Civil War." *North Carolina Historical Review* 75, no. 1 (January 1998): 29–69.

Watson, Harry L. "'The Common Rights of Mankind': Subsistence, Shad, and Commerce in the Early Republican South." *Journal of American History* (June 1996): 13–43.

Weil, François. *Family Trees: A History of Genealogy in America*. Cambridge, MA: Harvard University Press, 2013.

White, William Lindsay. *Lost Boundaries*. New York: Harcourt, Brace, 1948.

Wilkinson, A. B. *Blurring the Lines of Race and Freedom: Mulattoes and Mixed Bloods in English Colonial America*. Chapel Hill: University of North Carolina Press, 2020.

Williams, Walter L. "Southwestern Indians Before Removal: Prehistory, Contact, Decline." In *Southeastern Indians Since the Removal Era*, edited by Walter L. Williams, 3–23. Athens: University of Georgia Press, 1979.

Williamson, Joel. *New People: Miscegenation and Mulattoes in the United States.* New York: New Press, 1980.

Williamson, Joy Ann. *Black Power on Campus: University of Illinois, 1965–1975.* Champaign: University of Illinois Press, 2003.

Willis, Margaret. *The Guinea Pigs After Twenty Years: A Follow-up Study of the Class of 1938 of the University School Ohio State.* Columbus: Ohio State University Press, 1961.

Wilson, Emily Herring, and Susan Mullally. *Hope and Dignity: Older Black Women of the South.* Philadelphia, PA: Temple University Press, 1983.

Wilson, Mira B. "Colored Students Are an Asset." *Independent School Bulletin* 3 (February 1949): 13.

Woods, Naurice Frank, Jr. "Adaline and the Judge: An Ex-Slave Girl's Journey with Albion W. Tourgée." *Elon Law Review* 5, no. 1 (2013): 199–222.

Worthington, Leah, Rachel Clare Donaldson, and John W. White, eds. *Challenging History: Race, Equity, and the Practice of Public History.* Columbia: University of South Carolina Press, 2021.

Young, Amy L., and J. Baine Hudson. "Slave Life at Oxmoor." *Filson Club History Quarterly* 74 (Summer 2000): 189–219.

Zinsser, William, ed. *Inventing the Truth: The Art and Craft of Memoir.* New York: Houghton Mifflin, 1995.

Illustration Credits

All images not otherwise credited are courtesy of the author.

CHAPTER ONE

Nancy Bell, baptismal record, First Presbyterian Church of Danville, circa 1827. Courtesy of the First Presbyterian Church of Danville (KY).

Martha Ann, manumission, 1853. Courtesy of the Boyle County (NC) Courthouse.

Nancy Bell Graves, application for the veteran's pension of Edmund Graves, 1881. Courtesy of the National Archives and Records Administration.

CHAPTER TWO

Mary Haith and Elijah Jones marriage bond, 1827. Courtesy of the Orange County (NC) Courthouse.

Sidney D[allas] Jones from George Albright, land deed, 1864. Courtesy of the State Archives of North Carolina.

CHAPTER THREE

Bandon plantation, circa 1933. Courtesy of the Library of Congress.

Isabella Holley, Freedmen's Bureau complaint, 1867. Courtesy of the National Archives and Records Administration.

CHAPTER FOUR

Ledger of Ormond Beatty, entry for Susan (Penman) Davis, 1867. Courtesy of the Centre College Special Collections and Archives.

CHAPTER FIVE

Jennie (Mary Jane Holley Jones) to her son Robert E. Jones, The Bishop, circa 1902. Courtesy of the Amistad Research Center.

Broadside, circa 1890. Courtesy of the Greensboro (NC) History Museum.

CHAPTER SIX

Pattie Beatty Quisenberry address book with entry for Mr. Frank Williams (Fannie Miller Williams). Courtesy of the Filson Historical Society.

CHAPTER SEVEN

Musie (Susie Pearl Williams), University of Cincinnati yearbook, 1913. Courtesy of the University of Cincinnati.

Musie (Susie Williams Jones), hair sample, Caroline Bond Day Papers. Courtesy of the Peabody Museum of Archaeology and Ethnology at Harvard University.

Alsacious (Alsie Trammel), back row, last on the right, Bennett College High School Class, 1932. Courtesy of the Bennett College Archives and Special Collections.

CHAPTER EIGHT

Paul M. Jones, school board campaign ad. Courtesy of the Port Washington Public Library.

Epigraph Credits

INTRODUCTION

Zen koan.

CHAPTER ONE

James Baldwin, excerpt from *No Name in the Street.* Copyright © 1972 by James Baldwin, renewed © 2000 by Gloria Baldwin Karefa-Smart. Reprinted with the permission of The Permissions Company LLC on behalf of the James Baldwin Estate.

CHAPTER TWO

Zora Neale Hurston, excerpt from "How It Feels to Be Colored Me." Copyright © 1928 Fellowship of Reconciliation, www.forusa.org. Reprinted by permission. All rights reserved.

CHAPTER THREE

Harriet Jacobs, *Incidents in the Life of a Slave Girl: Written by Herself* (Boston: Published for the Author, 1861).

CHAPTER FOUR

Excerpt(s) from *Beloved* by Toni Morrison, copyright © 2007 by Penguin Random House LLC. Used by permission of Penguin Random House Audio Publishing Group, a division of Penguin Random House LLC. All rights reserved.

Martha S. Jones is the Society of Black Alumni Presidential Professor, professor of history, and a professor at the SNF Agora Institute at the Johns Hopkins University. A prizewinning author and editor of four books, most recently *Vanguard*, she is past copresident of the Berkshire Conference of Women Historians and has contributed to the *New York Times*, *Atlantic*, and many other publications. She lives in Baltimore, Maryland.